Early Praise for *Functional Programming: A PragPub Anthology*

If you've been wondering what all the functional hubbub is about, *Functional Programming: A PragPub Anthology* will satisfy. You can wet your whistle with several languages, get a feel for how to think functionally, and do so without overcommitting to one language or school of thought.

➤ **Ben Vandgrift**
Chief architect, Oryx Systems Inc.

Programming's last sea change was in the 1990s when object orientation went mainstream. It's happening again, but this time it's functional programming that's sweeping through our profession. Read this book to understand why and to learn how to ride the wave.

➤ **Paul Butcher**
Founder and CTO, writeandimprove.com

I really enjoyed the structure and flow of the book. The chapters stand on their own as essays but when put together make a strong argument for functional programming, regardless of the language. It's also a treat to see all these different familiar writers write about diverse languages.

➤ **Ben Marx**
Lead engineer, Bleacher Report

You're sure to find a way functional programming resonates with you with the wealth of approaches and languages covered. The treatment of Scala collection is superb: everything a beginner needs to know from the get-go!

➤ **Jeff Heon**
Research software developer, CRIM

Functional Programming: A PragPub Anthology

Exploring Clojure, Elixir, Haskell, Scala, and Swift

Michael Swaine
and the PragPub writers

The Pragmatic Bookshelf

Raleigh, North Carolina

Many of the designations used by manufacturers and sellers to distinguish their products are claimed as trademarks. Where those designations appear in this book, and The Pragmatic Programmers, LLC was aware of a trademark claim, the designations have been printed in initial capital letters or in all capitals. The Pragmatic Starter Kit, The Pragmatic Programmer, Pragmatic Programming, Pragmatic Bookshelf, PragProg and the linking *g* device are trademarks of The Pragmatic Programmers, LLC.

Every precaution was taken in the preparation of this book. However, the publisher assumes no responsibility for errors or omissions, or for damages that may result from the use of information (including program listings) contained herein.

Our Pragmatic books, screencasts, and audio books can help you and your team create better software and have more fun. Visit us at *https://pragprog.com*.

The team that produced this book includes:

Publisher: Andy Hunt
VP of Operations: Janet Furlow
Executive Editor: Susannah Davidson Pfalzer
Indexing: Potomac Indexing, LLC
Copy Editor: Nicole Abramowitz
Layout: Gilson Graphics

For sales, volume licensing, and support, please contact *support@pragprog.com*.

For international rights, please contact *rights@pragprog.com*.

Printed in the United States of America.
ISBN-13: 978-1-68050-233-6
Printed on acid-free paper.
Book version: P1.0—July 2017

Contents

Part VII — Going Deeper

Introduction

by Michael Swaine

This book shows how five different languages approach the paradigm of functional programming. The chapters were written by experts in the different languages and first appeared as articles in *PragPub* magazine. After publishing nearly one hundred issues of the magazine, it became clear that we were in possession of a wealth of information about functional programming, and we decided that some of the best articles would make an interesting book.

Functional programming is one of the major paradigms of programming. In functional programming, we approach computation as the evaluation of mathematical functions, and as much as possible we avoid changing state and mutable data.

Certain concepts and issues are sure to come up in any discussion of functional programming. Recursion. Lazy evaluation. Referential transparency. Eliminating side effects. Functions as first-class objects. Higher-level functions. Currying. Immutable data. Type systems. Pattern matching. The authors touch on all these concepts, looking at them from the perspective of different languages.

But functional programming is not an all-or-none thing. It is perfectly reasonable to write imperative code that uses functional techniques and practices and data structures. It is fine to mix and match styles, and some programming languages are designed as hybrids, allowing you to use the style that best fits your needs of the moment. Scala, for example, or Mathematica, or Swift. Our authors explore these different approaches in this book, and you can decide which works best for you.

We explore functional programming in five languages in this book, with articles by experts in each language. If this encourages you to look for a definitive guide to some of the languages, we can recommend Venkat Subramaniam's *Pragmatic Scala [Sub15]*, Stuart Halloway and Aaron Bedra's *Programming Clojure (2nd edition) [HB12]*, Dave Thomas's *Programming Elixir 1.3 [Tho16]*,

Chris Eidhof, Florian Kugler, and Wouter Swiersta's *Functional Swift* (https://www.objc.io/books/functional-swift/), and Miran Lipovaca's *Learn You a Haskell for Great Good!: A Beginner's Guide [Lip11]*. What you'll find here is an exploration of an important programming paradigm in five languages, written by a team of experts. That's what we set out to create.

I hope you will agree that the result is an interesting book.

Acknowledgements

Not for the first time, the editor is pleased to acknowledge his colleagues at the Pragmatic Programmers, who are a joy to work with, thorough professionals, and wonderful human beings. This book especially benefitted from the skills and judgement of publisher Andy Hunt who understood the vision, vice president of operations Janet Furlow who steered it to completion, executive editor Susannah Davidson Pfalzer who helped shape it, and copy editor Nicole Abramowitz who fixed its flaws.

Most of the chapters in this book first appeared as articles in *PragPub* magazine, and I am grateful to the authors not only for the original articles but for the editing—in some cases extensive—that they helped me with in the process of turning magazine articles into book chapters. Read Appendix 1, *Meet the Authors*, on page 247. I think you'll be impressed.

I also need to thank Gilson Graphics for its design and production work, Nancy Groth for original editing of the articles for magazine publication, and the technical editors who gave generously of their time and expertise, including Paul Butcher, Ian Dees, Jeff Heon, Ron Jeffries, and Kim Shrier.

I hope you enjoy this first in what I hope will be a line of *PragPub* anthologies.

Part I

The Functional Paradigm

Why functional programming matters, and how to think in the functional way

## CHAPTER 1

Functional Programming Is Big Again

by Michael Swaine

The summer I moved to Silicon Valley was the summer they decommissioned ILLIAC IV at Moffett Field.

We've Seen This Movie Before

In 1981, the center of attention in computing had shifted from massive machines programmed by a white-coated priesthood of programmers to cheap desktop crates built and programmed by scruffy hackers. I'd relocated from the Midwest to Palo Alto and signed on to help launch a new weekly news-magazine to cover the scruffy ones. Meanwhile, just down El Camino at NASA's Moffett Field, they were officially shutting down and disassembling the computer that had inspired Stanley Kubrick and Arthur C. Clarke's HAL 9000.

ILLIAC IV is a legendary pivotal point in computer design, and it holds a similar position in the long and complicated history of functional programming.

The idea behind ILLIAC IV was to break away from the sequential model that had dominated computing since the start. Certain problem domains, like fluid dynamics, were best approached by parallel processing, and ILLIAC IV was specifically designed for just this kind of parallel problems: problems where a single instruction could be applied in parallel to multiple sets of data. This is known as SIMD (single instruction, multiple data). The more general case—multiple instructions operating on multiple data sets, or MIMD—is harder. But every kind of parallel programming requires new algorithms and a new mindset. And is an invitation to functional programming.

Functional programming, or FP, "treats computation as the evaluation of mathematical functions and avoids changing state and mutable data," according to Wikipedia. That will do for a definition, although we will need to dig much deeper.

FP had been around since the 1950s when John McCarthy invented Lisp, but the drive for parallel processing provided a new impetus for functional programming. Avoiding changing state was a hard pill to swallow back then, but it was just right for the SIMD model. This led to the development of new FP languages and features in existing languages. Fortran was what most people doing scientific computing were using at the time, and it was natural to enhance it. Programmers of the ILLIAC IV could write in IVTRAN or TRANQUIL or CFD, parallelized versions of FORTRAN. There was also a parallelized version of ALGOL.

For the right kind of problems, ones that could be addressed with SIMD, ILLIAC IV was the fastest computer in the world, and it held the unofficial title of the fastest machine in the world up to its decommissioning in 1981. It was an order of magnitude faster than any other computer at the time, and was perfectly suited to its target applications and to functional programming.

But that era came to an abrupt end. On September 7, 1981, ILLIAC IV was shut down for good. You can still see part of it on display at the Computer History Museum in Mountain View, just down the road from Moffett Field.

Why did its era end? From Wikipedia: "Illiac IV was a member of the class of parallel computers, referred to as SIMD...Moore's Law overtook the specialized SIMD ILLIAC approach making the MIMD approach preferred for almost all scientific computing."

But along the way, it acquired another place in history, as the inspiration for HAL 9000 in *2001: A Space Odyssey*. Arthur C. Clarke was no neophyte regarding computers: he had talked with Turing at Bletchley Park and was an avid follower of developments in microcomputers. Clarke was intrigued when he learned of work on ILLIAC IV at the University of Illinois at Urbana-Champaign, and honored the campus in the movie as HAL 9000's birthplace.

Flash forward to the 00s. The use case that made FP worth learning was again parallel processing, but driven by the advent of multicore processors. "The chipmakers," I claimed at the time, "have essentially said that the job of enforcing Moore's Law is now a software problem. They will concentrate on putting more and more cores on a die, and it's up to you to recraft your software to take advantage of the parallel-processing capabilities of their chips."

The impetus for FP in the 2000s was again the desire to break free of the sequential model, and there were different approaches being offered. If you were heavily invested in Java skills and tools, and didn't want to toss aside the code libraries, the skills, and the tools you counted on, you could use Martin Odersky's Scala language, recently released on the Java platform. It was also offered on the .NET platform, although (oops) support was dropped in 2012. .NETters were better off looking to F#, created by Don Syme at Microsoft Research. If you wanted a more purely functional language, you had Erlang, developed for highly parallel programming by Joe Armstrong at Ericsson, or Haskell, or many other options.

What all these languages offered was the ability to work in the functional paradigm. The two defining features of the functional paradigm are that all computations are treated as the evaluation of a function and that you avoid changing state and mutable data. But there are some additional common features of functional programming:

- First-class functions: functions can serve as arguments and results of functions.

- Recursion as the primary tool for iteration.

- Heavy use of pattern matching.

- Lazy evaluation, which makes possible the creation of infinite sequences.

Iterative programmers who approached FP for the first time back then might have added: it's slow and it's confusing. It is in fact neither of these, necessarily, but it does require a different way of thinking about problems and different algorithms; and to perform adequately, it needed better language support than was common in the 2000s. That would change over the next decade, and along with it would change the very purposes for which people were drawn to FP.

New Arguments for Functional Programming

A decade later, the case is once again being made for functional programming. Now the language support is here and the case for FP is broader.

While parallelism was traditionally the driving force behind any push for functional programming, now when people talk about FP, they are more likely to reference the ability to think about problems at a higher level, or the virtues of immutability. Instead of FP being seen as the strange way you need to write in order to deal effectively with parallelism, the new argument is that it is the *more natural* way to write, closer to the concepts and terminology of your problem domain. People are using FP for apps that have no need for parallelism, merely because it allows them to program more efficiently and clearly, working closer to the way they think about their problems.

They say that rather than having to translate their problem to the programming language, they can adapt the language to the problem.

And if you have multiple cores available and parallelism can benefit your code, you might get the parallelism for free. "Recent clever innovations in the [Clojure] libraries have rewritten the map function to be automatically parallelizable, meaning that all map operations benefit from a performance boost without developer intervention," Neal Ford has said.

FP's recognized good fit for concurrency appeals to people writing multi-processor apps, high-availability apps, web servers for the social network, and more. FP's higher-level abstractions appeal to those looking for faster development time or more understandable code. FP's emphasis on immutability has a strong appeal for anyone concerned about reliability.

That sales pitch is a real change from the arguments made for functional programming in the time of ILLIAC IV. Today there are new reasons to look at FP, plus stronger language support for FP and a wider choice of approaches. That starts with language choice. You can comfortably stick with familiar languages and its tools, bringing in a functional approach just where you find it useful. Or you can go straight to a language built from the ground up for functional programming. You'll see both approaches in this book.

It's an exciting time to explore functional programming, and the rewards are significant. But it still requires a different way of thinking.

In the next chapter, Michael Bevilacqua-Linn invites us to think about programming in the functional way.

## CHAPTER 2

Functional Thinking for the Imperative Mind

by Michael Bevilacqua-Linn

It can be difficult to pin down exactly what functional programming is.

It's difficult because the term, although theoretically well defined, has in practice come to encompass several different, though related, ideas. If you talk to a Clojure hacker, you'll probably get an earful of macros. A Haskell programmer might talk about monads, and an Erlang programmer about actors.

These are all different concepts. Macros give programmers extremely powerful metaprogramming, monads allow us to model changing state safely, and actors provide a robust way of doing distributed and concurrent programming.

Yet all of these different ideas are seen as defining features of functional languages. The breadth of concepts can make it a bit difficult to figure out what it's all about. And yet, the core idea is very simple.

It's About Functions

At its core, functional programming is about programming with pure, side-effect-free functions.

This is a pure function:

```
f(x) = <raise power="2">x</raise>
```

So is this:

```
public int incrementCounter(int counter) {
  return counter++;
}
```

This is not:

```
private int counter = 0;
public void incrementMutableCounter() {
  counter++;
}
```

The first two examples increment a counter by returning a new integer that's one higher than the passed-in integer. The third example does the same thing but does it by mutating a bit of state that may be shared across many pieces of a program.

A definition: a function like incrementCounter that doesn't rely on mutating state is called a pure function. And this purity has many benefits. For instance, if you've got a pure function that does some expensive computation, you can optimize your program by only calling the function once and caching the result—a technique known as memoization.

Pure functions also make programs easier to reason about. An object-oriented program is a graph of objects, each with its own bundle of mutable state. Modifying one object's state can lead to another's state being modified, possibly many nodes in the graph away. In a program with only pure functions, this sort of action at a distance is impossible.

That's the simplistic description of functional programming.

It's About Immutability

Unfortunately, strict purity and the real world don't play well together. Pure functions can be used to model some domains well, others not so much. Compilers are pure functions. Google's search is not.

Practical functional programming languages *emphasize* immutability and functional purity, but they must have some means of modeling a changing world that stops short of total functional purity. In Haskell, probably the most strict functional language, you can model change using monads, and otherwise maintain strict purity.

Other functional languages have other techniques for minimizing and controlling state change that may not be quite as strict as Haskell's. Clojure, for instance, uses a software transactional memory system in combination with a set of reference types and fiendishly clever immutable data structures to maintain a high degree of purity while still letting programmers deal with a changing world.

It's a Way of Thinking

So to a first approximation, functional programming is about programming with pure functions and immutable state, unlike imperative programming, which relies heavily on mutability. Around this immutable core there is a set of language techniques and features that replace mutable imperative techniques. Examining these will give us a deeper feeling for what it is to think and program functionally.

Let's take a look at a simple example: filtering a list so it only contains odd numbers.

```java
public List<Integer> filterOdds(List<Integer> list) {
  List<Integer> filteredList = new ArrayList<Integer>();

  for(Integer current : list) {
    if(1 == current % 2) {
      filteredList.add(current);
    }
  }
  return filteredList;
}
```

This is fine imperative code. We iterate through a list, and for each element we check to see whether it's odd by computing its modulus. We could, perhaps, make its intent a bit clearer if we were to pull that check out into a helper function and name it.

```java
public List<Integer> filterOdds(List<Integer> list) {
  List<Integer> filteredList = new ArrayList<Integer>();

  for (Integer current : list) {
    if (isOdd(current)) {
      filteredList.add(current);
    }
  }
  return filteredList;
}
private boolean isOdd(Integer integer) {
  return 1 == integer % 2;
}
```

Now what if we want to create a function that allows us to filter evens instead of odds? The only bit of code that needs to change is calling an isEven instead of isOdd.

```java
public List<Integer> filterEvens(List<Integer> list) {
  List<Integer> filteredList = new ArrayList<Integer>();
```

```
  for (Integer current : list) {
    if (isEven(current)) {
      filteredList.add(current);
    }
  }
  return filteredList;
}

private boolean isEven(Integer integer) {
  return 0 == integer % 2;
}
```

This works, but we committed one of the cardinal coding sins. Most of filter-
OutEvens is cut and pasted from filterOutOdds. What we really want is a way to
have a filter that can use some arbitrary bit of logic to do its filtering.

Let's take a look at how we might accomplish this in Java. Both isOdd and
isEven take a single argument and return a boolean value. Let's define an interface that captures the essence of this computation. We'll call it Predicate, which
is a mathy name for a function that returns a boolean value.

```
public interface Predicate {
  public boolean evaluate(Integer argument);
}
```

Now we can rewrite filterEvens and filterOdds to be more generic.

```
public List<Integer> filter(List<Integer> list, Predicate predicate) {
  List<Integer> filteredList = new ArrayList<Integer>();

  for (Integer current : list) {
    if (predicate.evaluate(current)) {
      filteredList.add(current);
    }
  }
  return filteredList;
}
```

Then we define our two predicates.

```
class isEven implements Predicate {
  public boolean evaluate(Integer argument) {
    return 0 == argument % 2;
  }

}

class isOdd implements Predicate {
  public boolean evaluate(Integer argument) {
    return 1 == argument % 2;
  }
}
```

Now we can simply instantiate one of the predicates and pass it into the filter method. If we come up with a new way to filter our list—say we only want to keep integers that are perfect squares—we can just define a PerfectSquare predicate rather than having to cut and paste the entire filtering function.

What we've just done with the filter method and Predicate interface simulates a concept from the functional world: higher-order functions. A higher-order function is a function that can be passed into, or returned from, another function. Let's take a look at how we'd do similar filtering in Clojure—a modern, functional variant of Lisp.

```
(filter odd? [0 1 2 3])
(filter even? [0 1 2 3])
```

That's it! The first thing you probably noticed is that it's much shorter than that Java version. The second is probably that the parentheses aren't in their usual spot. Clojure, and other Lisps, use prefix notation for function calls. This means that the function that's being called is the first thing inside the parentheses, with its arguments coming afterward.

Syntactic differences aside, notice how the Clojure version uses all built-in functions and language features? There's no need for us to define a Predicate interface. odd? is a function that takes a number and returns true if it's odd, while even? does the same for even numbers. We can pass those functions directly into the filter function using the power of higher-order functions.

This turns our original imperative solution, in which we wrote code that was concerned with the nitty gritty details of iterating through a list, into a very declarative one. We're working at a higher level of abstraction that often lets us describe what results we want, rather than the details of getting them.

So when people talk about functional programming, they're generally talking about at least two separate, but very closely related things. First, they're talking about programming with pure functions. Since this is a pipe dream for most real world problems, practical functional programming languages generally settle for making it easier to use immutability than not, and for facilities that control mutation when you absolutely need to do it.

Second, they're talking about the style of programming that has grown up around this functional core. As we've seen, this style relies heavily on higher-order functions and other related techniques. These techniques often produce code that operates at a higher level of abstraction, such as using the filter function we saw above rather than explicit iteration.

These two facets of functional programming have significant benefits. The extreme emphasis on immutability makes programs easier to reason about. The behavior of a function can be understood just by reading the code in the function itself, rather than worrying about some bit of mutable state that it may rely on that's hundreds or thousands of lines away. The use of higher-order functions often leads to declarative code, which is shorter and more direct than the imperative equivalent.

So if you think of these two things when you think of functional programming, you won't be wrong: a preference for programming with pure functions, and a style of programming that involves higher-order functions in declarative code.

The next dozen or so chapters are organized by language, with several chapters devoted to functional programming in each language. After that you'll find a collection of chapters that go more deeply into functional programming with these languages. You can jump right to the language you're most interested in, or you can just read straight through. But you can't do better than to start with the next chapter, in which Venkat Subramaniam will show you how Scala, a hybrid functional language, implements the concepts we've discussed.

Part II

Scala: A Hybrid Language

Martin Odersky was doing deep theoretical work in functional programming when Sun Microsystems released Java. Realizing that Java changed the playing field for language development, he created Scala, a language that brought functional features to the Java infrastructure. The result was a language that leverages the JVM and its libraries and allows programmers to use object-oriented or functional approaches at will—a true hybrid language. Twitter and Foursquare were among Scala's early adopters.

## CHAPTER 3

Scala and Functional Style

by Venkat Subramaniam

When designing Scala, Martin Odersky took the bold, unconventional step of bringing together two different paradigms: the object-oriented and the functional. This is no trivial undertaking: these two styles are quite dissimilar, and this marriage of distinct paradigms poses some real challenges.

To see what Odersky was up against, let's first take a look at what it means to be functional. There are two defining aspects to the functional style of programming: the purity of functions, and programming with higher-order functions.

Functional Purity

Purity means that functions have no side effects. The output of a function is predictably the same as long as the input is the same. A pure function isn't affected by and doesn't affect anything outside; it also doesn't mutate any value.

There are two benefits of function purity. First, it's easier to understand and prove the correctness of a pure function. Second, pure functions promote referential transparency. Pure functions can be easily rearranged and reordered for execution on multiple threads, making it easier to program concurrency on multicore processors.

Scala does not enforce purity, though it makes it easy to detect where mutable variables are used—simply search for vars. It is good Scala practice to use immutability and specifically immutable vals as much as possible.

Higher-Order Functions

The other aspect of functional style is working with *higher-order functions*—this is the facility that treats functions as first-class citizens. It lets us pass functions to functions, create functions within functions, and return functions from functions. This in turn allows for functional composition, and a virtue of Scala is that we can design using both functional composition and object composition, as we desire or as appropriate.

Let's explore Scala's approach to functional programming with some examples. We'll start with some small examples that just manipulate numbers so we can easily grasp how to use higher-order functions in Scala. And then we'll look at a practical example where we apply the concepts we've learned.

A Simple Example

Let's start with a simple iteration: given a list of stock prices, we'd like to print each price on a separate line.

Initially, the traditional for loop comes to mind, something like this in Java:

```
for(int i = 0; i <= prices.size(); i++)
```

Or is it < instead of <= in the loop condition?

There is no reason to burden ourselves with that. We can just use the for-each construct in Java, like so:

```
for(double price : prices)
```

Let's follow this style in Scala:

```
val prices = List(211.10, 310.12, 510.45, 645.60, 832.33)
for(price <- prices) {
  println(price)
}
```

Scala's type inference determines the type of the prices list to be List[Double] and the type of price to be Double. The previous style of iteration is often referred to as an external iterator. Scala also supports internal iteration, so we could write the previous example using the foreach function of List.

```
prices.foreach { e => println(e) }
```

The foreach function is our first example of a higher-order function: it receives another function as a parameter.

Let's reflect on this code for a moment. In general, a function has four parts: name, parameter list, return type, and body. Of these four, the body is the most important. In the previous function that's passed to foreach, the body is between the => and the closing }. The parameter list has one parameter e and since Scala can infer type, we did not have to say e : Double, though we could. Scala already knows the return type of this function based on what foreach expects and this function is anonymous, so does not have any name. The anonymous function we passed previously is called a function value in Scala.

But Scala has the smarts to allow us to reduce the code even further. If we simply pass the parameter received in the function value to another function in the body, as in this example, we can let Scala do that job:

```
prices.foreach { println }
```

That reduced some noise in the code; the parameter was received in the function value and passed to println.

We can take this up another notch: Scala makes quite a few things optional, including dot, so we can refactor the previous code to

```
prices foreach println
```

Here we're sending the println function itself as a parameter to the foreach method instead of wrapping a call to it into a function value—the println function itself is treated here as a function value.

All right, we know how to use the functional style to iterate over elements: simply pass a function value that operates on an element to the internal iterator and it takes care of calling that function value with each element in the list as a parameter. And this can clearly produce some concise code.

We can explore this further. There are different flavors of internal iterators available on collections in Scala. Let's look at the benefits a few of these offer.

If we want to pick the first price that's greater than $500, we can do that without mutating any variables (functional purity):

```
prices find { price => price > 500 }
```

If we want all the prices that are greater than $500, we just replace find with the filter function.

```
prices filter { price => price > 500 }
```

If we have to compute ten percent of each of the prices given, we can achieve this elegantly using the map function.

```
println(prices map { price => price * 0.1 })
```

will print

```
List(21.11, 31.012, 51.045, 64.56, 83.233)
```

The map function applies the function value given, once for each element in the list, collects the result from the function value (which is ten percent of the price in this example) into a list, and returns the collected list.

Finally, say we're asked to total the prices given. We're quite familiar with how to do that in the imperative style.

```
var total = 0.0
for(price <- prices) {
  total += price
}

println("Total is " + total)
```

to get the output of

```
Total is 2509.6
```

However, a variable was tortured in the making of this example. We can avoid that with functional style again.

```
println("Total is " + prices.reduce { (price1, price2) => price1 + price2 })
//Total is 2509.6
```

The reduce function takes a function value that accepts two values. In the first call to the function value, price1 is bound to the first element in the list and price2 is bound to the second element. In each of the subsequent calls to the function value, price1 is bound to the result of the previous call to this function value and price2 to the subsequent elements in the list. The reduce function returns the result from the last call to the function value once it has been applied for each of the elements in the list.

Scala also provides a specialized version of the reduce function specifically to sum up values—the sum function. Here's how we can use it for the preceding example:

```
println("Total is " + prices.sum)
```

We've seen a few functions here that are typical of functional style: foreach, find, filter, map, and reduce. It's time to put these to a practical use.

A Practical Example

Functional programming emphasizes immutability, but it's equally about designing with state transformation and function composition.

In object-oriented programming, we strive for good object composition. In functional programming, we design with function composition. Rather than mutating state, state is transformed as it flows through the sequence of functions.

Let's construct an example to see what this difference between imperative and functional style looks like in practice. Let's say we're given a list of ticker symbols and our goal is to find the highest-priced stock not exceeding $500.

Let's start with a sample list of ticker symbols.

```
val tickers = List("AAPL", "AMD", "CSCO", "GOOG", "HPQ", "INTC",
    "MSFT", "ORCL", "QCOM", "XRX")
```

For convenience (and to avoid cryptic symbols in code), let's create a case class to represent a stock and its price (case classes are useful to create immutable instances in Scala that provide quite a few benefits, especially ease in pattern matching, a common functional style you'll see explored in depth in Chapter 10, *Patterns and Transformations in Elixir*, on page 69).

```
case class StockPrice(ticker : String, price : Double) {
  def print =
      println("Top stock is " + ticker + " at price $" + price)
}
```

Given a ticker symbol, we want to get the latest stock price for that symbol. Thankfully, Yahoo makes this easy.

```
def getPrice(ticker : String) = {
  val url = s"http://download.finance.yahoo.com/d/quotes.csv?s=${ticker}&f=snbaopl1"
  val data = io.Source.fromURL(url).mkString
  val price = data.split(",")(4).toDouble
  StockPrice(ticker, price)
}
```

We fetch the latest stock price from the Yahoo URL, parse the result, and return an instance of StockPrice with the ticker symbol and the price value.

To help us pick the highest-priced stock valued not over $500, we need two functions: one to compare two stock prices, and the other to determine if a given stock price is not over $500.

```
def pickHighPriced(stockPrice1 : StockPrice, stockPrice2 :
      StockPrice) =
  if(stockPrice1.price > stockPrice2.price) stockPrice1
      else stockPrice2

def isNotOver500(stockPrice : StockPrice) = stockPrice.price < 500
```

Given two StockPrice instances, the pickHighPriced function returns the higher priced. The isNotOver500 will return a true if the price is less than or equal to $500, false otherwise.

Here's how we would approach the problem in imperative style:

```
import scala.collection.mutable.ArrayBuffer

val stockPrices = new ArrayBuffer[StockPrice]
for(ticker <- tickers) {
  stockPrices += getPrice(ticker)
}
val stockPricesLessThan500 = new ArrayBuffer[StockPrice]
for(stockPrice <- stockPrices) {
  if(isNotOver500(stockPrice)) stockPricesLessThan500 += stockPrice
}
var highestPricedStock = StockPrice("", 0.0)

for(stockPrice <- stockPricesLessThan500) {
  highestPricedStock =
        pickHighPriced(highestPricedStock, stockPrice)
}
highestPricedStock print
//Top stock is AAPL at price $377.41
```

Let's walk through the code to see what we did.

First we create an instance of ArrayBuffer, which is a mutable collection. We invoke the getPrice() function for each ticker and populate the stockPrices ArrayBuffer with the StockPrice instances.

Second, we iterate over these stock prices and pick only stocks that are valued less than $500 and add to the stockPricesLessThan500 ArrayBuffer. This results in possibly fewer elements than we started with.

Finally, we loop through the second collection to pick the stock that is valued the highest among them, again mutating the highestPricedStock variable as we navigate the collection using the external iterator.

We can improve on this code further, use multiple collections if we desire, wrap the code into separate functions, and put them into a class if we like. However, that will not affect the fundamental approach we took: imperative style with mutable data structure. The state of the collection of stocks and their prices went through quite a few mutations.

Now let's write this code in functional style. Ready?

```
tickers map getPrice filter isNotOver500 reduce pickHighPriced print
```

We're done. That's it, small enough to fit in a tweet. OK, this conciseness does take some getting used to. Let's walk through it.

`tickers map getPrice` first transforms the collection of `tickers` into a collection of `StockPrice` instances. For each ticker symbol, we now have the name and price in this collection. The `filter` function then applies the `isNotOver500` on that collection and transforms that into a smaller collection of `StockPrices` with only stocks whose prices do not exceed $500. The `reduce` function takes that further to pick the highest-priced stock, which we finally hand over to the `print` method of `StockPrice`.

In addition to being concise, the code does not mutate any state. The state goes through transformations as it flows through the composed functions.

Granted that this functional code is elegant and concise, but what about other considerations, like ease of debugging and performance? These are two concerns I often see raised.

What About Debugging and Performance?

From the debugging point of view, functional style is a winner. Since there are no mutable states, there are fewer opportunities for errors than in code with several mutable parts. We can write unit tests on each of the intermediate steps separately and also on the collective results. We can step through the code individually or collectively. We can also store the intermediate values in immutable `vals` along the way so we can examine those.

But what about performance? Surely immutability comes at a cost of performance? Well, if the collection is fairly small, we won't see any significant performance impact, but if the collection is fairly large, we may indeed face some copy overhead, but don't assume. Languages and libraries may offer optimizations and perform lazy evaluations. It would be a mistake to blindly reject the virtues of functional style in the name of performance. Prototype and see if performance is a concern for what you have to implement. If the performance is adequate, then you have gained from what the paradigm has to offer. If performance is not reasonable, then you can explore options to improve it, and modern functional style offers such options. One such is to use data structures that perform intelligent selective copying to provide close to constant-time copy performance, like `Vector` in Scala.

In the next chapter, we'll see how Scala collections make use of this style to provide a concise and fluent interface.

## CHAPTER 4

Working with Scala Collections

by Venkat Subramaniam

In the preceding chapter, we looked at the object-oriented side and the functional side of Scala. These two programming styles interplay powerfully in *collections*—and that's what we'll see in this chapter.

A direct look at the Scala collections hierarchy[1] can be overwhelming. But when distilled down, each Scala collection can be viewed as belonging to one of two categories: *immutable* or *mutable*. Some Scala collections are also *lazy* (read: efficient).

For starters, in both the immutable and mutable flavors, Scala provides implementations of Seq, Set, and Map. Seqs (lists) are ordered collections, sets are unordered, and maps are collections of key-value pairs.

Immutable Collections

In order to promote programming with no side effects, Scala imports the immutable collections by default. One of the simplest immutable collections is the Scala list.

```
val prices = List(10, 20, 15, 30, 45, 25, 82)
```

We talked earlier about internal and external iterators on page 16. Scala allows us to iterate over the collections using an external iterator (where you control the iteration) or an internal iterator (where you only provide the action to perform for each element).

---

1.   http://www.scala-lang.org/docu/files/collections-api/collections.html

So, to print each of the elements in the list we created, we can use either

```
for(price <- prices) { println(price) }
```

or

```
prices.foreach { price => println(price) }
```

(or the concise form: prices foreach println)

Collections provide a wealth of functions to manipulate them. Here's how we can get the first element from the list:

```
println("The first price is " + prices(0))
```

In Java, we're used to the array syntax instance[index] to access elements and instance.get(index) to access elements from an ArrayList. In Scala we use instance(index). That's the syntax, but what's going on behind the scenes? Recall that Scala does not have operators, and performs operations using methods. Scala has two special methods, apply and update, that can go into stealth mode. So when you write instance(param), you are really calling instance.apply(param). For a collection, apply takes an index and returns the value at that position. Similarly, instead of writing instance.update(param) = value, you can write instance(param) = value. For a collection, the update method takes an index and returns a reference to the object at that position.

So to access the fifth element, we can write

```
println("The fifth element is " + prices.apply(4))
```

or, in short,

```
println("The fifth element is " + prices(4))
```

We could use this approach with the imperative style to select elements. However, functional style and internal iterators really shine for this operation as well. To select the first price greater than 40, we can write

```
println("First price > 40 is " + prices.find { price => price > 40 })
```

When we run this, the output will be

```
First price > 40 is Some(45)
```

OK, what's going on here? We expected 45, but instead got Some(45). This is Scala taking an extra step to protect us from accidental NullPointerExceptions. If there is no price greater than 40, instead of returning null and expecting us to remember to do the null check, Scala returns an Option type. The option may either be None (non-existent—think of this like DBNull) or a Some value. So, we're forced to consider the case where there may not be a valid value in response to the function call.

If we'd like all values greater than 40, we can write

```
println("All prices > 40 are " + prices.filter { price => price > 40 })
```

While find picks the first matching element, filter picks all matching elements.

The collection API is quite comprehensive. If we want to know if any element is greater than 90, we'd write

```
println("Any > 90: " + prices.exists { price => price > 90 })
```

To know if all the elements are less than 90, we'd write

```
println("All < 90: " + prices.forall { price => price < 90 })
```

If the previous prices represent prices for some items in another list

```
val items = List("A", "B", "C", "D", "E", "F", "G")
```

we can combine these two quite easily

```
println("items and prices: " + items.zip(prices))
```

to get

```
items and prices:
    List((A,10), (B,20), (C,15), (D,30), (E,45), (F,25), (G,82))
```

All these operations on a list (those above and a lot more) leave the list unmodified. If we want a new list, we will have to get a copy. For example, if we want to add a price to the beginning of the list, we'd write

```
val theNewPricesList = 5 :: prices
println(theNewPricesList)
println(prices)
```

The new prices list we created will have the element 5 at the beginning, followed by the elements from the old list. The old list, prices, however, is not affected.

Immutability here means we made a copy of the list, so you will naturally wonder, does that mean poor performance? As we suggested on page 21, not necessarily. In the preceding example, we add the new element to the head of the list. Scala List is smart enough to share the entire prices list in the creation of the theNewPricesList. Under the hood, the new collection theNewPricesList has one element (5) followed by a reference to the head of the prices list. So, even though it appeared to be a full copy, the list smartly avoided the overhead and reused the existing list in the creation of the new list.

So, the cost of creating a list with a new element in the head position is constant. However, that's not the cost if we want to insert the new element in any position other than the head. Such simple sharing of the existing list will not work for other positions. Fortunately, Scala collection provides Vector. This is an implementation of Phil Bagwell's *tries*, a smartly designed data structure (known as persistent data structures because their contents are immutable or persist over time) that allows efficient partial copying of elements to provide practically constant-time performance.

Tries are tree structures with large branching factors; each node has 32 or more children. So, a trie that's only four levels deep can hold a million elements. The nodes are referenced using a special convention: the path to the nodes represents the keys. If the keys are numbers, the trie forms a list. For other keys, the trie would represent a hashmap.

Tries make shallow copies and share most of the subbranches when an element is inserted or removed. So, using Vectors, which are immutable, we can insert (or remove) elements at any position, and a copy is made for us with constant-time performance.

Let's create a vector of prices.

```
val prices2 = Vector(10, 20, 15, 30, 45, 25, 82)
```

On this Vector, we can perform pretty much all the iterations, find, filter, and zip operations we did with lists.

To create a new vector with an additional element at the head of the vector, we can write

```
val theNewPricesList2 = 5 +: prices2
```

To create a new vector with an additional element at the end of the vector, we can write

```
val theNewPricesList3 = prices2 :+ 85
```

If we only want to create new collections with elements added to the head, a list is adequate. However, for inserts or appends, prefer a Vector. For example, to append an element to a list of a million elements on my machine, it took 0.25 seconds, while it took only 25 microseconds for a vector of the same size.

To store a key-value pair or a dictionary, we can use a Map implementation.

```
val langs = Map("Java" -> "Gosling", "Scala" -> "Odersky")
println("Scala was created by " + langs("Scala"))
```

The map created this way is immutable. We can create new maps like so:

```
println(langs + (("Lisp", "McCarthy")))
```

This new map will contain the key-values in the old map, plus the new key-value pair. Maps provide several convenience functions just like List and Vector.

Mutable Collections

We've only discussed immutable collections so far. As mentioned, we get this capability by default. To create mutable collections, we have to do an explicit import or reference to the class name.

```
val capitals =
  scala.collection.mutable.Map("New York" -> "Albany", "Texas" -> "Austin")
println(capitals)

capitals("Oregon") = "Salem"
println("After change: " + capitals)
```

The output from the preceding code is

```
Map(Texas -> Austin, New York -> Albany)
After change: Map(Oregon -> Salem, Texas -> Austin, New York -> Albany)
```

Unlike its immutable counterpart, the mutable version of the map provides ways to insert and remove keys from the collection. Likewise, a ListBuffer allows mutation as well.

From the concurrency point of view, immutable collections offer thread safety compared to the mutable versions. We have to select the appropriate implementation based on our need—both in terms of what the collections should do for us and the performance we desire out of them.

Lazy Collections

Scala also provides lazy collections, which allow us to postpone the creation to just in time or on-demand. This allows us to express some algorithms or logic in very succinct manner. Let's see how laziness can be useful.

The following code will help us determine if a given number is prime:

```
def isPrime(number : Int) = {
  val sqrtOfNumber = math.sqrt(number).toInt
  val hasFactorsOtherThan1AndItself =
    (2 to sqrtOfNumber).exists { i => number % i == 0 }
  number > 1 && !hasFactorsOtherThan1AndItself
}
```

Suppose we need to determine a list of prime numbers. We could express it like this:

```
//Won't work
def primes(number : Int) : List[Int] = {
  if(isPrime(number)) number :: primes(number + 1)
    else  primes(number + 1)
}
```

Given a number, we determine if it is a prime number. If it's prime, we prepend it to the list of all prime numbers greater than that number. Otherwise, we simply exclude that number and return all greater prime numbers. The code is quite expressive, but won't work. As we ask the primes to be computed, the code will enter into an uncontrolled recursion and fail with a StackOverflowError.

It would be useful if the list of primes could be expressed as above, but the list itself was not computed until we asked for a specific number of elements. Enter the lazy collection called Stream. Let's change the code to use a Stream.

```
def primes(number : Int) : Stream[Int] = {
  if(isPrime(number)) number #:: primes(number + 1) else primes(number + 1)
}

println(primes(1).take(10).toList)
```

In this version we replaced the List[Int] with Stream[Int] and the prepend operator :: of List with the operator #:: for Stream.

When we invoke the primes function with a parameter of 1, the code runs until it hits the first call to #:: and pauses, deferring the computation of the collection to a later time. When we invoke the take(10), we are asking the first ten elements of the collection to be returned. At this time, the Stream will execute the deferred code enough times to fill the collection to the requested count. The output from the preceding code is

```
List(2, 3, 5, 7, 11, 13, 17, 19, 23, 29)
```

The lazy list gives us two benefits. The code is highly expressive, and we're deferring computations until needed.

Here we used a special collection Stream instead of List. Streams exist to represent lazy collections, but the Scala API also provides easy ways to make straight collections into lazy ones. For this, we use view.

Now, let's consider a list of names and a function to determine the length of each name.

```
val names = List("Steve", "Susan", "Mac", "Brad", "Gill")

def len(n : String) = {
  println("Len for " + n)
  (n, n.length)
}
```

Suppose we want to create a tuple with the name and length, but then extract only the first name of a certain length. Here's the code for that, using the len function and the functions of the list.

```
println(names map len find { e => e._2 == 3 })
```

The function len returns a tuple, and the find function is asked to select a tuple where the second value (length) is 3. The output from the preceding code is shown next.

```
Len for Steve
Len for Susan
Len for Mac
Len for Brad
Len for Gill
Some((Mac,3))
```

The len function was evaluated for each element and then the find function was evaluated for the first three values, until it yielded true.

Using a lazy collection, we can eliminate wasted calls to the len function. It hardly takes any effort, as you can see next.

```
println(names.view map len find { e => e._2 == 3 })
```

The output from the preceding code is:

```
Len for Steve
Len for Susan
Len for Mac
Some((Mac,3))
```

The call to view turned the names list into a lazy collection. When you called map on the collection, rather than executing the given function, len, it cached away that computation for some later time. When find was invoked on the result, this was a call on a lazy collection that was produced by the call to map. So, rather than executing each function entirely from left to right on all the elements of the collection, the lazy collection executed them left to right entirely on one element, deciding along the way if it had to continue or not. So the computation was short-circuited and no further computation was done once find succeeded, selecting an element.

We've merely scratched the surface of the Scala collections API. Familiarize yourself with other classes and functions provided based on what your application may need or where your interests take you.

What's next? Well, so far we have *used* functions that accepted other functions. In the next chapter, we will see how we can create such functions.

## CHAPTER 5

Creating Higher-Order Functions in Scala

by Venkat Subramaniam

In Chapter 3, *Scala and Functional Style*, on page 15, we discussed higher-order functions in functional programming, and in Chapter 4, *Working with Scala Collections*, on page 23, we looked at the higher-order functions in the Scala collections API. In this chapter, we'll learn how to write our own higher-order functions.

Higher-order functions can accept other functions as parameters, can return functions, and can allow you to create functions within functions. In Scala, these functions that can be passed around are called *function values*.

You know that in OO programming, classes (or objects) abstract and encapsulate behavior and data. Well, function values also abstract and encapsulate behavior, but rather than holding on to state, they can help transform state.

Let's look at two examples where function values come in handy.

Creating a Higher-Order Function

Continuing with the stock prices example, you're asked to write a function that will total the prices given in a collection. You figure a simple iteration is sufficient, and you write:

```
val prices = List(10, 20, 15, 30, 45, 25, 82)

def totalAllPrices(prices : List[Int]) = {
  prices.foldLeft(0) { (total, price) =>
    total + price
  }
}
```

In the totalAllPrices function, the foldLeft method of the list is used to compute the total in a functional style with pure immutability. You pass a function value to the foldLeft method. This function value accepts two parameters and returns the total of these two parameters. The foldLeft method invokes the function value as many times as the number of elements in the list. The first time, total and price are bound to the value 0 (passed in as parameter to the foldLeft method) and the first element in the list, respectively. In the second call, total is bound to the total returned from the previous call to the function value, and price is bound to the second element in the collection. The foldLeft function iterates this sequence of calls for the remaining elements in the collection.

Exercise your totalAllPrices function to see the result.

```
println("Total of prices is " + totalAllPrices(prices))
//Total of prices is 227
```

Before you could declare this done, you're asked to write one more function, to total only prices that are greater than a given value. Clearly you could reuse most of the code from that little function you just wrote. Looking at your watch (you have those pesky meetings to attend), you say to yourself, "There's a reason God created copy and paste," and you end up with the following function:

```
def totalOfPricesOverValue(prices : List[Int], value : Int) = {
  prices.foldLeft(0) { (total, price) =>
    if (price > value) total + price else total
  }
}
```

Sadly, the demand for features seems to be relentless today, and you're asked for yet another function, this time to total only prices that are *less* than a given value. You know that copying and pasting code is morally wrong, but you decide to just make it work for now and refactor it to make it better right after that meeting you have to run to.

Right after the meeting, you stare at the following version of the code:

```
val prices = List(10, 20, 15, 30, 45, 25, 82)

def totalAllPrices(prices : List[Int]) = {
  prices.foldLeft(0) { (total, price) =>
    total + price
  }
}

def totalOfPricesOverValue(prices : List[Int], value : Int) = {
  prices.foldLeft(0) { (total, price) =>
    if (price > value) total + price else total
  }
}
```

```
def totalOfPricesUnderValue(prices : List[Int], value : Int) = {
  prices.foldLeft(0) { (total, price) =>
    if (price < value) total + price else total
  }
}
```

Let's exercise it.

```
println("Total of prices is " + totalAllPrices(prices))
//Total of prices is 227
```

```
println("Total of prices over 40 is " +
 totalOfPricesOverValue(prices, 40))
//Total of prices over 40 is 127
```

```
println("Total of prices under 40 is " +
 totalOfPricesUnderValue(prices, 40))
//Total of prices under 40 is 100
```

You have good intentions to make it work and make it better, but you want to quickly refactor it to remove the duplications before your colleagues accuse you of revealing your dark side through this code. Function values to the rescue here.

If you slightly modify the first function, to if (true) total + price, then you notice the only difference between the three function bodies is the conditional expression in the if statement. You can extract this condition as a function value.

This extracted function value would accept an Int as parameter and return a Boolean. You can express this as a mapping or transformation from Int to Boolean, or selector : Int => Boolean. Just as prices : List[Int] represents a reference prices of type List[Int], selector : Int => Boolean represents a reference selector of type function value that accepts an Int and returns a Boolean.

Now you can replace the three previous functions with one function:

```
def totalPrices(prices : List[Int],
 selector : Int => Boolean) = {

  prices.foldLeft(0) { (total, price) =>
    if (selector(price)) total + price else total
  }
}
```

The function totalPrices accepts as parameter a collection and a function value. Within the function, in the if condition, you call the function value with the price as parameter. If the selector function value returns a true, you add that price to the total; ignore the price otherwise.

Exercise the code and ensure that this version produces the same result as the three functions in the earlier version.

```
println("Total of prices is " +
  totalPrices(prices, { price => true }))
//Total of prices is 227

println("Total of prices over 40 is " +
  totalPrices(prices, { price => price > 40 }))
//Total of prices over 40 is 127

println("Total of prices under 40 is " +
  totalPrices(prices, { price => price < 40 }))
//Total of prices under 40 is 100
```

You pass both the collection and the function value as parameters, within the parentheses (), to the totalPrices function. You can also pass the function value outside of the parentheses; however, you have to do a bit more work for that.

Multiple Parameter Lists

It's time to meet *multiple parameter lists*. We're mostly used to single parameter lists with multiple parameters. However, in Scala you can also have multiple parameter lists, each with multiple parameters.

```
def totalPrices(
  prices : List[Int])(selector : Int => Boolean) = {
  prices.foldLeft(0) { (total, price) =>
    if (selector(price)) total + price else total
  }
}
```

In this version of the totalPrices function, rather than accepting two parameters in one parameter list, you have two parameter lists, each with one parameter. This allows you to invoke the method using the following syntax:

```
totalPrices(prices) { price => price > 40 }
```

You're attaching the function call to the end of the method call, like it is a parasite (in a good way) on the totalPrices function. This syntax is a common way to pass function values to functions.

Scala allows you to pass function names in place of function values. So, if you have to pass the same function value to multiple functions, you have a few options, as shown here:

```
Console println "Total of prices over 40 is " +
  totalPrices(prices) { price => price > 40 }
//Total of prices over 40 is 127
```

```
val returnTrue = { price : Int => true }
Console println "Total of prices is " +
 totalPrices(prices)(returnTrue)
//Total of prices is 227

def isLessThan40(price : Int) = price < 40

Console println "Total of prices under 40 is " +
  totalPrices(prices) { isLessThan40 }
  //Total of prices under 40 is 100
```

In the first call to totalPrices, you pass a just-in-time created function value. In the second call, you pass returnTrue, which is an immutable reference to a function value. In the third call, you use yet another way: you pass a function as a function value. You can use either the () or the {} syntax to pass returnTrue and isLessThan40.

You saw different ways to create function values and pass them to functions. Let's take a look at one more example of the use of function values.

Function Values and the Loan Pattern

Suppose you have a Resource class:

```
class Resource {
  println("Creating Resource")

  def someop1() { println("someop1") }
  def someop2() { println("someop2") }

  def close() { println("cleaning-up...") }
}
```

If an instance of Resource takes up significant resources outside the JVM, like database connections, open files, handles to external systems with significant memory usage, and so on, you'd want to clean up the resource quickly after use. You can't rely on the JVM's garbage collector (GC), as you can't predict when it would run, and your memory usage within the JVM may be too low to trigger the GC reasonably soon to clean up the external resources. Users of your class may be tempted to write code like this:

```
val resource = new Resource
resource.someop1()
resource.someop2()
//forgot to call close

//Creating Resource
//someop1
//someop2
```

In this case, forgetful programmers like me will omit the call to the close method. Even if they remember, a simple call to close is not sufficient. An exception before the code reaches close will prevent proper cleanup. So the right way to approach this would be:

```
val resource = new Resource
try {
  resource.someop1()
  resource.someop2()
} finally {
  resource.close()
}
//Creating Resource
//someop1
//someop2
//cleaning-up...
```

This is too verbose and taxes the forgetful programmers even more each time an instance of your Resource class is created.

(As an aside, Java 7 has a feature named Automatic Resource Management [ARM] to make this less verbose; however, it still requires the programmers to remember to do the right thing.)

If the resource has to be cleaned up quickly, why not do it for the programmers rather than expecting them to remember? You can do that using function values.

You can (kindly) force the programmer to use your class in a certain way, so they don't have to suffer the consequences of forgetting, but instead can be guided by the compiler to do the right thing.

First, let's make the constructor private. This will prevent the users of your class from creating an arbitrary instance. Make the close method private as well; that way they don't have to worry about calling it, as you'll take care of it. That leaves only the instance functions like someop1() and someop2() public.

```
class Resource private {
  println("Creating Resource")

  def someop1() { println("someop1") }
  def someop2() { println("someop2") }

  private def close() { println("cleaning-up...") }
}
```

With this change, calls like new Resource() will result in a compilation error. It's time to manage the creation and cleanup of the instances of Resource.

```
object Resource {
  def use[T](block : Resource => T) = {
    val resource = new Resource
    try {
      block(resource)
    } finally {
      resource.close()
    }
  }
}
```

You created a companion object for the Resource class. The use method accepts a function value, called block, as a parameter and returns whatever the block returns. You specify that the block should receive an instance of Resource and may return anything, expressed as parametric type T.

Within the use method, you create an instance of Resource. Remember companion objects have full access to the companion class, so the constructor and the close method being private is not an issue from within here. Then within the safe haven of the try-finally statements, you pass the Resource instance to the function value. In the finally block, you call close to clean up the instance.

Users of your Resource can now use an instance and have it automatically cleaned up with ease, as follows:

```
Resource.use { resource =>
  resource.someop1()
  resource.someop2()
}
//Creating Resource
//someop1
//someop2
//cleaning-up
```

By using the function value, you've made it easy for the programmers to do the right thing. They don't have to endure the consequences of forgetting to clean up; you've done it for them. This approach is called the *loan pattern*, and it also goes by the name *execute around method pattern*. Next time you write a method, add a little spice to your code, and see how you can benefit from function values.

JVM-based Scala bridges the gap from object-oriented to functional programming, allowing developers to work in the style they prefer, and even mix and match within a program. In the next four chapters, you'll see a different approach, and see how Clojure brings a purer functional style to the JVM.

Part III

Clojure: The New Lisp

Rich Hickey worked for years to connect the Lisp language with Java before developing Clojure. In Clojure he has created a modern Lisp for functional programming that works with the Java infrastructure. Walmart is among the big companies using Clojure for data management.

## CHAPTER 6

An Interview with Rich Hickey

by Michael Swaine

Clojure is one of the most interesting new languages to arrive on the scene. It's an elegant, clean, modern version of Lisp that was created for functional programming, designed for concurrency, and, like Scala, compiles into JVM bytecode.

Clojure addresses the issues that have held Lisp back (libraries, readability, performance) while preserving its virtues. But what's stirring all the interest in Clojure is its potential for concurrent programming. As Stuart Halloway and Aaron Bedra point out,[1] "Massively multi-core hardware is right around the corner, and functional languages provide a clear approach for taking advantage of it." This is the application for which Clojure was created, so we knew we had to talk with its creator, Rich Hickey.

Why Clojure?

MS: *I really appreciate your giving this time, Rich. I want to focus on basically one question: why Clojure? For programmers in various situations, I want to ask: what's in it for me? Why should I want to read about Clojure? Why should I invest the time to learn it? How would it benefit me to program in Clojure?*

RH: *Sure thing.*

MS: *Cool. So say I'm an independent software developer and while maybe I'm not personally feeling the pain of the economic crunch, I do see signs that the nature of my client list may be changing. I want to be constantly learning new languages and technologies that broaden my options. Why should Clojure be on my short list of career-enhancing technologies?*

---

1. *Programming Clojure (2nd edition) [HB12].*

RH: If you have not yet experienced functional programming, Clojure may offer the most approachable way to do so. Some have called it "the Python of functional programming," and I'll accept anything good that implies. Its seamless access to the Java ecosystem means you'll never be at a loss for libraries, and your applications can be delivered in an accepted environment. Clojure is new, but not disconnected. The infrastructure underlying it, the JVM, is excellent technology.

MS: The argument for functional languages these days is all about multicore processors and concurrent programming. Let's say I know something about functional programming and in fact have some very specific need for a functional language for concurrent programming. Why is Clojure that language?

RH: Clojure is designed for concurrent programming, and specifically advocates that a functional style and pervasive immutability are prerequisites for concurrency. The data structures are immutable, and the locals are not "variable." However, Clojure also recognizes the need for state in real applications, and provides language-supported mechanisms for managing state that avoid the locks-and-deadlocks headaches commonly found in other languages. Among functional languages (Haskell, ML, etc.), Clojure is relatively unusual in being dynamically typed, and in being connected to a mainstream infrastructure.

The Infrastructure

MS: Let's talk about that infrastructure. Say I'm a Java developer. I'm not afraid to learn a new language, but I'm not about to abandon the whole Java ecosystem. What does Clojure offer me?

RH: Clojure lets you do just that—learn something new and not give up your investment and knowledge. That's true of all of the JVM languages, though—Groovy, JRuby, Scala, etc. Clojure is unique there in giving you the performance of a compiled language and the flexibility of a dynamic language. Performance is closer to Java than to Python. Access to Java from Clojure, and Clojure from Java, is easy, wrapper-free, and fast.

MS: Clojure's performance may be close to raw Java, but the experience of programming in Clojure is very un-Java-like.

RH: Clojure may be the most different from Java of the popular JVM languages, and it is so for a reason—we are going to have to do things differently if we are going to leverage multicore, and our large OO programs have become spaghetti. If you really want to learn something new, rather than just do what you are currently doing slightly differently, Clojure is a good choice.

MS: OK, imagine you're talking to an old Lisp hacker from way back, which in fact you are. And let's say that I've moved on. Performance, libraries, fitting in with the crowd—for some reason, I left Lisp. Why is Clojure the reason for me to get back into it?

RH: As a Lisp dialect, Clojure offers everything you love about Lisp—interactive development, elegance, succinctness, extensibility, expressiveness. It is aimed *squarely at those areas that had caused people to leave, or not be able to use, Lisp in the past, in particular the library and poor citizenship issues. It is poised to leverage the huge amount of work done in Java, and in turn be leveraged by Java programs. In addition, Clojure moves Lisp forward in incorporating some of the best ideas developed over the years—building the core library on interface-based abstractions, lazy sequences, first-class associative data structures, etc. Lisps have been called functional programming languages, but Clojure embraces that more deeply than do Common Lisp or Scheme.*

MS: *Clojure is now at version one point something. That can mean different things. Beyond being good for exploring functional programming, is Clojure ready for prime time? Say I want to use it right now for production work. How solid is Clojure?*

RH: *Clojure is quite solid. It has a very small core that rarely changes, and thousands of users pounding on it. It integrates with the Java tool ecosystem, so JVM debuggers, profilers, etc. work right out of the box. And IDE integration efforts are well underway, with good plugins for NetBeans and IntelliJ.*

Compared to What?

MS: *Let's try some direct comparisons. Say I've devoted some time to learning Erlang. Why should I choose Clojure over Erlang?*

RH: *I'm loathe to engage in us vs. them, especially with Erlang, which I quite admire. If you truly have an application for which Erlang is best suited—for example, a low-level distributed communications app with high uptime requirements—it's hard to beat it. Clojure is more of a general-purpose language, has better compute performance, better in-process SMP concurrency support, and a much better library and interoperability story. For distribution, you can choose from many techniques and tools, including message queues, some of which are written in...Erlang.*

MS: *All right, the same question for the new Scala developer. Why should I choose Clojure over Scala?*

RH: *Clojure is simpler. It is dynamic. Having fewer paradigms to support, it is more focused on being functional. Being a Lisp, it has a regular syntax, and syntactic extensions are very consistent. Not being object-oriented, Clojure libraries have a different structure, encouraging a greater use of generic data structures, yielding higher interoperability. Clojure is based on the idea that immutability and functional programming are more important contributors to program robustness than is static typing. If these values resonate with you, you will likely prefer Clojure, but I certainly expect Clojure and Scala to peacefully coexist.*

MS: *Well, you've convinced me that Clojure is worth a look. Thank you for taking the time to chat with us.*

RH: *Sure. This was a good exercise. Thanks for suggesting it.*

In the next chapters, Michael Bevilacqua-Linn will introduce you to functional programming in Clojure, beginning by looking at its roots in Lisp.

## CHAPTER 7

Getting Clojure: Why Lisp Still Matters

by Michael Bevilacqua-Linn

Clojure is a dynamically typed, practical programming language that targets the JVM and other modern runtimes. It is a language in the Lisp tradition, and in this chapter we'll examine one of the things that makes Clojure—along with other Lisps—special.

Lisp is the second oldest high-level programming language. It was originally created in 1958 by John McCarthy, and has gone through more than fifty years of evolution. One of the most recent branches of this evolution is Clojure, a fairly new language targeted at working programmers.

Newcomers to Lisp—Clojure newbies included—are often put off by what seems like a strange syntax. Those oddly placed parentheses—and so many of them!

Given that Lisp's syntax actually has proven to be a barrier to widespread adoption, why would anyone decide to create a new Lisp in this day and age?

It turns out that the choice of syntax isn't arbitrary. It enables the most powerful metaprogramming system yet created. It's powerful enough that the majority of the language is implemented using it. Looking at it another way, a Clojure developer has the power of a compiler writer at their fingertips.

The REPL

A good way to get to know this system is to start with Clojure's interactive programming environment, the Read Eval Print Loop, or REPL.

You know what a REPL is: a user of the REPL types some code. The REPL reads it in, turning it from a string into another data structure. That data structure is then evaluated to produce a value, which is printed. Finally, the REPL loops back to the beginning, waiting for new input.

You will find instructions for installing a REPL in Chapter 20, *Clojure's Exceptional*, on page 163.

Let's start off in the classic style by running "hello, world" in the REPL.

```
=> (println "hello, world")
hello, world
nil
```

If we'd like to add two numbers together, the syntax looks the same. Here, we add 21 and 21.

```
=> (+ 21 21)
42
```

Even creating a function follows the same syntax. Here, we create a say-hello, which just prints "hello, pragmatic programmers".

```
=> (defn say-hello [] "hello, pragmatic programmers")
#'matters/say-hello
=> (say-hello)
"hello, pragmatic programmers"
```

There's a subtle difference between these examples, and it points to the important matter of evaluation. In the first example, we saw "hello, world" printed, followed by nil. In the second and third, there was no nil, and we only saw the results 42 and #'matters/say-hello, respectively.

The Eval in REPL takes our code and executes it. Evaluating a bit of code will always produce a value. Since a call to println has no interesting value, it being executed only to print something, nil is returned. Our other two examples do have interesting values: the value of two numbers added together and the name of a function we just defined.

Let's dig into the notion of evaluation in a bit more detail. We'll build up a simple model of how it works. Most things in Clojure evaluate to themselves. For instance, here we evaluate the integer 1 and string "foo" in the REPL.

```
=> 1
1
=> "foo"
"foo"
```

Some things don't evaluate to themselves, like the calls to println and + we saw earlier. With those, the arguments were first evaluated and then passed into the println function or + operator.

This is a bit more clear if we nest some calls, as we do below. First (* 10 2) is evaluated to get 20, then (+ 22 20) is evaluated to get the final value of 42.

```
=> (+ 22 (* 10 2))
42
```

We can nest these calls arbitrarily deep, by adding one more layer in the following snippet.

```
=> (+ 22 (* 10 (/ 4 2)))
42
```

Occasionally, it may be handy to turn off evaluation. We can do so by prepending our snippet of code with a single quote, as we demonstrate here.

```
=> '(+ 1 1)
(+ 1 1)
```

Now that we've got a better idea of what Clojure evaluation is, let's take a closer look at what's getting evaluated. When we type something into the REPL, we're typing in a series of characters, a string. This isn't what ultimately gets evaluated by Clojure. Instead, these characters are first passed into the R in REPL, the reader.

The reader takes a series of characters and turns them into some other data structure. To understand this a bit better, let's take a quick detour into a couple of Clojure's built-in data structures: vectors and keywords.

Vectors and Keywords

Keywords are used much as we would use a keyword in Ruby or an enum in Java, and are prepended with a colon.

```
=> :foo
:foo
```

Vectors give us fast positional access to their elements. They can be created by placing the elements of the vector inside of square brackets. We create a vector and name it some-keywords in the following snippet.

```
=> (def some-keywords [:foo :bar :baz])
#'matters/some-keywords
```

We can use first to get the first element of a vector.

```
=> (first some-keywords)
:foo
```

In the preceding example, the actions of the reader take place behind the scenes, as part of the REPL. Let's make things a bit more explicit by using read-string. This takes a string directly and reads it. Here, we're using it to read in a new vector and name it some-more-keywords.

```
=> (def some-more-keywords (read-string "[:foo :bar :baz]"))
#'matters/some-more-keywords
```

We can treat it just as we did our original vector.

```
=> (first some-more-keywords)
:foo
```

So far, the reader might remind you of something like JSON or YAML. It takes a string and turns it into some more complicated, probably nested, data structure. That's not far off, but something about it might strike you as odd. Here I am claiming that the Read in REPL reads in *data* that we can manipulate in our code, much like JSON or YAML parser would.

But aren't we typing code into the REPL? How does that work?

To find out, let's take a look at another Clojure data structure, the list. In Clojure, as in other Lisps, a list is a singly linked list. One way to create a list is to use list, as we do in the following code snippet.

```
=> (def a-list (list :foo :bar :baz))
#'matters/a-list
```

Another way is to simply enclose the list elements in round braces. Here we do that using read-string this time, just as we did with our earlier vector.

```
=> (def another-list (read-string "(:foo :bar :baz)"))
#'matters/another-list
```

These two lists are equivalent.

```
=> (first a-list)
:foo
=> (first another-list)
:foo
=> (= a-list another-list)
true
```

Let's take a look at another list. Here, we create a list with three elements: the symbol + and the integers 21 and 21.

```
=> (def funky-looking-list (read-string "(+ 21 21)"))
#'matters/funky-looking-list
```

And here, we use the first function to get the first element.

```
=> (first funky-looking-list)
+
```

Our first two list examples just contain keywords; our final one obviously contains code! Clojure code is just Clojure data, a property known as homoiconicity.

The evaluation rule that we hinted at earlier for function calls *is actually the evaluation rule for lists*. We can see this by evaluating funky-looking-list manually, as we do in the following snippet.

```
=> (eval funky-looking-list)
42
```

Because Clojure code is just Clojure data, we can manipulate it just as we would any other data. This gives us, the humble application or framework programmer, an incredible amount of power.

Macros

To see how, we'll need to understand Clojure's macro system. A macro is a special kind of function. It's intended to take a piece of data that represents code, also known as a form. A macro transforms one form into another before Clojure's compiler compiles it. Finally, the evaluation rule for a macro is special in that a macro does not evaluate its arguments.

Let's take a look at a simple macro. This macro takes two arguments, a name and a string to print. It then creates a function that prints the passed-in string.

```
(defmacro make-printer [name to-print]
  (list 'defn name [] (list 'println to-print)))
```

Here we'll use it to create a function named foo.

```
=> (make-printer foo "this is a foo")
#'matters/foo

=> (foo)
this is a foo
nil
```

If we'd like to see what this macro expands out to, we can use macroexpand-1 on a call to it, as we do in the following code.

```
=> (macroexpand-1 '(make-printer foo "foo"))
(defn foo [] (println "foo"))
```

In make-printer we constructed the list that our function definition consists of using list and '. Clojure has a feature that makes this easier: *syntax quote*, represented by a single backtick.

Syntax quote is much like regular quote. The main difference is that it allows us to turn evaluation back on inside of it using unquote, represented by a tilde. In addition, syntax quote will fully qualify any symbols it comes across, which helps avoid a common pitfall in macro writing known as unintentional name capture.

Here, we've got a simple use of syntax quote. As we can see, it evaluates the inner forms (+ 1 2) and (+ 3 4) as we've applied unquote to them, but leaves the outer form unevaluated.

```
=> `(+ ~(+ 1 2) ~(+ 3 4))
(clojure.core/+ 3 7)
```

Syntax quote is useful because it allows us to write macros that look like templates for the code that they'll generate. For instance, here's our make-printer rewritten to use syntax quote.

```
(defmacro make-printer-2 [name to-print]
  `(defn ~name [] (println ~to-print)))
```

And here's what it expands out to.

```
=> (macroexpand-1 '(make-printer-2 foo "foo"))
(clojure.core/defn foo [] (clojure.core/println "foo"))
```

Much of Clojure's core functionality is built using macros. For instance, defn expands to def and fn, as we show below.

```
=> (macroexpand-1 '(defn say-hello [] "hello, pragmatic programmers"))
(def say-hello (clojure.core/fn ([] "hello, pragmatic programmers")))
```

In summary: Clojure code is just Clojure data. We can use the macro system and syntax quote to write code templates that look like the code they generate. This makes macro programming, an inherently difficult activity, about as easy as it'll ever get. In fact, the macro programming so enabled is powerful enough that much of Clojure's functionality is implemented using it.

A couple of final notes on Eval. First off, the model of Eval that we built up here is incomplete in several ways. Most notably, Clojure supports a form of lazy evaluation, which defers the evaluation of a form until it's needed. Second, it's tempting to think that the Eval in other languages, such as JavaScript, is the same as the Eval in a Lisp like Clojure.

Don't be fooled by those imitators! In JavaScript and most other languages, Eval operates on strings. This means writing any significant program must be done by string manipulation, an extremely error-prone and difficult proposition for large problems.

In the next chapter, we'll examine another thing that makes Clojure special. Clojure has a unique, intuitive view on state and identity that makes it ideal for concurrent programming.

## CHAPTER 8

Identity, Value, and State in Clojure

by Michael Bevilacqua-Linn

In the preceding chapter, we took a look at one language feature that makes Clojure special: its Lisp-style macro system and the syntax that enables it. This *code as data* style is a very old characteristic of languages in the Lisp family, and Clojure is one modern instance of it.

Clojure's Lisp-style macro system isn't the only trick it's got up its sleeve. In this article, we'll take a look at another one of its defining characteristics. Clojure embodies a novel philosophy on identity, value, and state. While this philosophy makes Clojure uniquely suitable for concurrent programming, I've found that it also reduces the complexity of non-concurrent programs.

In this chapter, we'll explore Clojure's philosophy on identity, value, and state. Then we'll take a look at what this philosophy means for programs without a lot of concurrency, and some of the technology that makes it feasible.

Clojure's approach to identity, value, and state represents a fresh take on some very old computing concepts. Let's start by taking a look at the model Clojure is trying to improve on, the traditional object-oriented approach to state. In one very important way, this approach has a lot more to do with the way computer memory works than with how humans think and model problems.

The Object-Oriented Model

To understand why, let's take a look at simplified computer memory. It consists of a series of eight memory cells, each of which holds a bit of information. Every cell has an *address*, which represents a *place*. You can reach into that place and change what's there, but once you change it, any notion of what was there in the past is lost as shown in the figure on page 52.

Memory Values

1	0	0	1	1	0	0	0
1	2	3	4	5	6	7	8

Memory Address (Places)

To change a value, the bit at a particular location is flipped. For instance, in the following dramatic re-enactment, we change the value at memory location 8 from 0 to 1.

This simplified model is similar to the model presented by even modern computer memory. Modern memory holds many more bits, and the addressing schemes it uses are more complex, but the core model of memory as a series of cells with an address still holds.

One core abstraction we work with as developers in popular object-oriented languages is mutable object references to mutable objects. This makes memory friendlier to work with in many ways. However, in one important respect, the model that they provide is much like the computer memory we just looked at.

Traditional object-oriented models encourage us to program as if we were using places to store our data, just like the cells in our simple memory model. Many object references may refer to the same place; however, if we modify an object through any of those references, *all* of the references may eventually see the modification.

For instance, the following diagram is a simple data model of a person, which represents your humble author. Here, I'm modeled as an object with three references pointing at it, which stand in for Java-style object references. For the sake of the model, let's say I commit a heinous crime involving three yaks, a razor, and an industrial-sized can of shaving cream.

On the run from the law, I need to change my name and address. Doing so using standard object-oriented tools would mutate the object that represents me. This means that my old name and address would be lost, as the following diagram demonstrates!

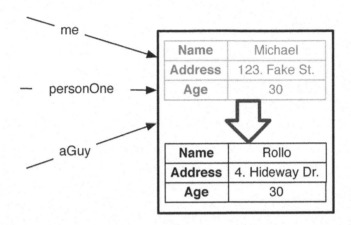

This is *not* how human memory works. Just because I changed my name now, doesn't mean that my past name is just wiped away. We're used to computers working this way, so the strangeness inherent in this model isn't readily apparent to the seasoned developer.

This model can have surprising effects. For instance, let's say that we modified the object through the reference labeled me. What do the other references see?

In the simple case, our program is single-threaded and we might reasonably expect that once the person is modified, all subsequent attempts to view it through any of the references will see the modified value. Even this simple case can be fairly complex, especially for large software systems. Two pieces of code far apart in the codebase may modify the same data without realizing it, which can cause errors that are difficult to debug.

Worst of all is when the references reside in separate threads. In this case, two threads may attempt to modify the person concurrently. This causes all sorts of problems; we'll discuss how Clojure helps solve them in Chapter 9, *Concurrent Programming in Clojure*, on page 59. The traditional solution to these problems involves locks. Programming with locks is notoriously difficult, and has driven many a noble developer to the brink of insanity, or at least a career in marketing.

The Clojure Model

Clojure provides a different model. To explain it, let's revisit the terms *value*, *state*, and *identity* and give them definitions that might be a bit different from the ones you're used to.

In Clojure's world, a *value* is an immutable piece of data, or a composite of immutable pieces of data. This differs from what we might consider a value in most object-oriented languages, where we'd consider both immutable data, such as integers and strings, and mutable data, such as most objects, to be values.

Next up is the notion of an *identity*. An identity is an entity that's associated with a series of values over time. An identity is not a place, like a mutable memory cell, or the mutable objects we saw earlier. Neither is an identity a name, though it may be named, or have several names. For instance, I might refer to myself as "me," but you, gentle reader, might call me "Mike."

Finally, Clojure's idea of *state*: in Clojure's model, state is just the value of an identity at a point in time. This may seem like a strange definition of state at first blush, but it's fairly intuitive. The state of a system is whatever value the system holds when it's queried.

The following figure lays out our first cut at representing my run from the law in our new model. We'd make our person immutable. To change the name and address, we create a new immutable person that starts with the old one as a base. Then when we create a new person, we'd assign our reference to the new person:

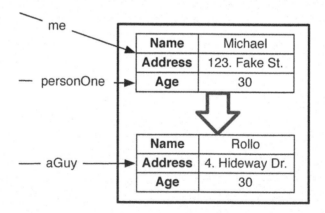

This allows us to have some references refer to the new person and some to the old person, so if one thread is using the data while another thread attempts to modify it, it can simply use the old value.

Persistent Data Structures

The first bits of technology that help make this style of programming a reality are Clojure's persistent data structures, maps, vectors, and sets. A persistent data structure is a data structure that preserves its previous version when it's modified, making it appear to be immutable.

A deep explanation of how Clojure's persistent data structures work is beyond the scope of this article, but let's dig into them just a bit. Closure's persistent data structures use a technique called structural sharing to avoid copying all of the data in the data structure. In addition, behind the scenes they're built on top of trees with very high branching factors.

The upshot of this is that while there is a slight memory and performance penalty associated with Clojure's persistent data structures, they're both memory efficient enough and performant enough for most uses.

Let's take a look at defining a persistent map to represent a person. It's common in Clojure to use a map to carry data, rather than defining a new type as we would in an object-oriented language. We can create a map by putting a series of key-value pairs between curly braces, as we do in the following code snippet.

```
(def mike
  {:name "Michael"
   :address "123 Fake St."
   :age 30})
```

Since the map referred to by mike is immutable, we can't modify it directly. Instead, we can use assoc to create a new, immutable map. The assoc function takes a map-like data structure and a variable number of key-value pairs, and associates them with the map. If the keys have values existing in the map, they are overwritten.

In the following code snippet, we use assoc to create a new map based on the one referred to by mike, and we create a new reference to mike. As we can see, the existing new-mike is not affected.

```
=> (def new-mike (assoc mike :name "Rollo"
                             :address "4 Hideway Dr."))
#'examples/new-mike
=> mike
{:age 30, :name "Michael", :address "123 Fake St."}
=> new-mike
{:age 30, :name "Rollo", :address "4 Hideway Dr."}
```

In addition to the persistent maps we just saw, Clojure has several other persistent data structures—most notably vectors, which give us fast lookup by index and fast appends all while remaining immutable, and sets, which are just immutable versions of normal sets.

Managed Reference Types

Now that we've seen how Clojure handles immutable data, let's revisit the simple model of personasvalue. While it gets at the intuition behind Clojure's approach to state, value, and identity, it's got a fairly large problem. What is responsible for ensuring that the references are updated when the person takes on a new value, or ensures that the reference isn't updated if a thread is working with the current value?

As with all problems in computer science, this can be solved with an additional layer of indirection. Enter the second bit of Clojure technology we'll see: Clojure's managed reference types. Clojure's managed references can sit between an immutable data structure and the references to it and manage state changes. This ensures that all of the references being managed point at the latest value for a given identity.

To see a value, the reference that points to it must be de-referenced. De-referencing returns the state that the reference refers to, which captures it at the point in time it was de-referenced.

The following diagram shows one last model of our person. Here, we've got a managed reference through which our person is accessed. As we can see, this adds an additional layer of indirection. Both the personOne and aGuy references go through the managed references, while the me reference does not:

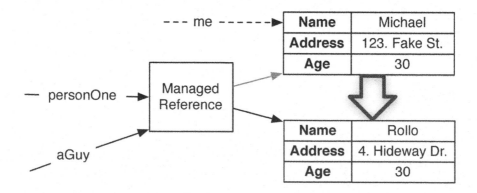

Clojure has several different types of managed references, which are useful for handling different types of concurrency problems. The three types of references we'll go over are atoms, agents, and refs. Atoms are generally all you need when you're not dealing with a highly concurrent problem, so we'll cover them in detail now and we'll go over agents and refs in Chapter 9, *Concurrent Programming in Clojure*, on page 59.

Atoms provide a way to manage independent state synchronously. This means that they're good for managing state that only involves a single managed reference, and where the calling thread wants the changes to happen synchronously.

To create a new atom, we use the atom. To modify the reference and have it so it points at a new value, we can use swap!. The swap! function takes an atom, a function to call on the value it refers to, and additional arguments for the function.

The swap! function then runs the passed-in function on the value of the atom and the additional arguments, returning the new value. This is easiest to see by example. Here, we create an add-to-int-atom, which adds an integer to the atom we just defined.

```
(def int-atom (atom 0))
(defn add-to-int-atom [value]
  (swap! int-atom + value))
```

Now we can use add-to-int-atom to add the number 42 to the number that the atom refers to.

```
=> (add-to-int-atom 42)
42
```

To de-reference the atom, we use the @ symbol. Here, we de-reference it into int-atom-snapshot.

```
=> (def int-atom-snapshot @int-atom)
#'cim-clojure-class.2-state/int-atom-snapshot
=> int-atom-snapshot
42
```

Now we can create another reference, another-int-atom-reference, which refers to the same managed reference that int-atom does.

```
=> (def another-int-atom-reference int-atom)
#'cim-clojure-class.2-state/another-int-atom-reference
=> @another-int-atom-reference
42
```

Now we'll be able to see the results of the addition when we de-reference both int-atom and another-int-atom-reference.

```
=> (add-to-int-atom 68)
110
=> @int-atom
110
=> @another-int-atom-reference
110
```

However, the snapshot we took earlier remains unchanged.

```
=> int-atom-snapshot
42
```

This gives developers an additional degree of control and certainty even in programs without a high degree of concurrency. If you've de-referenced a piece of data from an atom, you can be sure it won't change out from under you. This can be important even in a single-threaded application.

This is because traditional object-oriented programs consist of a graph of mutable data structures. Making a modification at one node in the graph can mutate a piece of data many hops away. Even though these mutations are done through a well-defined interface, this can still lead to the sort of spooky action at a distance most commonly associated with global variables and quantum physics, two fairly obtuse phenomena.

Since Clojure's approach gives us a way to ensure that this action at a distance can't take place, it helps with the non-concurrent case as well as the concurrent one. That said, Clojure's take on value, state, and identity was designed to give the programmer a better model for solving concurrent problems, so in the next chapter we'll take a closer look at them.

We'll dig deeper into atoms, to see how they behave in the face of concurrency, and we'll explore Clojure's other managed reference types. We'll also introduce the *software transactional memory* system that they work in concert with. Together, these form a powerful model for concurrent programming.

## CHAPTER 9

Concurrent Programming in Clojure

by Michael Bevilacqua-Linn

In the previous chapter, we learned about Clojure's take on value, state, and identity. In this chapter, we'll take things a bit further and see how Clojure's philosophy makes it ideal for concurrent programming. As we do so, we'll take a closer look at Clojure's managed references—atoms, agents, and refs —as well as the software transactional memory system they work with.

A concurrent program is one where multiple processes, or threads, may be run in parallel. The main difficulty with concurrent programming is coordinating access to shared resources. As we'll see, this can have strange effects even in seemingly simple situations.

Let's start off with a look at a simple concurrent programming problem in Java. We just want to increment counters from multiple threads running concurrently. We use two counters: the first is a plain old int, and the second is a much more impressive sounding AtomicInteger.

A "Simple" Concurrent Programming Problem

Next, we create a thread pool with five threads in it using Java's ExecutorService, and we submit 10,000 tasks to the service. Each task increments both our normal counter and our atomic counter. The full code snippet follows.

```
public class ConcurrencyExamples {

  private static int counter = 0;
  private static AtomicInteger atomicCounter =
      new AtomicInteger(0);

  public static void main(String[] args)
      throws InterruptedException {
    ExecutorService executors = Executors.newFixedThreadPool(5);
```

```
    for (int i = 0; i < 10000; i++) {
      executors.execute(new Runnable() {
        public void run() {
          counter++;
          atomicCounter.incrementAndGet();
        }
      });
    }

    // Shut down the pool and block until all tasks have executed.
    executors.shutdown();
    executors.awaitTermination(60, TimeUnit.SECONDS);

    System.out.println(
      String.format("Normal int counter: %s",
          counter));
    System.out.println(
      String.format("AtomicInteger counter: %s",
          atomicCounter));
  }
}
```

If we've handled our concurrent counter manipulation properly, both counters should have the value 10,000. As we can see from the following output, that's not the case.

```
Normal int counter: 9815
AtomicInteger counter: 10000
```

So what happened? It turns out that incrementing an integer isn't an atomic operation. It's actually broken up into multiple steps when compiled into bytecode, so the thread doing an increment can see the int it's incrementing in an inconsistent state.

To make this a bit more clear, let's take a look at a simpler example that just increments an int a single time.

```
public class JustIncAnInt {
  private static int i;

  public static void main(String[] args){
    i++;
  }
}
```

Once we compile the preceding code, we can use a command-line tool that comes with most JDKs to get a readable representation of the bytecode it's compiled to:

```
> javap -c JustIncAnInt
Compiled from "JustIncAnInt.java"
public class JustIncAnInt extends java.lang.Object{
```

```
public JustIncAnInt();
  Code:
    0:  aload_0
    1:  invokespecial  #1; //Method java/lang/Object."<init>":()V
    4:  return
public static void main(java.lang.String[]);
  Code:
    0:  getstatic  #2; //Field i:I
    3:  iconst_1
    4:  iadd
    5:  putstatic  #2; //Field i:I
    8:  return

}
```

As we can see, that single increment is actually compiled to multiple bytecode operations. Without going too far into the weeds, the 0: getstatic #2; //Field i:I is responsible for loading the current value of the counter. It's not until 4: iadd that the increment is performed, and 5: putstatic #2; //Field i:I that it's written back into the variable.

This, combined with subtleties involving when a write that one thread makes becomes visible to other threads, leaves plenty of opportunity for two threads to read and increment the variable at the same time. One solution would be to use one of Java's locking mechanisms to protect the counter variable to ensure that only one thread can access the counter at a time, and that any modifications made to it are visible when the lock is relinquished.

None of this is a surprise to any developer versed in concurrency on the JVM, but it's a nice illustration of the difficulties in concurrent programming. Programming with locks is low level and fraught with peril.

Another higher-level solution is the one that we demonstrated using AtomicInteger. The AtomicInteger class provides an incrementAndGet, which atomically increments an internal counter, ensuring that no thread can see it in an inconsistent state.

Two main downsides to the AtomicInteger solution are that it can only be used for integers, and it can only deal with coordinating changes to a single object. What if, for instance, we needed to change a map and an integer in lock step? To do so with Java, we'd probably need to fall back to locks.

Clojure's Solution

Clojure's immutable data structures, managed reference types, and software transactional memory system combine to provide a model that's both high level and much easier to use than locking concurrency. Let's dig in with a look at an atom, which I find to be the simplest to understand of the reference types Clojure provides.

Atomic Power

As we saw in Chapter 8, *Identity, Value, and State in Clojure*, on page 51, atoms are good for managing state that's independent and to which we want to make synchronous changes. Here, independent means we can make the change without coordinating a change to any other piece of state. Synchronous means we want to block the thread that triggered the change until it's done.

We can create an atom out of any immutable data structure using atom, and make a change to the atom's state by passing the atom and function into the swap! function. The swap! function applies the passed in function to the value wrapped by the atom, swaps the old value for the new one, and returns it. Here, we create a simple atom counter, and a function to increment it.

```
(def atom-counter (atom 0))
(defn increment-atom-counter []
  (swap! atom-counter inc))
```

To de-reference an atom, or any of Clojure's managed references, we can use the @, as we show below.

```
=> @atom-counter
0
=> (increment-atom-counter)
1
```

So far, so good, but how does that help us with concurrency? When multiple threads attempt to modify an atom concurrently using swap!, Clojure first reads the current value out of the atom. Then it uses a lower-level function over atoms called compare-and-set!.

The compare-and-set! function takes an old value and a new value, and it atomically sets the atom to the new value only if the current value of the atom equals the passed in old value. If swap! is unable to set the value of the atom using compare-and-set!, it will continue to retry until it is successful.

Here, we've rewritten our original Java example to something similar in Clojure, which takes advantage of atoms.

```
(defn concurrent-atom-modification []
  (let [executors (Executors/newFixedThreadPool 5)
        counter (atom 0)]
    (dotimes [_ 10000]
      (.execute executors (fn [] (swap! counter inc))))
    (.shutdown executors)
```

```
    (.awaitTermination executors 60 TimeUnit/SECONDS)
    @counter))
```

Running concurrent-atom-modification sets our counter to the correct value.

```
=> (concurrent-atom-modification)
10000
```

This gives us a high-level approach to concurrency, much like the one we saw with Java's AtomicInteger, but we could wrap any immutable data structure, like a Clojure vector or map, in one so it's more general.

One consequence of the way that atoms work is that the function passed into swap! can't have any side effects, or at least no side effects that can't be repeated. This is because the function may be retried if the compare-and-set! fails the first time around.

Get an Agent

Next up, let's take a look at Clojure's agents. Like atoms, agents let us manage changes to independent state, but they're designed to do so in an asynchronous way. To modify the value referred to by an agent, we can use the send function.

Like swap!, it takes an atom to modify and a function that modifies it. Unlike swap!, it returns immediately. Operations are queued if necessary and applied to the agent serially. Here we create an atom version of our counter, and a function to increment it.

```
(def agent-counter (agent 0))
(defn increment-agent-counter []
  (send agent-counter inc))
```

Calling increment-agent-counter doesn't return the value of incrementing the counter; instead, it returns a reference to the agent. At some point in the future, the counter will be incremented. Since incrementing the counter a single time is very fast, by the time we de-reference the counter, it's already been done.

```
=> (increment-agent-counter)
#<Agent@64889c4e: 1>
=> @agent-counter
1
```

Since agents are guaranteed to be applied serially, any side effects that they execute will only execute once, unlike atoms.

Working the Ref

The final managed reference type we'll look at is the ref. These can be used when we need to make coordinated changes across more than one data structure.

In the example we'll see below, we'll take a look at a tiny system that keeps track of television series and episodes. An episode of a series is represented as a map with an id, a name, and a nested map that represents the series it's attached to. The nested series has a series id and name, as we show below.

```
{:id 42
 :name "Fragged"
 :series {:id 10 :name "Battlestar Galactica"}}
```

As episodes are added to the system, we want to populate two maps, one of episodes keyed off of episode id and one of series keyed off of series id. To add the series to our series map, we'll pick the embedded series out of an episode when it's added, and add it to the series map if it's not already there.

We'd like to ensure that we never see our data in an inconsistent state, where we've added an episode but not its corresponding series, and we'll do so using Clojure's refs and software transactional memory system.

Let's start by creating a couple of refs to hold our maps.

```
(def all-episodes (ref {}))
(def all-series (ref {}))
```

The meat of our solution involves adding episodes using assoc. Much like the swap! function does for atoms, and the send function does for agents, alter takes a reference, function, and arguments.

Unlike swap! and send!, alter must be called inside of a transaction. To create a transaction, we wrap our calls to alter inside of dosync. This acts like a database transaction, and it turns our multiple calls to alter into one atomic unit.

If one thread was to modify either map while another was in the process of doing so, one thread would win and its transaction would commit. The other would roll its transaction back and try it again. This means that, just like with the atoms we saw earlier, we need to avoid side effects in our transactions.

```
(defn add-new-episode [current-episode]
  (let [current-series (:series current-episode)]
    (dosync
      (alter all-episodes
        #(assoc % (:id current-episode) current-episode))
      (alter all-series
        #(assoc % (:id current-series) current-series)))))
```

Now we can create a few test episodes, and add them to our system.

```
(def e1 {:id 1
         :name "33"
         :series {:id 10 :name "Battlestar Galactica"}})
```

```
(def e2 {:id 2
         :name "Water"
         :series {:id 10 :name "Battlestar Galactica"}}})
(def e3 {:id 3
         :name "The Target"
         :series {:id 11 :name "The Wire"}}})
=> (add-new-episode e1)
{10 {:name "Battlestar Galactica", :id 10}}
=> (add-new-episode e2)
{10 {:name "Battlestar Galactica", :id 10}}
=> (add-new-episode e3)
{11 {:name "The Wire", :id 11},
 10 {:name "Battlestar Galactica", :id 10}}
```

Both of our maps contain the correct value, and they got there in a thread-safe way!

```
=> @all-episodes
{3 {:name "The Target",
    :series {:name "The Wire", :id 11},
    :id 3},
 2 {:name "Water",
    :series {:name "Battlestar Galactica", :id 10},
    :id 2},
 1 {:name "33",
    :series {:name "Battlestar Galactica", :id 10},
    :id 1}}
=> @all-series
{11 {:name "The Wire", :id 11},
 10 {:name "Battlestar Galactica", :id 10}}
```

That wraps up our look at Clojure's concurrency. We've only scratched the surface here. Clojure's API docs[1] present an excellent, if concise, description of the reference types we've seen here and they're a great place to look for more information. And to dig deeper into Clojure, have a look at Chapter 20, *Clojure's Exceptional*, on page 163, where Stuart Halloway talks about Clojure's handling of exceptions.

As you can see, Clojure and Scala both rely on the JVM and have some similarities and some differences in syntax and in their implementation of functional principles. In the next chapter, Dave Thomas introduces Elixir, a functional language with a very different approach to all of that.

---

1. http://clojure.github.io/clojure/

Part IV

Elixir: Making Programming Fun Again

José Valim developed Elixir with high extensibility and productivity in mind, building it on top of the rock-solid VM of the Erlang functional language. Its modern syntax makes functional feel fashionable. Pinterest is among Elixir's early users.

## CHAPTER 10

Patterns and Transformations in Elixir

by Dave Thomas

Fifteen years ago. That was the last time I was this excited by a programming language, and that language was Ruby. I hadn't found anything as exciting since.

It wasn't for lack of trying. I explored them all as they came out, but none grabbed me—none made me feel like I'd enjoy spending years digging in.

Then I discovered Elixir. Twice. The first time I thought it was very nice, but not compelling. But Corey Haines pushed me to look again. He was right. Elixir is special.

Here's what you need to know:

Elixir is a functional programming language that runs on the Erlang virtual machine. It has a Ruby-like syntax, and features protocols (for extending modules without changing their source), macros, and very good metaprogramming support. It has many modern features, too, the benefit of learning from other languages' experience. For example, macros are lexically scoped, so metaprogramming no longer risks messing up the global execution environment.

Running on the Erlang VM, called Beam, Elixir is fully compatible with existing Erlang code. This means you can take advantage of the high availability, high concurrency, and distributed nature of Erlang. It also means you can use all the thousands of existing Erlang libraries, both built-in and third-party. In particular, Elixir can run within the OTP framework. (OTP is a collection of useful Erlang libraries and tools, as well as an acronym that apparently no longer stands for anything. It's just OTP.)

So let's look at some code.

If you want to follow along at home, this would be a good time to download Elixir. The instructions are on the Elixir site.[1]

The following code calculates the sum of the elements in a list.

```
elixir/sum.ex
defmodule MyList do

  def sum([]), do: 0
  def sum([ head | tail ]), do: head + sum(tail)

end

IO.puts MyList.sum [1,2,3]    #=>  6
```

Our sum function lives in a module called MyList. The function is defined in two clauses. So how does Elixir know which to run?

Pattern Matching

This is where *pattern matching* comes in. The parameter list of the first function clause is just the empty list. When you call sum, this clause will *match* if and only if you call it with an empty list. If it *does* match, the function returns 0.

The second clause has a complicated parameter list: [head|tail]. This pattern matches a list (the square brackets tell us that). The list must have a first element (the head) and a tail (the remainder of the list). If the list we pass in has only one element, the head will be set to that element, and the tail will be the empty list.

So let's call MyList.sum with the argument [1,2,3]. Elixir looks for the first clause whose pattern matches the argument. The first clause doesn't match—the argument isn't the empty list—but the second clause does. head is set to 1 and tail to [2,3]. Elixir evaluates the body, head+sum(tail), which means that the sum function is called again, recursively. On the last call, the first clause matches, there is no further recursive call, and the result is returned. The sequence of calls looks something like this:

```
sum([1,2,3])
1 + sum([2,3])
1 + 2 + sum([3])
1 + 2 + 3 + sum([])
1 + 2 + 3 + 0
```

Pattern matching is at the core of Elixir. In fact, it's the only way of binding a value to a variable. When we write what looks like an assignment:

```
a = [1,2,3]
```

---

1. http://elixir-lang.org

Elixir is busy trying to work out how to have the left-hand side match the right. In this case, it does this by binding the list [1,2,3] to the variable a.

Once a has this value, you can write:

```
[1,2,3] = a
```

And Elixir will be perfectly happy—the value on the left matches the value on the right. But if you then write:

```
99 = a
```

Elixir will complain that it can't find a match. That's because Elixir will only change the value bound to a variable if it is on the left-hand side of the match operator.

Pattern Matching Structured Data

Matching goes further—Elixir will look at the structure of the two sides when making a match:

```
[ a, b, c ] = [1, 2, 3]     # a = 1, b = 2, c = 3
[ head | tail ] = [1, 2, 3]   # head = 1, tail = [ 2, 3 ]
```

Once bound, a variable keeps the same value for the duration of the pattern match. So the following match will only succeed if the variable list is a three-element list where the first and last elements have the same value:

```
[ a, b, a ] = list
```

You can mix constants and variables on the left-hand side. To illustrate this, I'm going to introduce a new Elixir data type, the *tuple*. A tuple is a fixed-length collection of values. We write tuple constants between braces:

```
{ 1, 2, "cat" }
{ :ok, result }
```

(The :ok in the second line of code is an Elixir symbol. You can think of it as a constant string, or as a symbol in Ruby. You can also think of it as a constant whose value is its name, but that can lead to catatonic states.)

Many library functions return two-element tuples. The first element will be the status of the result—if it is :ok, the call succeeded; if it is :error, it failed. The second value will be the actual result of the call, with more information on the error.

You can use pattern matching to determine if a call succeeded:

```
{ :ok, stream } = File.open("somefile.txt")
```

If the File.open succeeds, then stream will be set to the result. If it doesn't, the pattern won't match, and Elixir will raise a runtime error. (Although in this case, you're better off opening the file with File.open!(), which will raise a more meaningful error on failure.)

Pattern Matching and Functions

Our MyList.sum example shows that pattern matching also applies to calling functions. Do you see that? The function parameters act as the left-hand side of the match, and the arguments you pass act as the right-hand side.

Here is another (hoary old) example: it calculates the value of the nth Fibonacci number.

Let's start with the specification of Fibonacci numbers:

```
fib(0) -> 1
fib(1) -> 1
fib(n) -> fib(n-2) + fib(n-1)
```

Using pattern matching, we can turn this specification into executable code with minimal effort:

elixir/fib.ex
```
defmodule Demo do

  def fib(0), do: 1
  def fib(1), do: 1
  def fib(n), do: fib(n-2) + fib(n-1)

end
```

Elixir comes with an interactive shell called iex. This lets us play with our fib method:

```
elixir % iex fib.ex
Erlang R15B03 ...
Interactive Elixir (...)
iex(1)> Demo.fib(0)
1
iex(2)> Demo.fib(1)
1
iex(3)> Demo.fib(10)
89
```

The wonderful thing about this is how easy it is to convert a specification into runnable code. And once that code is written, it's easy to read it and see what it does.

Something else to note: there are no conditional statements in the implementation of our function. This also makes the code easier to read (and maintain). In fact, many fairly large Elixir modules are written with few or no conditional statements.

Transformation Is Job #1

You might be thinking that this is all very well, but you don't write mathematical functions as part of your daily job.

But functional programming isn't about mathematical functions.

Functions are things that transform data. The trig function *sin* transforms the value 90 degrees to the value 1.0. And that's the hint.

Programming is not about data. It's about *transforming* data. Every program we write takes some input and transforms it into some output. The input could be a web request, some command-line parameters, or the weather in Boise. Whatever it is, our code takes it and transforms it multiple times on the way to producing the desired result.

And that's why I think functional programming is a natural successor to object-oriented programming. In OO programming, we're constantly concerned about the state of our data. In functional programming, our focus is on the *transformation* of data. And transformation is where the value is added.

In the next chapter, we'll look at functions, both named and anonymous. And we'll explore the pipeline operator, which lets us write things like:

```
request |> authenticate |> lookup_data |> format_response
```

Which looks a little bit like magic.

## CHAPTER 11

Getting Functional with Elixir

by Dave Thomas

In the preceding chapter, we looked at the basics of pattern matching and saw how it is universal in Elixir—it's the only way to bind a value to a variable or parameter. That may have seemed like an unusual way to start talking about functional programming, but it's very natural for Elixir. And pattern matching really shines when we apply it to functions, which we'll explore in depth in this chapter.

Anonymous Functions

Elixir has a nice set of built-in modules. One of these, Enum, lets you work on enumerable collections. One of its most commonly used functions is map, which applies a function to a collection, producing a new collection. Let's fire up the Elixir interactive shell, iex, and try it.

```
iex> Enum.map [2,4,6], fn val -> val * val end
[4,16,36]
```

The first argument we pass to map is the collection: in this case, a list of three integers. The second argument is an *anonymous function*.

Anonymous functions (I'm going to call them *fn*s from now on) are defined between the keywords fn and end. A right-facing arrow, ->, separates a list of zero or more parameters on the left from the body of the function on the right.

We passed map the function fn val -> val*val end. This fn takes a single parameter, val, and the body of the function multiplies that value by itself, implicitly returning the result.

A fn is just another Elixir value, so we also have written this code as:

```
iex> square = fn val -> val * val end
#Function<erl_eval.6.17052888>
iex> Enum.map [2,4,6], square
[4,16,36]
```

You can call fns using something like a regular function call:

```
iex> square.(5)
25
```

The period and the parentheses are required.

Boy, that's way too much typing, you say.

No it's not, and we don't reward whining around these parts anyway.

That said, Elixir does have a shortcut.

```
iex> Enum.map [2,4,6], &( &1 * &1 )
[4,16,36]
```

When Elixir sees a unary &, it knows that it needs to generate an anonymous function. The function will have from 1 to n parameters, denoted in the expression that follows as &1 to &n. So, &(&1*&1) is logically the same as fn p1 -> p1*p1 end, and &rem(&1,&2) becomes fn p1,p2 -> rem(p1,p2) end.

Because fns are just values, you can even write the code as:

```
iex> square = & &1 * &1
#Function<erl_eval.6.17052888>
iex> Enum.map [2,4,6], square
[4,16,36]
```

This is a fantastically useful shortcut, but there is a gotcha. When deciding what code to make the body of the fn, Elixir starts at the ampersand term and looks up the parse tree for the immediately enclosing expression. With &(&1*&1), it's the multiplication operator. With &rem(&1,&2), it's the function call to rem.

Named Functions

Anonymous functions tend to be used for callback work—they are typically short and localized in their use. Named functions, however, are where the real work gets done.

Named functions can only exist inside Elixir modules. Here's an example:

```
elixir/ascii.exs
defmodule AsciiDigit do
  def valid?(character) do
    character in ?0..?9
  end
end

IO.inspect AsciiDigit.valid? ?4    # => true
IO.inspect AsciiDigit.valid? ?a    # => false
```

To follow this code, you first have to know that the syntax ?x returns the integer character code for x (so ?0 is 48).

Our example defines a module called AsciiDigit containing a single function, valid?. This takes a character code and returns true if it is a digit from 0 to 9. We use the range operator .. to define the first and last valid character, and the in operator to check for inclusion.

As we saw in *Patterns and Transformations in Elixir*, Elixir supports pattern matching when determining which function to run. You can use def multiple times for the same function, each with a different pattern of parameters. Elixir will dynamically choose one where the parameters match the arguments passed.

Let's take another look at our Fibonacci function.

```
elixir/fib.exs
defmodule Fibonacci do

  def fib(0), do: 1
  def fib(1), do: 1
  def fib(n), do: fib(n-2)+fib(n-1)

end

Enum.map 0..10, &Fibonacci.fib(&1)    #=> [1,1,2,3,5,8,13,21,34,55,89]
```

Despite appearances, there's just one definition of the fib function in there. It just has three *heads*—three patterns of arguments that select different bodies.

The first two heads select the cases where the argument is 0 or 1. They use the abbreviated form of the body, do: expr to return 1. The third form is the recursive step. If neither of the first two match, the third one executes.

What happens if we pass our function a negative argument? Right now, it will loop until we run out of stack or patience—subtracting 1 or 2 from a negative number will never reach 0. Fortunately, Elixir has *guard clauses*, which allow us to put additional constraints on pattern matching.

```
elixir/fib1.exs
defmodule Fibonacci do

  def fib(0), do: 1
  def fib(1), do: 1
  def fib(n) when n > 1, do: fib(n-2)+fib(n-1)

end

Fibonacci.fib(10)    #=> 89
Fibonacci.fib(-10)
# => ** (FunctionClauseError) no function clause matching in Fibonacci.fib/1
```

Now, when we call fib with a negative number, Elixir can't find a function clause that matches, so it raises an exception. If you really wanted to, you could handle this case in code, giving a more application-specific error:

```
elixir/fib2.exs
defmodule Fibonacci do

  def fib(0), do: 1
  def fib(1), do: 1
  def fib(n) when is_integer(n) and  n > 1, do: fib(n-2)+fib(n-1)
  def fib(x), do: raise "Can't find fib(#{x})"

end

Fibonacci.fib(10)      #=> 89
Fibonacci.fib(-10)     #=> ** (RuntimeError) Can't find fib(-10)
Fibonacci.fib("cat")   #=> ** (RuntimeError) Can't find fib(cat)
```

We extended our guard clause to check that the parameter is an integer, and then added a fourth function head that accepts any parameter and reports an appropriate error.

But understanding how Elixir does functions isn't the same as understanding how to do *functional programming* in Elixir. As we are about to see.

A Practical Example

Most of the long number strings we deal with every day (credit card numbers, IMEI numbers in your phone, and so on) have a check digit. This is normally the final digit of the number, and it is calculated using some algorithm that combines all the previous digits. So, when you enter your credit card number, the web page can recalculate the check digit, and verify that it is the same as the last digit in the number you gave. It isn't a check against fraud; it's simply a quick way of picking up typos.

Probably the most widely used technique is the Luhn Algorithm.[1] It reverses the digits in the number, and splits them into two sets: digits at odd positions in the string, and digits at even positions. It sums the odd digits. For the even digits, it multiplies each by two. If the result is ten or more, it subtracts nine. It then sums all the results. Adding the sum of odd and even positions will yield a result that's divisible by ten for valid numbers.

When I first started with Elixir, my head was still full of conventional ways of doing things. As a result, I'd write something like the following:

elixir/nf1.ex
```elixir
defmodule CheckDigit do

  import Enum

  def valid?(numbers) do
    numbers = reverse(numbers)
    numbers = map(numbers, fn char -> char - ?0 end)
    numbers = with_index(numbers)
    { odds, evens } =
        partition(numbers, fn {_digit, index} -> rem(index, 2) == 0 end)
    sum_odd = reduce odds, 0, fn {number, _index}, sum -> sum + number end
    sum_even = reduce evens, 0, fn {number, _index}, sum ->
      result = number * 2
      if result >= 10 do
        result - 9 + sum
      else
        result + sum
      end
    end
    rem(sum_odd + sum_even, 10) == 0
  end

end
```

Ugh! Let's step through it (hopefully you're wearing boots).

The Enum module has lots of functions for dealing with collections. We'll be using many of them in this code, so we import the module. This means we can write map instead of Enum.map.

Our valid? function is passed a list of UTF-8 digits. By coincidence, that's exactly what the single quoted string literal generates.

Using the description of the Luhn algorithm, we reverse the digits, and then convert the UTF representation to the actual integer value (so ?1, which is 41, gets mapped to 1). At this point, given the argument '123', we'd have a list of integers [3, 2, 1].

---

1.   http://en.wikipedia.org/wiki/Luhn_algorithm

Now it gets messy. We need to partition the digits into those on an even position and those at an odd position. To prepare to do that, we use map, passing it the function fn number, index -> {number, index} end. This function takes the actual digit value, along with its index in the list, and maps it to a tuple containing each.

At this point, alarm bells should be ringing. This is just too damn hard. But we plow on, because that's what programmers do.

The partition function takes a collection and a function. It returns a tuple where the first element is a list of values for which the function returned true, and the second element is the rest of the values.

Now we have to sum the odd values. Whenever you need to reduce a collection to a single value, you'll probably want to use the reduce function. It takes the collection, an initial value, and a function. This function receives each element of the collection in turn, along with the current value. Whatever the function returns becomes the next current value. So, summing a list of numbers can be done with

```
Enum.reduce list, fn val, sum => val + sum end
# or
Enum.reduce list, &( &1 + &2 )
```

But what we have is a list of {value, index} tuples. This means we need to use pattern matching on the first parameter of the function to extract just the value. (The underscore in front of _index means we're ignoring this field.)

Summing the even numbers is similar, but we have to do the doubling, and the conversion of numbers ten or above.

At the end of all this, we can test this in iex. I'm using a standard Visa test credit card number here, so don't go booking a trip to Tahiti using it.

```
$ iex validate_cc.exs
iex> CheckDigit.valid? '4012888888881881'
true
iex> CheckDigit.valid? '0412888888881881'
false
```

Refactor to Functional Style

Our solution works, but the style isn't very functional. (That's a polite way of saying it's butt ugly.) To tidy it up, I look for places where there's clearly something wrong, and see if I can fix them.

The first problem I see is the first three lines. I'm transforming the given number into a reversed set of digits, each with an associated index.

The word *transform* is the clue. Functional programming is all about transforming data. It's so important that Elixir has a special operator, |>. This lets us build pipelines of functions, where each transforms the results of the previous. It lets us compose functionality.

Using the pipeline operator, we can rewrite the first three lines as

```
numbers
  |> reverse
  |> map(fn char -> char - ?0 end)
  |> map(fn digit, index -> {digit, index} end)
```

We take the original list and transform it by reversing it, then by converting character codes to integers, and then by adding the index.

The pipeline operator looks like magic, but it's actually quite simple. It takes the value of the expression on its left, and inserts it as the first argument of the function call on its right, shifting all the other arguments down.

Now the second ugliness is all this partitioning and summing. Our problem is that we're thinking imperatively, not functionally. We're telling Elixir each step of what to do, when instead we should be thinking of the specification of what we want and letting Elixir work out the details.

Think back to our Fibonacci example. There we implemented our specification as three function heads, which matched the two special cases and the one general case. Can we do the same here?

Rather than processing our list of digits one element at a time, what if we process it in twos? This means we're working with a pair of digits—the first will be the one at an odd position, the second at the even position. We know how to calculate the Luhn number for these two digits, and then we can add the result for them into the result for the remainder of the list. That's our recursive step.

When we finally empty the list, we will have calculated the required sum, so we can simply return it.

There's one other case to consider. If the list has an odd number of digits, then when we get to the end, we'll only have a single element. But we know that element is at an odd position, so we can simply add it to the accumulated sum and return the result.

So, here's the new version of our code:

```elixir
elixir/nfx.ex
defmodule CheckDigit do

  import Enum, only: [ reverse: 1, map: 2 ]

  @doc """
  Determine if a sequence of digits is valid, assuming the last digit is
  a Luhn checksum. (http://en.wikipedia.org/wiki/Luhn_algorithm)
  """

  def valid?(numbers) when is_list(numbers) do
    numbers
      |> reverse
      |> map(&(&1 - ?0))
      |> sum
      |> rem(10) == 0
  end

  defp sum(digits), do: _sum(digits, 0)

  defp _sum([], sum), do: sum
  defp _sum([odd], sum), do: sum + odd
  defp _sum([odd, even | tail], sum) when even < 5 do
    _sum(tail, sum + odd + even*2)
  end
  defp _sum([odd, even | tail], sum) do
    _sum(tail, sum + odd + even*2 - 9)
  end

end
```

The pipeline at the top is now a lot simpler—there's no messing with indexes and no temporary variables. It reads like a code version of the spec.

The sum function is an example of a common pattern. We need to set the initial value of the thing we're summing, but we don't want the code that calls us to know about that detail, so we write a version of sum that just takes the numbers and then calls the actual implementation, passing in the list and a zero for the initial value. We could give the helper functions the same name, but I prefer using _sum to differentiate them. (Many Elixir programmers would have called them do_sum, but that always strikes me as too imperative.)

The _sum function has four heads:

- If the list is empty, we return the sum that we've been accumulating in the second parameter.

- If the list has one element, add its value to the sum so far and return it. This is the terminating condition for a list with an odd number of elements.

- Otherwise, we extract the first two elements from the list. This uses the pattern [odd,even|tail]. The first element is bound to odd, the second to even, and the remainder of the list is bound to tail.

  Looking back at the Luhn algorithm, we have two cases to consider. If the result of multiplying the even number by two is less than ten, then that's the number we add into the sum. We use a guard class to check for this.

- Otherwise, we have to subtract nine from the product. That's what the fourth function body does.

Notice how we're passing the updated sum around as the second parameter to the function—this is a universal pattern when you want to accumulate a value or values across a set of recursive function calls.

What's Different About This Code

When you write in a language such as Java, C#, or Ruby, you're working at a number of levels simultaneously. Part of your brain is thinking about the specification—what has to get done. The other part is thinking about the implementation—the nuts and bolts of how to do it. And that's where things often get bogged down.

But look at that last example. We're iterating over a set of digits. We're selecting those with odd or even positions. We're performing conditional calculations. We're summing the result. *And there isn't a single control structure in the program.* No ifs, no loops. The code pretty much reflects the specification of what we want to happen.

And that's one of the reasons I'm a fan of functional programming in general, and Elixir in particular.

The value of functional programming, though, shows up in parallel processing, so let's start getting parallel. In the next chapter, we'll see how we can use Elixir to run hundreds of thousands of processes, and how to coordinate their work.

## CHAPTER 12

Getting Parallel with Elixir

by Dave Thomas

In the preceding chapter, we rounded out a look at the basics of sequential Elixir code by looking at functions. So let's expand our world out into a second dimension by introducing some concurrency.

The Actor Model

The actor model of concurrency is actually fairly old. It probably dates back to a couple of hundred thousand years ago, when humans first started communicating and remembering things. Fred would ask Wilma if she'd seen Barney, and Wilma would respond back to Fred, but only after she'd first told Bamm-Bamm to stop teasing Dino.

The essence of the actor model is just that—independent, asynchronous *actors* that communicate only by sending each other messages. The word *only* is significant—there is no state shared between actors.

Step forward to the mid 1970s, and Carl Hewitt proposed[1] actors as a model of computation. In his mind, actors weren't simply a means of achieving concurrency. They were instead a fundamental building block of software systems, much as objects are to OO programmers.

In fact, there's a lot of similarity between an actor and an object. Both maintain their own independent state, which they encapsulate behind an API. But the two also differ. The obvious difference is that objects interact sequentially (threading notwithstanding), while actors can operate in parallel. But there's another, deeper, difference implicit in this distinction. Actors do not have to

---

1. http://en.wikipedia.org/wiki/Actor_model

process messages in the order they arrive. In fact, you don't necessarily *know* the order in which messages arrived. And it turns out that this is liberating.

Actors and Elixir

Elixir runs on the Erlang virtual machine, and Erlang has support for actors built into the language. In fact, the actor model is one of Erlang's defining characteristics.

And, perhaps surprisingly for something so rich, it's really simple.

An actor in Elixir is called a *process*. You create new processes using one of the variants of the spawn function, send messages to it using the <- operator, and receive messages using a receive expression.

Let's start with spawn:

```
elixir/spawn1.exs
process_id = spawn fn ->
                       IO.puts "In process #{inspect self()}"
                    end
IO.puts "Spawned process #{inspect process_id}"
```

The spawn function runs the function you pass it as a separate process, returning the process id (from now on, we'll use *pid*).

Notice that we use self inside the process we create. Anywhere in Elixir, self returns the current pid. Called in the spawned process, it will return that process's pid. Called in the main process, we'll get the main process's pid instead.

If you run this code, you'll likely see:

```
$ elixir spawn1.exs
Spawned process #PID<0.36.0>
In process #PID<0.36.0>
```

However, you might also see:

```
$ elixir spawn1.exs
In process #PID<0.36.0>
Spawned process #PID<0.36.0>
```

It's up to the process scheduler whether the spawned process runs before the main process continues.

There's another way of looking at spawn—it's a function that transforms another function into a process. And indeed you can write the code that way.

```
elixir/spawn2.exs
process_id = fn -> IO.puts "In process #{inspect self()}" end |> spawn

IO.puts "Spawned process #{inspect process_id}"
```

Messages

The expression

```
pid <- expression
```

sends the value of the expression to the process with the given pid. This value
is queued in a per-process mailbox, and the sender continues to run.

When a process wants to retrieve a message from its mailbox, it calls receive.
This takes a block containing one or more clauses. Each clause consists of
a pattern and an expression. Elixir looks at each message in the process's
mailbox in turn. For each message, it tries to match it against the patterns
in the receive block. Once a match is found, it runs the corresponding code.
If no match is found, Elixir waits until a new message arrives in the mailbox,
and tests it. (This process means that any particular execution of receive will
only inspect any message in the mailbox one time. However, if you call receive
a second time, it will once again scan the entire mailbox.)

Let's extend out an example, and have the spawned function wait for a message. When it receives it, it will write it in a cheery message.

```
elixir/spawn3.exs
cheery = fn ->
  IO.puts "In spawned process #{inspect self()}"
  receive do
    msg -> IO.puts "Well, hello #{msg}"
  end
end

pid = cheery |> spawn

IO.puts "Spawned process #{inspect pid}"

send pid, "world!"

IO.puts "Message sent"
```

Running this, you may see output like:

```
$ elixir spawn3.exs
Spawned process #PID<0.36.0>
In spawned process #PID<0.36.0>
Message sent
Well, hello world!
```

How would we get our process to send the message back to us, rather than just print it? The trick is to pass it *our* pid as part of the message we send it:

```elixir
elixir/spawn4.exs
cheery = fn ->
  IO.puts "In spawned process #{inspect self()}"
  receive do
    { from_pid, msg } ->
        send from_pid, "Well, hello #{msg}"
  end
end

pid = cheery |> spawn

IO.puts "Spawned process #{inspect pid}"

send pid, { self(), "world!" }

IO.puts "Message sent"

receive do
  msg -> IO.puts "The process said: #{inspect msg}"
end
```

See how we defined a simple protocol for our message? Rather than passing a single value, we now pass a tuple containing our pid and message. The receiver uses pattern matching to break this message apart, allowing it to send the response back to the original process.

We can take this further. Let's support different (human) languages. We'll add a language code to our protocol, and match multiple clauses in the receiving process.

```elixir
elixir/spawn5.exs
cheery = fn ->
  IO.puts "In spawned process #{inspect self()}"
  receive do
    { from_pid, :en, msg } ->
        send from_pid, "Well, hello #{msg}"
    { from_pid, :fr, msg } ->
        send from_pid, "Bonjour #{msg}"
    { from_pid, :es, msg } ->
        send from_pid, "Hola #{msg}"
  end
end

pid = cheery |> spawn

IO.puts "Spawned process #{inspect pid}"

send pid, { self(), :es, "mundo!" }

IO.puts "Message sent"
```

```
receive do
  msg -> IO.puts "The process said: #{inspect msg}"
end

$ elixir spawn5.exs
Spawned process #PID<0.36.0>
In spawned process #PID<0.36.0>
Message sent
The process said: "Hola mundo!"
```

We're on a roll, so let's try sending a second message. (We'll also remove some of the tracing.)

elixir/spawn6.exs

```
cheery = fn ->
  receive do
    { from_pid, :en, msg } ->
        send from_pid, "Well, hello #{msg}"
    { from_pid, :fr, msg } ->
        send from_pid, "Bonjour #{msg}"
    { from_pid, :es, msg } ->
        send from_pid, "Hola #{msg}"
  end
end

pid = cheery |> spawn

send pid, { self(), :es, "mundo!" }
receive do
  msg -> IO.puts "The process said: #{inspect msg}"
end

send pid, { self(), :fr, "world!" }
receive do
  msg -> IO.puts "The process said: #{inspect msg}"
end
```

When we run this, we get the Spanish message, but then our process just hangs forever (modulo your patience). The problem is that our subprocess is no more—once it received the first message, it left the receive block and terminated. There was nothing around to receive the second message we sent. We'll need to make our greeter loop, receiving requests. The easiest way to do this is to make it into a named function in a module.

elixir/spawn7.exs

```
defmodule Greeter do
  def loop do
    receive do
      { from_pid, :en, msg } ->
        send from_pid, "Well, hello #{msg}"
      { from_pid, :fr, msg } ->
        send from_pid, "Bonjour #{msg}"
```

```elixir
        { from_pid, :es, msg } ->
          send from_pid, "Hola #{msg}"
      end
      loop()
    end
end

pid = spawn &Greeter.loop/0

send pid, { self(), :es, "mundo!" }
receive do
  msg -> IO.puts "The process said: #{inspect msg}"
end

send pid, { self(), :fr, "tout le monde!" }
receive do
  msg -> IO.puts "The process said: #{inspect msg}"
end
```

The key here is the function loop. It handles a message, and then immediately calls itself, recursively, so it can handle the next message. Because Elixir turns tail recursion into a simple jump, this function can recurse forever without using any process stack.

Our code here is pretty poorly structured, though. Let's give our module a proper API, and hide the implementation details (the loop) by making it private.

```elixir
elixir/spawn7.exs
defmodule Greeter do
  def loop do
    receive do
      { from_pid, :en, msg } ->
        send from_pid, "Well, hello #{msg}"
      { from_pid, :fr, msg } ->
        send from_pid, "Bonjour #{msg}"
      { from_pid, :es, msg } ->
        send from_pid, "Hola #{msg}"
    end
    loop()
  end
end

pid = spawn &Greeter.loop/0

send pid, { self(), :es, "mundo!" }
receive do
  msg -> IO.puts "The process said: #{inspect msg}"
end

send pid, { self(), :fr, "tout le monde!" }
receive do
  msg -> IO.puts "The process said: #{inspect msg}"
end
```

One of the cool features of this code is in the get_response function. We pass it the language for which we want a response, and use that language in the receive block to match only a message with that language code. Putting an up arrow in the pattern (^language) makes the pattern use the value in the variable, rather than assigning to it.

The main body of the code makes use of this. See how we submit requests for Spanish, French, and English (in that order), but we ask for the results in the order French, Spanish, English. And, sure enough, that's what we see.

```
$ elixir spawn8.exs
Bonjour tout le monde!
Hola mundo!
Well, hello world!
```

Monitoring Your Processes

Remember the example where our child process didn't loop and we sent it two messages? The first was processed, but the child exited, and we never got a response to the second message.

We can handle this by linking our original process and the child process. If we do this, and one of the processes dies, the other will be sent a message. Let's go back to that example, and change our spawn call with spawn_link.

elixir/spawn9.exs
```
cheery = fn ->
  receive do
    { from_pid, :en, msg } ->
        send from_pid, "Well, hello #{msg}"
    { from_pid, :fr, msg } ->
        send from_pid, "Bonjour #{msg}"
    { from_pid, :es, msg } ->
        send from_pid, "Hola #{msg}"
  end
end

Process.flag(:trap_exit, true)
pid = cheery |> spawn_link

send pid, { self(), :es, "mundo!" }
receive do
  msg -> IO.puts "The process said: #{inspect msg}"
end

send pid, { self(), :fr, "tout le monde!" }
receive do
  msg -> IO.puts "The process said: #{inspect msg}"
end
```

Run this, and you'll see:

```
$ elixir spawn9.exs
The process said: "Hola mundo!"
The process said: {:EXIT, #PID<0.36.0>, :normal}
```

Have a look at the second message we received. Rather than getting a French greeting, we get a tuple {:EXIT, pid, :normal}. This is Elixir sending us a message to notify us that the process exited normally.

In fact, all state information in Elixir is sent as messages. You can choose which processes you want to monitor, and you can create trees of these processes where each level monitors the processes below them. This is a large part of the ability of the Erlang VM to deliver 9-nines availability in highly concurrent systems.

A Final Example

Let's use our knowledge of actors to write one final example program. This is a library that implements the map function. (The map function takes a collection and applies a function to each element, returning a new collection containing the results of each function call.) However, we'll make this example more interesting by running each computation in a separate process. Without further ado, here's the code:

elixir/pmap.exs
```elixir
defmodule Parallel do

  import Enum, only: [map: 2]

  # Parallel map
  def pmap(collection, fun) do
    collection |> spawn_children(fun) |> collect_results
  end

  defp spawn_children(collection, fun), do: collection |> map(&spawn_child(&1, fun))

  def spawn_child(item, fun),    do: spawn(__MODULE__, :child, [item, fun, self()])

  def child(item, fun, parent), do: send parent, { self(), fun.(item) }

  defp collect_results(pids),    do: pids |> map(&collect_result_for_pid/1)

  defp collect_result_for_pid(pid) do
    receive do
      { ^pid, value } -> value
    end
  end
end
```

The basic idea is a really nice example of the way functional languages express code. The main pmap function takes a collection, transforms it into a set of processes, and then transforms those processes into their results. The only new thing in this code is the use of spawn in the spawn_child function. Because we want to pass arguments, we use the variant of spawn that lets us specify a module, function, and argument list.

To give our code something to work on, we'll write a deliberately inefficient function to calculate Fibonacci numbers.

elixir/pmap.exs
```elixir
defmodule Sequence do
  def fib(0), do: 0
  def fib(1), do: 1
  def fib(n), do: fib(n-1) + fib(n-2)
end
```

Some simple unit tests verify that it works:

elixir/pmap.exs
```elixir
ExUnit.start

defmodule MyTest do
  use ExUnit.Case

  import Parallel
  import Sequence

  test "basic fib works" do
    assert fib(10) == 55
    assert fib(30) == 832040
  end

  test "parallel map works" do
    assert pmap([1,2,3,4,5,6], &fib/1) == [1, 1, 2, 3, 5, 8]
  end
end
```

But that isn't the whole story. Let's see if we can watch the parallelism at work. I'll calculate some Fibonacci numbers. The graph shows the CPU utilization on my 4-core laptop.

```
iex> c "pmap.exs"
iex> Parallel.pmap [42,41,40,39,38,42,41,39,38], Sequence.fib(&1)
[267914296, 165580141, 102334155, 63245986, 39088169, 267914296,
165580141, 63245986, 39088169]
```

We're pegging all four cores until the end, when the code runs out of work and ends up finishing up a calculation using just one core.

Concurrency Is the Core of Elixir

The functional aspects of Elixir are the most obvious external features. And they are what drew me to the language. But, after a while, you realize that they are really there to support the inherent concurrency in the environment.

And, for me, that's been both the most difficult and the most rewarding aspect of adopting Elixir. Now, when I write code, I try to think of a decomposition not into objects, but rather into actors, or services. And given that Elixir can run literally millions of processes on even a modest laptop, these actors can be very fine-grained.

It's an exciting time to be writing code, and Elixir is a gratifying language to use to write that code.

In Chapter 21, A Testing Framework for Elixir, on page 169 and Chapter 22, Building Test Data with Elixir, on page 177, Bruce Tate will use Elixir to build some useful tools.

If you've been reading this book sequentially, you've now seen how Scala, Clojure, and Elixir bring functional programming techniques to the mainstream. In the next chapter, we'll step back and explore the functional paradigm in greater depth in Haskell, a no-compromises pure functional language.

Part V

Haskell: The Researcher's Playground

Haskell was developed as a common open source platform for research in functional language design. One of its more distinctive features is its rich type system. Although foremost a research tool, Haskell has found a home in commercial applications, including Facebook's anti-spam programs.

## CHAPTER 13

Functional Thinking and Haskell

by Paul Callaghan

How do functional programmers think? I aim to give you a glimpse into the programming style and mindset of experienced functional programmers, so you can see why we are so passionate about what we do. Few of these ideas get the exposure they deserve in textbooks or tutorials, and in my view they are essential for coming to grips with a functional language and using it productively in real apps.

Most of what I'll say will refer to Haskell, though many of the ideas do apply to other functional languages as well.

What It's All About

The most important idea in modern functional programming is this:

It's all about data.

Functional programmers put data first. We start by thinking about what kinds of data we have in a problem domain, and what kinds of transformations we want to perform on the data. Once we have a handle on this, we start building up the data structures and the code to do the transformations.

Functional programming is *not* all about coding with pure functions. What modern functional *languages* are about is developing ever-better tools to help in this data-first style of programming. It's about providing easier ways to specify powerful data types, to manipulate them at a high level, to break them apart and recombine them, and to do all this with a degree of safety and reusability and without too much syntactic baggage or implementation detail cluttering up the code.

Because that's what they're designed for, remembering to put data first is absolutely key if you want to use these tools well. Taking a fully imperative approach in a functional language doesn't end happily. The tools aren't designed to work that way.

Ever used pipes in Unix shells? They are a very good introduction to functional thinking, and it's worth lingering a moment in Unixland before jumping into Haskell.

For example, suppose you want the three most memory-hungry processes owned by users whose login names begin with "foo." There's no magic Unix command for this, but you can easily build one by assembling smaller pieces. This is a key idea in Unix, which provides small tools to perform steps on data, and a way to glue the steps together. I'll leave the fine details of this example to you, but you'll probably use ps to list processes, grep to select matching rows, sort on a particular column, and finally head to grab the first few rows.

Another example: how do you count how many processes run by users Fred or Joe use more than 100M in virtual memory? You might need wc to count rows, and awk (or perl or ruby) to do the numeric filtering. The details aren't important.

What is important is to notice *what data we're using* (rows of lines, each with certain fields) and *how we're transforming that data* through a pipeline of steps, one simple step at a time. Look at the code, too—it tends to say pretty clearly what it's doing.

A Quick Exercise

Let's see how much Haskell you can understand just by first grasping an informal, hand-wavy solution and then looking at the corresponding code. It's very much a "think in data" solution, but also probably quite different from how you've seen this kind of problem approached before. Without modulo division or if statements, I give you "Functional Fizz Buzz."

The task is this: you want Fizz every three steps, and Buzz every five steps. We note that sometimes the cycles coincide. Let's talk cycles then.

```
threes = cycle ["", "", "Fizz"]
fives  = cycle ["", "", "", "", "Buzz"]
```

cycle is defined like this (the real library def is more efficient, but less clear):

```
cycle xs = xs ++ cycle xs    -- SIMPLE version of lib
```

So threes just spits out ["","","Fizz","","","Fizz",...] until we stop it, and similarly for fives. Next, we want to merge two streams into one: this is quite common, so there's a library function for it. zipWith pairs up elements and uses some operation to combine each pair:

```
zipWith g [a,b,c,...] [d,e,f, ...]  ===>
    (computes to) [g a d, g b e, g c f, ...]
eg zipWith max [1,2,3] [2,2,2] ===> [2,2,3]
eg zipWith (*) [1,2,3] [2,2,2] ===> [2,4,6]
```

Think zippers in clothes. Now, that's just what we want for merging our streams. It works for infinite streams too (why shouldn't it?).

```
fizzbuzz = zipWith (++) threes fives
```

(++) is string concatenation, and then we just push the list of lines to the screen. And hit ^C when we get bored.

```
main = putStr (unlines fizzbuzz)
```

If we want numbers in there between the Fizzes and Buzzes instead of blanks, we can just zip in another list that contains the numbers from 1 up to infinity, and just add in a number if the string would otherwise be empty.

So, it's a short piece of code that obviously works, built from small pieces and glued together in a simple way (think Unix pipes), and there's no worry about loops, division, variables, memory limits...

This isn't a one-off trick. Programming with Haskell is generally like this.

Data Types Are Cheap

As I said at the outset (and will say again), all we did here was to identify the kinds of data we had in the problem domain, and what kinds of transformations we wanted to perform on it, and then we built up the data structures and the code to do the transformations.

Let's look at the tools that modern functional languages provide for doing this.

The first "tool" is the sheer flexibility for declaring new data types and the scope for reusing them. This is very important: rather than encoding some data in a hash and hoping that you remember to keep the encoding consistent, Haskell allows—even encourages—you to add a new type that expresses exactly what you want to store. Such type declarations are much shorter than the equivalent in imperative or OO languages. *And* Haskell can automatically generate certain standard functions to use with the type, such as ordering tests or conversion to strings. I'll say it again—it's very quick and easy to add the data type that fits your problem domain well, and the close fit really helps code quality and clarity.

Some Examples

Some examples now.

```
data Bool = False | True
```

That's right—Bool isn't baked into the language, but the language is powerful enough to add such "primitive" notions directly into the core language. The various Boolean operators, including shortcut semantics, are just standard Haskell definitions. The "core" of Haskell is a surprisingly small language, and the rest of the standard language is defined in straightforward Haskell.

```
data RGB = Red | Blue | Green deriving (Eq, Ord, Show, Enum)
```

This defines three constants (Red, Blue, Green) and automatically generates equality and ordering tests, a show (i.e., to_s) function, and the ability to use .. notation; for example, [Red .. Green] is the list [Red, Blue, Green].

```
data Maybe a = Nothing | Just a
```

This is a little different. This is a (parametric) polymorphic type, and represents a box that is either empty (Nothing) or contains a single value of some type. This has various uses—for example, passing in an optional value or returning a value that is absent or a sensible value. The parametric polymorphism means it can be used with any value (and any type) we choose, so it's not limited, say, to just containing strings.

Note that parametric polymorphism is not the polymorphism seen in OO (though Haskell has a version of the latter, as explained below). A quick explanation is: parametric polymorphism means using the same code for everything, whereas the main kind of polymorphism in OO is more about allowing different values to be treated the same by virtue of calling object-specific code.

```
data Person = Person { name :: String, age :: Maybe Int,
                       fav_col :: RGB, address :: [String] }
```

Here's a simple record that stores a name, an optional age, a favorite color, and zero or more lines of an address (square brackets mean lists in Haskell). Notice that a record field can contain an arbitrarily complex value, so not just primitive types. An example value is

```
joe = Person "Joe" (Just 25) Red ["Durham Cathedral", "Durham"]
```

Haskell also has syntactic sugar for accessing and updating record-style values, which uses the names provided for the fields, in effect giving us accessors and setter functions.

We can also have recursive types like lists or trees, like the following (polymorphic) binary tree, which has values of some type at the leaves, and its internal nodes each have a left tree and a right tree.

```
data PTree a = PLeaf a | PNode (PTree a) (PTree a)
```

Lists are defined in a similar way, with a [] case and a cons case. Again, this isn't baked in, apart from a bit of syntactic sugar that Haskell provides to allow a simpler notation. Haskell also allows more complex examples, such as the following, which is effectively parameterizing which type holds the subtrees. This allows us to vary how the child trees are stored; for example, we could have zero or more (c = lists), or precisely one for each of the RGB colors (with c a as a function from RGB to some polymorphic a). Not an everyday construct, but it does have its uses!

```
data X c a = XLeaf a | XNode (c (X c a))
```

We're able to combine constants, records, recursion, and polymorphism quite freely, and to mix these with types in the standard libraries, like arrays, hashes, and lists. This gives us a lot of flexibility and convenience to model data in our problem domains, and to do it without much code. This modeling can be very accurate, too, which helps to eliminate certain classes of errors. That is, if we can use these data type definitions to precisely say what is allowed, then our code need only deal with those cases, and we can easily check coverage of those cases. For example, representing optional values with Maybe forces us to explicitly handle the "nothing" case vs. the "something" case. Compare this to Ruby, where nils are often used for this, but it's quite common to forget to check for nils before calling a method.

In fact, Haskell does not have nil values (and does not need them), so that's one class of error we never see.

Don't underestimate how important this flexibility and accuracy is!

A Very Important (and Under-Appreciated) Type

Like most functional languages, Haskell has first-class functions, meaning we can treat functions like almost any other piece of data—build them, pass them around, use them. We should not forget how such functions sit with the preceding data types. The notation for the type is A -> B, indicating a conversion from some type A to some other type B. Tests on color values will have type RGB -> Bool, for determining the max of two colors with RGB -> RGB -> RGB. Values of these types can appear in record fields, etc.; for (a very contrived) example, each person could include a mapping from an int to a color that expresses what color that person associates with a number.

We can also represent "waiting for an X" as a function value; for example, if you have a person record but are waiting for their address to come from somewhere, this could be represented as a function of type [String] -> Person, which is supplied with the address when it is available, and will return the complete person thereafter. Using the previous example, we can do it like this, using Haskell's syntax for anonymous functions:

```
\address -> Person "Joe" (Just 25) Red address
```

Pattern Matching

Doing stuff with values in the preceding types is easy: we just write clauses in our functions to deal with the various patterns we expect to see.

For example, mirror-reversing a tree—there are two main cases (leaf or node), and each clause says what to do with the contents of the tree.

```
mirror (PLeaf x)   = PLeaf x
mirror (PNode l r) = PNode (mirror r) (mirror l)
```

Notice that we're covering all possible cases of tree here. A value which is of tree type is either a leaf or a node, and we provide code to handle both cases in full. We'll never get a runtime error when an unexpected input is received. Some of the compilers track this "totality" for us, and can give warnings when functions don't cover all cases. Also, it doesn't matter what kind of data is on the leaves— this operation is just manipulating the tree structure. So quite naturally, this function is (parametrically) polymorphic and can be used on any PTree value.

Also note, we don't need if statements so much now. Pattern matching does most of the checking work for us, and usually more succinctly—hence, easier to follow. We can still have the traditional Boolean-conditional tests; for example, if 2 > 3 then a else b, and there's a shorthand for combining these with the preceding patterns. Patterns can also be nested, allowing us to match complex conditions very easily. The following example snippet is from a toy compiler for Java, part of the code that flattens high-level code to simpler sequential low-level code. This case handles the lifting of a side effect out of a binary operator expression, where it is safe to do so. This is much easier to read than a load of nested if-statements, with less chance to make mistakes, too.

```
rwE (BINOP op l (ESEQ s r))
  | commutes s l
  = chg $ ESEQ s (BINOP op l r)
  | otherwise
  = chg $ ESEQ (MOVE (TEMP t) l)
     (ESEQ s (BINOP op (TEMP t) r))
  where t = new_tmp_var
```

Recursion, Control, and Higher-Order Functions

Pattern matching gives us decision making, but what about loops and so on? Most of the time, we don't really need them either.

Again, think data and transformations. When we have a collection of things to process in some way—say, a list of numbers that we want to turn into a list of colors, or a tree containing strings for which we want the leaf count—most of the transformations we want fall into two main patterns: *mapping* and *folding*.

Mapping is about applying the same operation to everything in a collection, but keeping the shape the same. For example, we can add 2 onto elements in the list [1,2,3] to get [3,4,5]. The order and count of elements stays the same. The operation to perform is supplied as a function. Ruby programmers will know this pattern already, and know how convenient it is for replacing an explicit loop.

The other and more powerful pattern is *folding*. Ruby programmers will know this for arrays as inject. For example:

```
[1,2,3].inject(1, &:*)
```

This gets the product of a list of numbers, and it works exactly the same. Another way to think of folding is to replace the "nodes" of some data structure with functions (or constants). Writing [1,2,3] in Lisp style (cons 1 (cons 2 (cons 3 nil))), then [1,2,3].inject(i,f), will give us (f 1 (f 2 (f 3 i))). In the product example, this is (* 1 (* 2 (* 3 1))). Notice that we're collapsing or folding the data into a different type (list of numbers into a single number), though with appropriate choice of f and i, we can produce a list of numbers again, or even produce more complex values—like lists of trees of numbers.

Now, this folding idea, of replacing constructor nodes with functions, applies to any data structure, so we can easily adapt it to other types, like trees or records. Here's folding on the simple trees explained previously.

```
foldPTree node_case leaf_case (PLeaf x)
 = leaf_case x
foldPTree node_case leaf_case (PNode l r)
 = node_case (foldPTree node_case leaf_case l)
             (foldPTree node_case leaf_case r)
```

So a leaf count can be done with foldPTree (\x y -> x + y) (_ -> 1); in other words, count one for each leaf value, then add up the results from subtrees. Once you understand the folding pattern, then such definitions suddenly become a lot clearer than the explicit version. Compare with this:

```
leaf_count (PLeaf x)   = 1
leaf_count (PNode l r) = leaf_count l + leaf_count r
```

The code is simple enough, but you still need to check each line carefully to see that it has all the details right and doesn't contain mistakes, like calling leaf_count l instead of leaf_count r. In a sense, mentally you have to rewrite it as a fold! It's similar to explicit loops in Ruby, when you realize that they can be written more directly as a map or an inject. Isn't it nice to shorten and simplify the code, to make it say what you mean more directly? Yes.

So these maps and folds are a natural way to transform your data, and thus are highly useful tools for programming, in terms of both saying simply what you mean and avoiding verbose code. In fact, explicit recursion in FP is a bit of an anti-pattern, particularly when it's not needed. It can be annoying to read extra code when a more direct version works. Plus, more code means more chance of slipping up.

Tony Hoare famously contrasted code with obviously no deficiencies vs. code with no obvious deficiencies—it helps to aim for the former!

How do functional programmers solve problems? We think about what kinds of data we have and what kinds of transformations we want to perform on them, and we build the data structures and the code to do the transformations, often using maps and folds. Now, you might not be able to spot the maps and folds in some piece of code right away—it takes practice—but when you have sketched out an explicit version, do go back and think about whether it has bits of mapping, bits of folding, or particular sub-cases like filtering, and see if you can simplify the code. Also think in terms of data and transformations, and the opportunities might become more obvious. Don't feel compelled to use folds and so on if you're not confident, but do try to reflect on your code afterwards and see if you can refactor. There will be cases when your pattern of recursion does not fit a fold, or will look worse if coded as a fold, but these are pretty rare. Similar advice applies for loops in other languages too: look for the mapping aspects, filtering, and folding, and try to use the higher-level operations instead. Again, you should find that explicit loops aren't required that often (and if they are, perhaps wider refactoring would help; for example, is there a bad design choice upstream that is forcing your hand?).

Three last technical points. First, folding corresponds to the "vanilla" pattern of processing values in a data type, and this pattern is inherently connected to how the data type is defined. It's not a coincidence. Second, we're passing functions into the maps and folds to control what happens in the various cases—hence, maps and folds are examples of higher-order functions. That just means functions that do stuff with functions. Third, mapping can be defined in terms of folding (exercise: try to write map in Ruby in terms of inject).

Further Features

Understanding how a functional programmer thinks also means seeing how to build bigger pieces from smaller ones. Understanding Haskell means understanding its syntax. And sizing up functional and Haskell programming involves looking at performance. So we'll touch on all three of these topics next, briefly.

Functional Glue

The other side of higher-order function use is how we use the building blocks to create larger blocks. Haskell is sometimes called an excellent "glue" language, because of the ease with which code units can be assembled. You've already seen pipelining—building large transformations from a sequence of smaller transformations, each contributing some piece towards the final result. Here's a Haskell example, written in various styles.

```
foo1 input = unlines  (map (\line ->
    unwords  (map reverse  (words line))) (lines input))
foo2 input = unlines $ map (\line ->
    unwords $ map reverse $ words line)  $ lines input
foo3 = unlines . map (unwords . map reverse . words) . lines
```

This reverses each word on each line of the input. Conceptually, we split the input into lines, then each line into words and then reverse each word, then reassemble the words and lines. The first version is the explicit version, the second cuts down some of the parentheses by using a syntactic trick, and the third shows the idiomatic version. Clearly, the first two still have some noise, but the third says very concisely what we are thinking. Reading right to left, we split the lines, do something to each line, and reassemble. And for each line, we split into words, reverse them, then reassemble. Again, no trickery—just using the language to say what we mean.

The dot deserves special mention. It is functional composition in Haskell, and basically means joining the output of one function to the input of another, so forming a bigger function. It is defined like this, as a piece of Haskell, and not baked in either:

```
f . g = \x -> f (g x)
```

So, foo . bar is a new function that takes some value x, applies g to it, then applies f to the result. The two functions can be anything (providing their input/output types are compatible, of course). For example, show . (\x -> x + 3) shows the result of adding 3 to a value (assumed numeric). Or, not . (\x -> x > 10) . (\x -> x + 3) tests for a number + 3 being more than 10, and inverts the result. We're not stuck with this definition of composition, either; we can define and use "reverse composition" too, where f gets applied first, then g—whatever we find most useful.

Here's an example that often annoys me in Ruby. Sometimes I want to do one mapping on a list, then another mapping, so I have to write

```
stuff.map(&:foo1).map(&:foo2)
```

In Haskell, it looks like this: map foo2 $ map foo1 $ stuff. But often, conceptually it is nicer to have one map doing two operations, so we can rewrite it to map (foo2 . foo1) $ stuff. Ruby doesn't support this kind of rewrite without a lot of extra syntax. (I suggest this flexibility is the acid test of full functional support in a language.)

Finally, if we need other kinds of glue, we can just define them ourselves.

Digression: Are Haskell Instructors Missing a Trick?

Many Haskell books introduce the operators (.) and ($) quite early, but this could be hindering rather than helping beginners by being too big a step. I'm steadily warming to the idea that the |> from Elixir and F# is a much better choice, and much easier for beginners to deal with.

Elixir's operator is a tool for chaining together a sequence of operations on some data, also known as *building a pipeline*, and it gives rise to code like this:

```
words "here is some text"
|> map reverse
|> sort
|> unlines
```

Haskell has a similar operator called $, but it is used the other way round. The previous example becomes:

```
unlines
$ sort
$ map reverse
$ words "here is some text"
```

Which one is easier to understand? If you've been using Haskell for ages, you might think the second version is fine because it's what you've grown used to. But I suspect the rest of the world would prefer the first.

When I was teaching Haskell at a university, I would talk a lot about complex programs being made up of pipelines, of sequences of transformations. Then

I'd try to convince my captive audience that they could build such pipelines with ($) (dollar) and (.) (function composition), and next try to explain how to read code with such pipelines. Not everyone got it. Very few did.

After seeing what Elixir uses, I'm a convert to |>. I'm sure that using that operator in pipelines would have been much easier to digest: it maps more easily to prior experience (like Unix pipes), and there's a much more immediate sense of it being a pipeline, thus reinforcing one of the key idioms in the paradigm. I don't have the luxury of testing this theory on undergrads anymore (phew).

```
x |> f = f x
```

The preceding code is all you need to define |> in Haskell: nothing else required, certainly no voodoo like macros. The type is also straightforward: (|>) :: a -> (a -> b) -> b. It literally says, pass in a value of type a and a function of type a -> b, and you'll get a value of type b.

One final point in favor of using |>: when you eventually do need to introduce monads (and this is the only time I'll mention them in this book), you can present monads as a generalization of |>: as providing the basic pipeline pattern but with some useful extra stuff added. Just compare the type signatures!

Clean Syntax

Haskell's syntax is one of its key features, and a model for other languages to follow. Several aspects are deliberately designed to cut down on syntactic baggage and allow more focus on the ideas in the code. This really emphasizes the declarative style of programming. Some key points:

- Function application is kind of Lisp style, but without so many parentheses; for example, map reverse (words "foo bar"), where map takes two arguments and words takes one.

- Partial application is natural and unobtrusive; for example, map (\x -> x * 2) is a function that applies some function (\x -> x * 2) to any list it is supplied later. Compare other languages, where we'd have to write something like ->(list) {map (\x -> x * 2) list} to get the same effect.

- Modern precedence and associativity rules for operators, which can be extended to include new user-defined operators—which really helps in the design of embedded domain-specific languages (DSLs).

- Semicolons. Yes, semicolons. And braces (curly brackets). The Haskell grammar actually requires these elements to delimit and separate groups of expressions, and most implementations of the language have a pre-processing stage that inserts braces and semicolons according to how indentation is being used in the code, typically through a variant of Landin's "off-side rule." (Key point: Haskell's use of layout is more flexible than Ruby's.)

Performance

You may have been worried by the seemingly infinite loop in the Fizz Buzz example. However, Haskell compilers generate "lazy" code, which means (as a first approximation) that work is only done when needed, so we only generate as much of the list as we need (here, until ^C is used), plus garbage collection reclaims unused space.

Note that there are several kinds of "lazy" available, including a few options we can set during compilation, and that the Haskell language definition only requires "non-strict" rather than "lazy."

Put another way, the language passes more control over execution order to the compiler and runtime. We don't have to micromanage the steps of computation, and the compiler is free to transform our code in powerful ways to improve performance. It's quite common for FP compilers to optimize away some of the intermediate data structures in a chain of functions (called "deforestation"), saving on memory and time. Some FP compilers (OCaml in particular) can even match the top C compilers in performance now because of the complex optimizations they can do when side effects are less of an issue.

The key point from this is the silver rule: "Trust your compiler." Your job is to write good code, and you can let the compiler deal with some of the lower-level details. It is much better at complex optimizations than you are—and less error-prone! If the program runs slowly, there is a good range of tools for profiling and analyzing that help to pinpoint bottlenecks. You can then work on optimizing the crunch points. Haskell's GHC compiler offers several simple techniques for speeding up bottlenecks, from reduction of laziness, through user-supplied rewrite rules, to even making it easy to code key steps in C. Meanwhile, most of your code can remain high-level and clear.

I hope you now have a clearer view of how functional programmers think: that most of it is about deciding which data structures you need, then coding up various transformations. And how we use the language to program at a high level and use it to express the big ideas in a straightforward and clear way. It is kind of addictive. You have a lot of flexibility and convenience, but you also get strong tools to do even more complex stuff and keep control of it. In the next chapter, we'll dive into Haskell coding.

## CHAPTER 14

Haskell Hands-On

by Paul Callaghan

The preceding chapter was a glimpse into the mindset of an experienced Haskell programmer. Now it's time to do some programming. Let's try a kata.

We're going to use Dave Thomas's word-chain kata,[1] and through it we'll explore how functional programmers approach a problem, we'll learn some Haskell syntax and libraries, and we'll touch on performance and optimization of Haskell code.

The objective of the kata is to find a series of steps from one word to another, where in each step a single letter is changed such that the resulting string is also a valid word. For example, turning "lead" into "gold" with the path ["lead", "load", "goad", "gold"]. For simplicity, I'll assume four-letter words and lower-case throughout.

Before we begin, remember the golden rule: it's all about data. So our approach will be all about identifying relevant data structures and transformations, and about decomposing big problems into smaller problems until we can solve them in a straightforward way. Remember the silver rule too: "Trust your compiler." So we'll focus on clear code first without worrying too much about efficiency.

So let's get you set up. I'm going to use the Glasgow Haskell Compiler (GHC)[2] as the main development tool here. GHC is the most advanced implementation of Haskell, covering the standard language (Haskell-98) and many experimental extensions and libraries, including some based on cutting-edge research. As well as compiling Haskell to fast native code, it also provides a REPL-style

---

1. http://codekata.com/kata/kata19-word-chains/
2. http://www.haskell.org/ghc/

tool called GHCi.[3] The Haskell Platform[4] provides an easy-to-install package of the main Haskell tools for standard platforms, including GHC and GHCi, Cabal (similar to Ruby's Gem tool), and other build tools, plus many of the popular extra libraries (cf. Gems) already installed. Such additional libraries can be found on Hackage.[5] Also, there are some IDEs for Haskell, but I just use vi. The full code for this chapter is in a Github Gist.[6] To play with the code, save it to a file with a .hs extension and run ghci on the file (or hugs, if you're using that), then run various bits of code as you wish.

One Step at a Time

All right, we're looking to construct paths, and paths contain steps, so how about starting with the step operation? We want this operation to take a word and return all of the valid words that are reachable in one step from that word. For example, from "lead" we want to get the list

```
["bead","dead","head","mead","read","load","lend","lewd",
        "leaf","leak","leal","lean","leap","lear","leas"]
```

and we want it to exclude non-words like "xead."

A key idea in functional programming is to split big problems into smaller ones. We use it all the time. So how can we apply it here?

At some point we probably need to use the dictionary to filter out invalid words like "xead," but does the filtering need to be tied into the word generation? Let's try splitting the problem right at this point. In fact, this is a common way to split problems in functional programming as well as elsewhere: via the "generate and test" pattern, where one component suggests results and the other one discards invalid ones. So let's try creating one component to generate a list of candidate words, and another to filter out the bad candidates.

Thinking About Types

A quick thought about types first: our basic step needs to have the type String -> [String], or from a word to a list of words. You might be itching to use more complex types after Chapter 13, *Functional Thinking and Haskell*, on page 97, but let's keep it simple for now. What do we have so far? Let's write it down.

```
one_step :: String -> [String]
one_step = filter is_valid_word . generate_candidates
```

---

3.   http://www.haskell.org/ghc/docs/latest/html/users_guide/ghci.html
4.   http://hackage.haskell.org/platform/
5.   http://hackage.haskell.org/packages/hackage.html
6,   https://gist.github.com/3733182

Of course, this won't compile because some code is missing (*aka*, we have at least one failing test).

What does this code mean? The definition uses function composition (the dot) and says directly that the one_step operation is a composition (or combination) of *generating candidates* and *filtering* them. Recall that f . g is defined in the Haskell Prelude as \x -> f (g x), so the composition is a new function (the \x -> ... bit) that applies f to the result of g x. Programming wise, we're building a bigger transformation from two smaller ones.

You can read function compositions in any direction—whatever makes more sense or another version that you are happier with. For example, right to left as a series of steps (generate the candidates, then filter them) or left to right for a more "transformational" view (filtering the results from the candidate list). Notice that we don't need to mention any parameters here: practically because the definition of function composition handles that for us, and philosophically because we want to say that the big operation is a composition of two others and that's all.

I'm going to leave word filtering for a bit, so I will just define the following and move on to the other missing code.

```
is_valid_word = error "Need to finish"
```

You can see what that line means, but I should pause briefly to explain it a bit, because it reveals something about programming in Haskell. The function error :: String -> a takes a string and causes a runtime exception when the expression is evaluated. That is, if the program ever tried to use is_valid_word, then there would be a runtime error whose message included the "Need to finish" string. This function is useful for stubbing out unfinished code, and for signaling serious problems at runtime. (It is a bit like throw for exceptions, and indeed, some exception support is built into Haskell—though not often used because we have other, softer alternatives.)

Note the type of error: it takes a string and the result type is a, but there's absolutely no constraint on a. In other words, it really does mean *anything*. This is sensible, because it allows us to flag errors anywhere; for example, we can use it where a list of Ints is expected because the type variable matches anything. Plus, if you think about it, there's no sensible operation that could have this type, so it kind of has to be this error functionality!

Telling It Like It Is

As long as we're paused, notice that I used the expression filter is_valid_word rather than some other single (yet to be defined) function name. There are some important points about language use here.

First, I'm making the positive choice that I want to use filtering on the candidate list, because I know what data structures are in play at the time, and have decided that filtering is going to be appropriate. So instead of a simple decomposition into two stages, I've gone a bit further on the particular detail.

Second, I'm using the language to say this *directly* rather than making up a new function name and adding another definition of that name. Compare these expressions: map (\x -> 2 + x) [1..10] vs. map add_two [1..10]. Haskell is flexible enough that quite often the code itself is the clearest explanation of the programmer's intent, and adding in extra definitions can make the code harder to follow. In this case, you would have to check elsewhere in the code to see what add_two *actually* does, whereas 2 + x is immediately obvious. Of course, there are cases where such new definitions can be justified—but Haskell gives you the choice. (You can be even more terse, like map (2+) [1..10].)

Third, what does the expression filter is_valid_word actually mean? Conceptually, it's taking the general idea of filtering a list with some predicate and then fixing the predicate to be a certain test: the result is an operation that picks out the valid words from a list. The important point here is that *in Haskell, this kind of expression is meaningful* and hence a key part of the coding style. Let's consider a simpler example.

```
foo = filter (\x -> reverse x == x)
bar = foo ["ada", "fred", "bob"]
```

The first line names a combination of filter and a test for a list being a palindrome. (Haskell strings are a list of characters, though this test for palindromes will work with a list of anything that has an equality test.) The combination can then be used with a list of words, as in the second line.

You Don't Have to Like Curry

What's the type of foo? Well, filter :: (a -> Bool) -> [a] -> [a]; in other words, it takes a predicate (takes some a value, returns a Bool) and a list of such a values and returns a list of the same. For the type of \x -> reverse x == x, we have to do some type inference, but it comes out as Eq a => [a] -> Bool; in other words, testing a list of a values as long as we can do equality tests on a values themselves. Putting these together—which means matching the first parameter of filter with the predicate—we get filter (\x -> reverse x == x) :: Eq a => [[a]] -> [[a]], hence converting a list of a values into a similar list (assuming equality is known).

A nested list of something might be a bit abstract if you are new to it, but it's fine to consider concrete examples, so in the context of bar, it's going to take and return a list of strings.

Some people like to use the word "currying" at this point. I don't. I think it's a bit of a misleading distraction that adds little. Conceptually (and theoretically; i.e., the lambda calculus), all functions in Haskell take one argument at a time, and either return a new function or a concrete value, and it's important to understand this. How filter behaved in the preceding code is a direct consequence of this.

Pragmatically, we often define and use multi-argument functions as if they were just like their equivalents in (say) Ruby, but underneath, Haskell is still using the preceding mechanism. The compilers will optimize such multi-argument functions so they behave efficiently, so we don't have to worry about how the functions are actually implemented.

Generating Candidates

Let's see, we're *generating* and *filtering*, right? So let's consider the operation that generates potential words for later filtering. Type-wise, we want generate_candidates :: String -> [String], so that from a given word we get all possible next steps.

It's always good to start with some concrete examples, especially if the operation doesn't seem obvious.

From generate_candidates "", we expect no candidates, since there's no way to change a single character in an empty string.

From generate_candidates "a", we expect ["b", "c", ... "z"], because we change the character to every other character except "a".

From generate_candidates "ba", we expect ["aa", "ca", "da", ... "za", "bb", "bc", ... "bz"], which is the list from changing the first character, plus the list from changing the second character.

There's a *bit* of a pattern here (which we should look to exploit in the code), but it's not obviously a map or a filter or a fold, so what do we do now? The functional programmer's next tactic is usually to start thinking about the *main cases of the input*. (The editor, who learned Lisp at a tender age at the feet of the legendary Dan Friedman, waves his hand and says, "Ooh, ooh, I know this one!") Uh, yes. This means thinking about (a) the empty list case and (b) the cons case.

One benefit of thinking via patterns is that we can think about the cases independently, and looking at the preceding examples, we've already done the first case (there are no candidates) so let's fill it in. This leaves:

```
generate_candidates []
 = []
generate_candidates (c:cs)
 = error "don't know"
```

Progress!

OK, the cons case requires some thought. It is highly likely to involve recursion somewhere, and the trick of writing recursive code is to think about possible recursive calls and what they give you, and from the results think of how to construct what you actually want. In this case, we can call generate_candidates on any string we like, but it's likely to be the tail of the input (or maybe a substring of it). Let's guess a call to generate_candidates cs (to produce all candidates from the tail string) and see where it gets us, specifically thinking about how we can use c, cs, and the result from generate_candidates cs to build the result.

But let's also think about the concrete examples for "ba" and "a" from the preceding code. The latter will be the result from the recursive call when processing "ba", so can we do something to ["b", "c", ... "z"] to get (part of) the overall result? Well, if we put character b at the front of each of the strings, we get the last part of the result list. Let's fill this in.

```
generate_candidates []
 = []
generate_candidates (c:cs)
 = error "don't know"
  ++ [ c : xs | xs <- generate_candidates cs ]
```

Syntax [expr | pattern <- list] indicates a "list comprehension," also seen in CoffeeScript, Python, and certain branches of set theory. It is a very convenient shorthand for combinations of maps and filters on lists, and it translates to a combination of map, filter, and list concatenation. The preceding code produces a new list by looping through the elements produced by the recursive call and sticking head character c on the front of each—it's a map, in other words.

The first case isn't too hard either: it's the result of putting any letter *except* for c at the front of the list tail cs. We can use a list comprehension here too, with a filtering step that skips the original character.

```
generate_candidates []
  = []
generate_candidates (c:cs)
  =   [ x : cs | x <- ['a'..'z'], x /= c ]      -- new at front
   ++ [ c : xs | xs <- generate_candidates cs ] -- old at front
```

Observe that when we're dealing with a one-character string, the recursive call will return an empty list, and mapping over it also produces an empty list, which is safe to append to the rest of the result. In short, we don't have to handle this situation as a special case—it just naturally slots into place.

We can test generate_candidates on the concrete examples and confirm that we get the expected outcome.

But our purpose here is understanding, not just correctly executing code. So let's pause a bit to consider whether the code makes sense, and whether it gives a clear enough view of how this part of the program works. I don't give cut-and-dried answers here, and I encourage you to think about what you want from the code and not just to accept current limitations on our understanding!

We've reached this version of the code by a few careful steps of reasoning, filling in pieces at a time, and we did understand each step. Are we therefore confident that the code is correct, with or without testing? Is confidence alone enough? On the other hand, how can we be confident that our tests are sufficient?

What about alternative coding approaches? This is a book on functional programming, and I have been cheerleading functional thinking, but let's ask: what would an imperative or OO programmer do here? Would we be happier with an imperative or OO version? One possibility is an outer loop on the string position and an inner loop on the replacement letters, generating a new candidate word on each iteration. Here's a version of the code that works along such principles.

```
generate_v2 w = [ before ++ d : tail after
                | (before, after) <- all_splits_of w
                , not (null after)
                , d <- ['a' .. 'z']
                , d /= head after ]

all_splits_of :: [a] -> [([a], [a])]
all_splits_of w = zip (inits w) (tails w)
```

The all_splits_of function returns all ways of splitting a list into two while keeping the original element order; for example, all_splits_of "lead" will give [("","lead"),("l","ead"),("le","ad"),("lea","d"),("lead","")]. We then loop over this list, replacing the head of the second part with a different character and rebuilding the string (except when the second part is empty). Is this clearer? Or can you find another version that does make more sense?

In the words of the immortal Tim Toady, TMTOWTDI.

It's worth noting that this version touches on recent FP research on *views*: the idea is that we choose a view of the data that simplifies the code, rather than always working with a particular physical representation. (It has some relationship with the concept of views in databases.) So we view a list as the join of two lists, and then loop through the various ways of splitting the list to get our answer. The FP work in views started with Philip Wadler, and has been expanded significantly by Conor McBride in the context of dependently typed programming (for example, in Epigram).[7]

Dictionary Filtering

We're not quite finished with the program that has been the motivator of this chapter. Now for the dictionary filtering. We'll do this bit by loading a list of words into a hash-like structure and then testing whether a word is present. Here's the code. I'm sure you could write this code in several brilliant ways, and it won't advance our understanding of Haskell or functional programming much to examine it in detail, so I'll be brief.

```
-- import lines should go at the top
import Data.Set(Set, fromDistinctAscList, member)
import System.IO.Unsafe(unsafePerformIO)

dict = fromDistinctAscList
    $ lines
    $ unsafePerformIO (readFile "fours.txt")

is_valid_word w = member w dict
```

The previous code loads a list of words from a file, splits the file into lines, and then builds a lookup table from it. I'm using Haskell's Set library, which uses efficient binary trees, but the implementation isn't important, as long as it gives reasonable performance. We can always switch to hash-based tables later if performance here ever becomes an issue. The key detail is that we can test word validity by testing membership of the set, as shown in the new definition of is_valid_word.

(Syntactic detail: the $ operator is a neat trick to save writing too many right-nested parentheses; in other words, instead of f (g (h x)), one can write f $ g $ h x. You can think of $ as a kind of pipeline symbol, similar to how function composition is sometimes used, though it's not building new functions or anything freaky. Its definition is f $ x = f x (boring), and the magic works entirely through the symbol being declared as a *right associative* operator. In

---

7.   http://sneezy.cs.nott.ac.uk/darcs/Pig09/web/

contrast, division is declared as left associative; for example, 1.0 / 2.0 / 3.0 is equivalent to (1.0 / 2.0) / 3.0 rather than 1.0 / (2.0 / 3.0). So this $ is just a useful bit of shorthand.)

But what's that unsafe doing (you ask)? You got me. It's a Haskell programmer cutting a corner, basically doing some unofficial IO (the file read) at an arbitrary point in the code and turning the dictionary into a global variable. (What's that sound? A fairy dying? No!) Normally, we should be careful about ordering IO actions so we don't try to read before writing and so on, but this idiom is kind of excusable since the dictionary is being used as a constant.

Breadth-First Searching

What's next? We can call one_step "lead" to get a list of next steps, and call one_step on any of the new words and so on. But we're after the *shortest* path between two words, so we need a controlled way of exploring how steps are related in order to find such a path. The obvious thing is to try all one-step paths, then all two-step paths, then three, etc.

This kind of process is called a "breadth-first search" (BFS). I'll show you a version of BFS that is phrased in terms of exploring a "state space." This framework also makes it easier to experiment with other kinds of searching, like best-first search. The parent-to-list-of-children relationship suggests a tree, so let's program it this way. (More generally, it could be a graph too, but let's keep it simple for now.)

First, we need a type. Haskell's standard library contains a module Data.Tree[8] that provides a suitable type and some useful related functionality.

```
-- contained in the Data.Tree module
data Tree a
 = Node { rootLabel :: a,        -- label value
          subForest :: Forest a   -- zero or more child trees
        }
type Forest a = [Tree a]
```

This is a tree with only one kind of node, and the node holds a value or label plus a list of zero or more child trees. The line type Forest a = [Tree a] defines a *type synonym*, providing a possibly more meaningful name for some type expression; i.e., a forest is a list of trees. The tree is (parametrically) polymorphic, of course. Concrete values look like this:

```
eg1 = Node "foo" [Node "bar" []]
eg2 = Node True [Node False [Node True []], Node True []]
```

---

8. http://downloads.haskell.org/~ghc/latest/docs/html/libraries/containers-0.5.7.1/Data-Tree.html

The library contains drawTree :: Tree String -> String, which shows a simple text picture of the tree, so we can run putStr $ drawTree eg1 right away. How do we convert eg2 to something showable? Well, we want to convert all of the Boolean values to strings, without changing the tree structure, and this sounds like a mapping operation. To cut a long story short, the Tree library implements the Functor interface too, which allows use of the overloaded fmap function for mapping over container types (like lists or trees), hence we can call putStr $ drawTree $ fmap show eg2.

Next, we'll create the state space as a tree, where each node contains a state plus the trees that are reachable from that state. Notice the type first and what it describes: from a state-generating function and an initial state, we can produce the tree. It's polymorphic too, because the tree-building process doesn't care what's in the tree. The implementation is straightforward: start a new tree at the current state and then collect the state space trees produced by all of the children. When a state has no children, there's nothing to recurse on, hence no subtrees—just an empty list in the node.

```
import Data.Tree -- put at top of file

state_tree :: (s -> [s]) -> s -> Tree s
state_tree children_of state
 = Node state [ state_tree children_of s | s <- children_of state ]
```

Now you would not run this code directly in a conventional setting, but it is fine in a lazy language because we will only need to generate enough of the tree to satisfy what the caller code requires—even if the tree's depth was not finite.

Still, if we tried drawTree on an infinite tree, it would just keep on going or maybe run out of memory eventually. OK, let's define another function to help us get sensible output: prune n t returns the structure from t down to a depth of n and discards anything deeper than level n.

There are two main cases, a depth of zero (or below) and a positive depth. When we hit zero, then truncate the tree by dropping its children. Otherwise, build a new tree based on the pruned child trees.

```
prune :: Int -> Tree a -> Tree a
prune d (Node x cs)
 | d <= 0    = Node x []
 | otherwise = Node x [ prune (d - 1) c | c <- cs ]
```

With this, code like putStr $ drawTree $ fmap show $ prune 3 $ state_tree (\s -> [s+1, s+1]) 0 now generates something useful. (Nothing significant here—it's just a test value. The state generator here just says, from each state—which happens to be a number—it has two child states of that number with one added, hence it generates a tree that shows the depth at each level and has a fan-out of two children at each step.)

Now for BFS, we need to go through the state tree in breadth-first order. To keep things general—in other words, free from any application-specific details—we are going to write a traversal function (to visit all of the states in order) and later filter the resulting state list for goal states. The traversal function will have the type bft :: Tree a -> [a]. It's a bit trickier, but the technique here is to get a second function (here called bft_) to handle a *list of trees* at a time, then the main function calls it with the original tree in a singleton list.

```
bft :: Tree a -> [a]
bft t = bft_ [t]
bft_ :: [Tree a] -> [a]
bft_ trees =    [ x | Node x _ <- trees ]
            ++ bft_ (concat $ map subForest trees)
```

You can think of bft_ as taking the next list of trees, skimming off the root values of the trees, and adding on the result of traversing the various child trees. The child traversal works by taking all of the children, flattening the lists of children to a flat list, and then running bft_ on this new list. If it helps, draw the picture and check how the code mirrors an informal level-by-level sweep.

The last step is to identify when we have found "goal" states—states that solve the required problem. We can do this by passing in a predicate of type a -> Bool and using it when filtering the output of bft. Putting this all together, we get the following.

```
breadth_first_search :: (s -> Bool) -- goal test
                     -> (s -> [s]) -- state generator
                     -> s          -- initial state
                     -> [s]        -- solutions out
breadth_first_search is_goal children_of
 = filter is_goal
 . bft
 . state_tree children_of
```

To recap: we build the state tree, then do a breadth-first traversal of it to get a list of states to try, then return the ones that correspond to solved goals.

That's our solution. Now compare this to implementations in your favorite language. Is this more modular? More reusable?

Using the Search

OK, let's plug the word-chain code into the preceding and see what happens; for example, let's define the following and run word_chain "lead" "gold".

```
word_chain a b = breadth_first_search (\w -> w == b) one_step a
```

You should see the word "gold" popping out every few seconds, which corresponds to each successful path being found. (There might be a short delay while the dictionary is loaded into memory on the first run.)

Oh. This confirms that paths exist, but we really want to know the intermediate steps. The way to get those is to change the state type from a String to something that keeps track of where it's been—in other words, a list of previous words. The following code lightly wraps up the basic code to maintain this list, testing against the head word in the list, and creating child states by expanding the head word and prepending the new child words to the previous path.

```
type Path = [String]

goal_path :: String -> Path -> Bool
goal_path target ws = target == head ws

child_paths :: Path -> [Path]
child_paths (w:ws)
 = [ s : w : ws | s <- one_step w, s `notElem` ws ]

init_path :: String -> Path
init_path w = [w]

word_chain_path a b
 = breadth_first_search (goal_path b) child_paths
 $ init_path a
```

Running word_chain_path "ruby" "code" now gets us a list of results, each a valid path, and the paths increase in length as the search enters deeper levels.

We're learning about Haskell and functional programming here, so note that it's fairly usual functional practice to wrap such code up in a better abstraction. For example, the combination of goal test, state generator, and initial state do effectively define a search problem, so it seems sensible to hold them in a record. It's easy to adjust the search code to expect this as input. From this, we can recast the move to paths as converting a simple search problem object into a more complex one—for example, convert_to_path_search :: SearchProblem s -> SearchProblem [s]. We could also encapsulate the path inside a new type so it's not just a bare list anymore.

Performance and Optimization

So is this code fast enough? Using the GHC interpreter, it takes around a second or two to do the lead-gold example (both directions), and a few seconds more for the ruby-code example (also both directions). With the GHC compiler, this reduces to a fraction of a second—even without turning on the optimization options of the compiler. It's probably fast enough.

GHC provides some good profiling tools to help diagnose and track performance issues. The following snippet is part of the standard time and space profile produced by running the ruby-to-code search 1,000 times (taking around 10 seconds, so 0.01 seconds per search). This is without any compiler optimizations.

The profiler result indicates that seventy-eight percent of the time was spent looking up words, and fourteen percent of the time calculating the candidates. For memory, eighty-four percent of the total allocation was spent on the generated words. A similar pattern is seen when searching the reverse direction, albeit some twenty times slower(!)—though this could be a quirk of these words (we'd have to see this pattern on a bigger test set before concluding it was really a code problem).

	CALLS	time	space	TIME	SPACE
state_tree	655000	0.8	4.3	95.9	93.7
child_paths	58000	0.5	3.1	95.2	89.4
one_step	0	2.3	1.7	94.6	86.3
is_valid_word	5703000	77.9	0.0	77.9	0.0
generate_candidates	286000	14.4	84.6	14.4	84.6

Now that we know this, if time or memory really were an issue, then we could start analyzing the offending operations, maybe even *fusing them together* in some way to reduce overheads, or adding in cheaper word validity tests (like reject words with no vowels). Until then, we can stick with the clear code.

We've not used many complex types, but types have still been useful in the process to describe what data we're manipulating, and as a guide for how certain operations should behave. There's room for a bit more type use in this Haskell-98 code, maybe wrapping up search problems as bundles, or perhaps wrapping valid words inside a new type to distinguish them from unchecked words.

But can we do better? What about dependent types? What details are we worried about that we'd like the extra confidence for? I'll let you think about this, but you might like to think about confirming that all candidate words are the same length, or conditions on the state generation to ensure that the states don't inadvertently cause infinite loops or repeat work, or that the state space is finite (which would confirm that a tree-based approach is adequate rather than needing the full graph-based approach).

I've not said much about testing either. We can certainly add tests to double-check that code is doing what we expect, but we've also managed to split various concerns apart so it's clear how each part works—indeed reflecting Hoare's comment on "obviously no deficiencies" vs. "no obvious deficiencies." Testing these smaller, more self-contained pieces is generally easier. With simpler code, it's also easier to exercise the relevant pathways.

At this point, I hope you have some appreciation of how we can use the language to keep the details simple and modular, and what a difference it makes to the final program. This isn't just a happy coincidence—many functional programs do develop like this, and it really does help us work with much more complex programs. In Chapter 23, *Haskell's Type System*, on page 185 and Chapter 24, *A Haskell Project: Testing Native Code*, on page 211, you can dig deeper into Haskell. But in the next chapter, you'll see a different approach to functional programming with Apple's Swift language.

Part VI

Swift: Functional Programming for Mobile Apps

Chris Lattner and others at Apple developed Swift as a replacement for Objective-C, the default language for all Apple platform development. It is a new language, just released in 2014. Swift is not a functional programming language, but it incorporates some key functional features, and depending on developer input, could evolve into a language that truly embraces the functional paradigm.

## CHAPTER 15

Swift: What You Need to Know

by Mark Chu-Carroll

The motivations behind the development of computer languages matter. Haskell was developed for research in functional language design. Clojure was designed around the idea that functional style and pervasive immutability are prerequisites for concurrency. Elixir was designed with high extensibility and productivity in mind. But in Swift, we are looking at a replacement for an existing language, created for a base of developers who may be interested in getting the benefits of functional programming, but who don't necessarily want to shift to an entirely new paradigm. The PragPub *authors examined Swift shortly after its release with this hybrid purpose in mind.*

In 2014, Apple announced a new programming language called Swift for iOS, macOS, watchOS, tvOS, and Linux development. For people like me, that was big news. I did my PhD in programming language design and implementation. I'm utterly obsessed with programming languages. The last time I set out to count how many languages I'd learned, it was over 120—and I've at least read the specifications of another 30 or so since then. I'm into programming languages. I was excited.

Since the dawn of OSX, the bulk of software development on the Macintosh has been done in a language called Objective-C. Objective-C is a lovely programming language (for its time), which never really caught on outside of OSX and its predecessor, NeXTSTEP. Objective-C was a hybrid between old-fashioned procedural imperative programming and object-oriented programming; Swift is also a hybrid, combining object-oriented programming and functional programming. In this it is like Scala (see Chapter 3, *Scala and Functional Style*, on page 15 to compare).

Objective-C dates back to around 1984 or so. Back then, the main programming languages that were used for developing applications were predominantly procedural imperative languages, like Pascal and C. Now we're at the cusp of another big change in programming. Functional programming is hot. And the way that functional programming is catching on is very similar to the way that object-oriented programming did before: by hybrids. If you look at many of the popular functional programming languages—such as Scala—what you'll find is basically a subset that is the old familiar object-oriented language, plus a bunch of functional stuff integrated into it.

With Objective-C really starting to look pretty crufty, Apple did the obvious thing: it made a break, and it introduced a new hybrid functional/object-oriented language, which it named Swift.

Hello, Swift!

Let's get a feel for Swift with a concrete example. It's traditional to start with "hello world," but to demonstrate functional programming, it makes more sense to start with the factorial function.

```
func fact(n: Int) -> Int {
  if n == 0 {
    return 1
  } else {
    return n * fact(n - 1)
  }
}

let x = fact(10)
println("The factorial of 10 is \(fact(10))")
```

This code is pretty unsurprising. The only thing that's at all unusual is that if you look inside the println, you can see that Swift does string interpolation: if you put \ (expression) into a string, then the result of that expression is converted into a string, and inserted into the enclosing string. That's been common in scripting languages for a long time, but it hasn't been a standard thing in systems programming languages like Swift. It's a small thing, but it's a good one.

The first big surprise in Swift is how you can test that function. In Objective-C, you would have had to create a full program, compile it, and run the executable. That's not the case in Swift. In Swift, you can open a *playground*, which is a fully interactive scripting environment. It's not that Swift comes with an interpreter; this is something different. A playground is a workspace with full access to the compiler, and it can compile and evaluate expressions on the fly! And the playground isn't limited to just text: you can create UI elements, interface builder-based UIs, interactive games, and more. Just put the code into a workspace and edit it. As the code changes, the moment it becomes syntactically valid, the playground will dynamically compile it using the LCC back end, and execute the generated code for you!

All I can say is: it's about time! I've been seeing toy versions of this kind of interactivity since I was an undergrad in the 1980s. And with Swift, we've finally got that in a full-blown systems language. Just this one little feature makes me excited about Swift.

All well and good, but now let's look at the details of Swift syntax to see how it operates as an object-oriented and as a functional language.

Functional Swift

The really cool new stuff in Swift is all functional programming features. There are two main facets to Swift's version of functional programming: managing mutability, and first-class functions and closures.

Managing Mutability

In programming, you can't avoid mutable state. It's a fact. Most of the time, it's the reason that we're using a computer. For example, say I'm using a program called Atom to write a blog post. There wouldn't be any point in using Atom if I couldn't modify the file I'm writing.

But mutable state makes things complicated. In a large, complex software system, code that avoids mutating things is usually easier to understand, less prone to errors and unexpected side effects, and easier to interact with.

That's the driving force behind the new hybrid languages: we want to be able to minimize mutability, but it's a mutable world. The trick is, you want to be able to glance at some code and say, "This is not going to change anything," or "This might change stuff." It's less about making it impossible to change stuff than it is about making it clear just where stuff could be changed, and making sure that it can't change unless you specifically declare its mutability. I'm a big fan of keeping things functional whenever it's reasonable.[1]

Swift does a bunch of things to realize that guarantee:

- Identifiers are declared with either let or var. If they're declared with let, then the identifier names a constant that cannot be altered by assignment.

---

1. http://scientopia.org/blogs/goodmath/2009/11/10/philosophizing-about-programming-or-why-im-learning-to-love-functional-programming/

If the value of a constant identifier is a struct or enum, its fields cannot be altered by assignment either.

- Methods on structs cannot alter the underlying struct unless the method is specifically annotated as "mutating." Without that annotation in the declaration, the object cannot be altered by any of its methods.

- Function parameters are, by default, immutable. To allow a parameter to be changed, you need to specifically annotate it with var or inout in its declaration. If it's a var, then changes to the parameter won't affect the original value in the caller; they will be made on a local copy.

- structs and enums are passed by value. That means that the structure is (conceptually) copied when it's passed as a parameter to a function. Unless you annotate the function parameter as an output parameter, the parameter cannot be modified; even if you call a mutating method, the mutation will be on the local copy of the value, not on the caller. (The reason for the "conceptually" up there is that the object is copied lazily; if you try to alter it, the copy happens at the point of the first alteration, so passing complex structures by value doesn't incur a copy cost unless you modify them.)

Functions and Closures

The other side of the functional programming support isn't about restricting things, but about enabling *new* things. And here Swift really shines. Swift has support for first-class functions (function parameter and return values), anonymous functions, curried functions, and full closures. Here's where Swift enables you to program in ways you couldn't in Objective-C.

Swift's support for first-class functions means that functions are just values, like any other value type. A Swift function can be assigned to a variable, passed to a function, or returned as the result type of a function.

For example, suppose you wanted to write a generic sort function—that is, a sort function that didn't just compare values using the standard less-than operator, but that could take any function that a user wanted to use to do comparisons. In Swift, you could write:

```
func sort_generic<T>(list: Array<T>, comparator: (T, T) -> Bool)
  -> Array<T> {
  ...
  if comparator(v, w) { ... }
  ...
}
```

This is something that those of us with experience with Lisp have been absolutely dying to have in a mainstream language for decades.

Closures are a closely related concept. A closure is a function value with one really interesting property. It closes over the environment in which it was declared. To understand what I mean, let's look at a really simple example from the Swift specification:

```
func makeIncrementor(amount: Int) -> () -> Int {
  var runningTotal = 0
  func incrementor() -> Int {
      runningTotal += amount
      return runningTotal
  }
  return incrementor
}
```

This function returns a value that is itself a function. The interesting thing is that the function can use any variable defined in any of the scopes enclosing its declaration. So the function incrementor can access the amount parameter and the runningTotal variable, even after the makeIncrementor function has returned. Since those are local to the invocation, each time you call makeIncrementor, it creates new variables, which aren't shared with other invocations.

So let's look at what happens when you run it:

```
let f = makeIncrementor(2)
let g = makeIncrementor(5)
f()        2
f()        4
g()        5
f()        6
g()        10
```

Anonymous functions make it really easy to work with first-class functions. You don't need to write a function declaration and then return it the way the preceding example did. Anytime you need a function value, you can create it in place as an expression.

```
func makeAnonIncrementor(amount: Int) -> () -> Int {
  var runningTotal = 0
  return {
    runningTotal += amount
    return runningTotal
  }
}
```

If the anonymous function takes parameters, you declare them before the function body with in:

```
sort_generic(mylist, { (x: Int, y: Int) -> Bool in return x > y})
```

Currying, finally, is a shorthand way of writing function values. The idea is that if you have a two-parameter function, you can rewrite it as a one-parameter function that returns another one-parameter function. That sounds confusing until you see it:

```
func add_numbers(x: Int, y: Int) -> Int {
    return x + y
}
func curried_add_numbers(x: Int) -> Int -> Int {
  return { (y: Int) -> Int in return x + y }
}
```

If you want to add 3+2, you can either call add_numbers(3, 2) or curried_add_numbers(3)(2): they do the same thing.

Swift provides a special way of declaring curried functions:

```
func better_curried_add_numbers(x: Int)(y: Int) -> Int {
  return x + y
}
```

You'll find out even more about Swift's functions in Chapter 25, *The Many Faces of Swift Functions*, on page 221.

Pattern Matching

I know, I said there were just two main facets to Swift's version of functional programming. Pattern matching isn't, strictly speaking, a functional language thing, but it's an idea that was introduced to most programmers by its inclusion in functional programming languages. The idea is simple: you can write assignments or conditionals that automatically decompose a data structure by matching the structural pattern of that data structure.

As usual, that becomes a lot clearer with an example.

```
let (x, y, z) = (1, 2.7, "three")
```

The right-hand side of that assignment structure is a tuple with three values. The first one is an integer, the second is a floating point number, and the third is a string. The left-hand side of the assignment has exactly the same structure—so the Swift compiler will match the pieces. That's equivalent to:

- let x = 1
- let y = 2.7
- let z = "three"

That's particularly useful for multiple return values. Strictly speaking, Swift doesn't really have multiple return values: every function returns exactly one value. But that one value may be a tuple containing multiple values. So you can write things like:

```
let result, error_core = my_function(parameters)
```

Pattern matching also happens in switch statements, where each branch of the switch can be a different pattern, as we saw earlier in the ParseResult example.

All of this stuff means that you can write beautiful functional code in Swift. In the next chapter, Tony Hillerson will show you how to really exploit Swift's functional capabilities by thinking functionally in Swift.

## CHAPTER 16

Functional Thinking in Swift

by Tony Hillerson

When Apple announced a new programming language for iOS and Mac development, a lot of developers immediately started geeking out over Swift. At Tack, where I work, we were no exception: most of us on the iOS side of the aisle started filling our chat room with "Sweet!," "What the heck?," and "Dude, check this out!" in equal measures. Now that the noise has settled down, we can analyze just how this language works, particularly in its functional style.

As you find your way around Swift, pay attention to the features that fit the functional paradigm. If you do, you'll be better able to take advantage of the things a functional language does well, like handle concurrency better, express yourself in code more clearly and expressively, and easily generalize complex problems to create flexible, reusable solutions.

But here's the thing: you really do have to think in a different way to realize the benefits of functional programming. It's not just a new set of tools, it's a different way of thinking about problems. So here are some "functional thinking" tips to keep in mind as you're learning Swift.

Avoid Nil, Unless You Mean It

Most languages we've used have had the concept of a null reference, like Objective-C's nil. They've also famously been called a Billion Dollar Mistake.[1] The main problem with nil is that it's usually an exceptional condition. A variable contains, or a function returns, either something useful or nil. How are we supposed to interpret nil? Does it mean that there is no data? Does it mean there was an error? Languages usually don't help us here. We're left to

---

1. https://en.wikipedia.org/wiki/Tony_Hoare#Apologies_and_retractions

clutter our code with defensive if statements, or forget to do that and track down strange errors later.

Maybe this isn't technically a functional feature, but it *is* part of your functional thinking toolkit. Functional languages typically have a way to explicitly state that some data can either contain some meaningful data or have no value. Just like Scala's Option/Some/None, for instance (see Chapter 4, *Working with Scala Collections*, on page 23), Swift has the concept of an *optional value*.

In fact, to say that a variable may not have a value, you must be explicit about this exceptional case and declare it as Optional with the ? syntax. Once you do this, you're making a clear statement that anyone using this variable should deal with the case that it has no value.

Later, when dealing with the Optional value, developers can take advantage of explicit or implicit unwrapping of the Optional value or the Optional binding syntax, like this:

```
var optionalValue:String?
if let s = optionalValue {
  // do something with s
} else {
  // handle the nil value
}
```

That looks like the if statement checks we're used to in Objective-C or other languages, but the key difference is that it's explicitly the case that optionalValue may not have a value.

Like other functional languages, Swift also has pattern matching capabilities, although these are fairly rudimentary. You can use them to deal with Optionals like this:

```
var x:String? = "Foo"
switch x {
case .None:
  println("This string is empty")
case let s where s!.hasPrefix("B"):
  println("it could be Bar")
case let s where s!.hasPrefix("F"):
  println("it could be Foo")
default:
  println("No idea what this is")
}
```

It's a bit strange that Optional binding doesn't work as well in switch statements as in if statements, and still requires explicit unwrapping in the where guard clause, but calling out the .None case is a win for readability. Note that having .None as the first case guarantees that the explicit unwrapping will not fail in the subsequent cases.

Again, Optionals aren't strictly a functional feature, but avoiding nil is becoming more popular as more functional languages come on the scene, and Swift, too, comes out of the box with these powerful, expressive Optional values.

Another way Swift helps us keep things more explicit and safe is by helping us get a handle on mutable state or avoid it altogether, and now we're really getting into the functional programming mindset.

Avoid Mutable State

A necessary feature of a purely functional language is that it has no *side effects*; functions are supposed to return an answer based on arguments, but nothing in the system should be changed by executing a function.

This often strikes programmers new to functional programming paradigms as strange, because to them, *the point* of a program is to change or "mutate" some state somewhere and record it or show the new state to the user. And this hints at some of the differences in the types of problems pure functional language programmers want to solve compared to "the rest of us." But there are benefits to avoiding mutable state in *any* system.

One of the most relevant benefits of having no mutable state in a function is that concurrency problems don't occur. No matter how many threads, or cores, or whatever, are running the code, there's no chance that something gets the program in a bad state, because *state never changes*. Writing code with no mutable state makes concurrency much easier to deal with no matter what paradigm you're working in.

The object-oriented programming paradigm treats mutable state as a matter of responsibility. A well-architected class exposes methods to allow objects of that type to have control over mutating their own state. It's the object's responsibility to mutate its state and to not allow mutation by other objects.

A multi-paradigm language, as opposed to a purely functional language, has both options available. So Swift has a few ways to deal with state. Thinking about the implications of these decisions will take you a good way down the road of functional thinking.

The most basic is the choice between let and var. Using let to define a value means that you never expect that value to change. Wherever possible, try to use let instead of var. This is a small win to readability and communicating explicit design goals: if you declare something a var, you're explicitly stating that you expect the value to change.

Of course, for us non-academic, working programmers, it's usually the case that we don't know values up front. More interesting than immutable variables is the ability collections have to be mutable or immutable. Just like Objective-C has both mutable or immutable arrays and dictionary, Swift does too, but it makes the syntax of dealing with them a lot nicer.

Immutable dictionaries, or those declared with a let, don't allow changes to either their keys or values. Immutable arrays don't allow changes to their length, but do allow values already defined to be changed. When passing around these simple data structures, using the immutable versions can help make code more explicit and deterministic. Make sure you understand how Swift deals with copying collection types by reading up on *Assignment and Copy Behavior for Collection Types* in the Swift reference.

Swift also has Structures, which, as opposed to objects, are copied by value instead of reference. This is a possible way to avoid mutating state, but may be strange to object-oriented developers. When something seems strange to you, it *sometimes* means you have an opportunity to learn. In this case, it's an opportunity to get more familiar with the functional way of thinking.

Immutable variables and copying by value are important for dealing with avoiding mutable state, but where the functional paradigm really gets traction on cutting down on mutation problems is with higher-order functions.

Use Higher-Order Functions

Another defining feature of a functional language is making functions first-class citizens. That means that not only is it possible to have functions attached to objects or structures or enums (or even inside of functions), it is also possible to have variables or constants that point to functions, to pass functions into other functions, and to return functions from functions. It is not something languages like Java can do at all. Objective-C made great strides with block syntax, and has always had use of C functions, but Swift provides even more power and much clearer syntax for dealing with functions.

The point of this power and clarity is to attack problems at a higher conceptual level. Instead of thinking about looping through lists of data and performing some actions on each item, there is a subtle shift to using higher-order functions of a collection to take action on the collection as a whole. This action will in fact do what is needed to each item, one at a time, achieving the same effect as the looping approach, but it spares you the details. You operate at a higher conceptual level.

Let me make the difference more clear with an example. Suppose we wanted to loop through a list of numbers and find their square, or find out which were odd, or sum them up. We could use a for-in loop and build up some mutable local variables and do the work. The functional way, however, looks like this:

```
let numbers = [1,2,3]
let squares = numbers.map { $0 * $0 }
let odds    = numbers.filter { $0 % 2 == 1 }
let sum     = numbers.reduce(0) { $0 + $1 }
```

That's pretty concise, I suggest. You could fit that entire program in a single tweet. It's only slightly longer than the English sentence in which I described the problem.

I made this as terse as possible, using Swift's trailing closure syntax, short-hand argument names, and implicit return syntactic sugar. But syntax is not the only interesting thing going on here.

Take notice of a few things here—things crucial to functional thinking:

First, we don't have any mutable state to worry about. Instead of calculating an answer using temporary variables, we use functions to give us the answers *directly* and place these into constants.

Second, we use methods already on the collections to do the high-level iteration work. These functions are:

- map, which produces a new collection with new values for each of the values in another collection.

- filter, which returns only the values we specify from a collection.

- reduce, which turns a collection of values into a single value.

Notice that these definitions don't specify *how* the mapping or filtering or reducing is to be done: they are high-level functions. Using these high-level collection functions, which are common to almost all functional languages in one guise or another, allows us to separate the problem of iteration—a general problem—from the specific problem of deriving the answer that we want in particular.

The answer we want in particular is derived by passing a closure, but we could just as easily have passed a function reference. The point is that the heavy lifting is done one item at a time by a small chunk of composable, reusable functionality that deals with solving a particular problem.

This idea is worth another example. In Chris Eidhof, Florian Kugler, and Wouter Swiersta's *Functional Swift*,[2] around page 125, there's a little tutorial involving a list of scene titles from Shakespeare's *Romeo And Juliet*. There's an example of a for-in loop walking through this list to decide if the scene falls into Act 1 or not. Here's what that looks like:

```
var act1SceneCount = 0
for scene in romeoAndJuliet {
  if scene.hasPrefix("Act 1 ") {
    ++act1SceneCount
  }
}
```

And now here it is done in a functional way:

```
func countIfAct1(accumulator: Int, title: String) -> Int {
  if title.hasPrefix("Act 1") {
    return accumulator + 1
  } else {
    return accumulator
  }
}
let act1SceneCount =
  romeoAndJuliet.reduce(0, countIfAct1)
```

Unlike my ultra-terse preceding example, this functional solution actually has more lines of code than the procedural one. Lines of code or terse syntax really isn't the point. The benefit to functional thinking demonstrated here is that reduce handles the iteration part, while the reusable function countIfAct1 handles the counting logic. Not much in the procedural approach is reusable. It also requires us to manage our own mutable state, where the functional approach does not.

By having countIfAct1 be a reusable chunk of functionality, we can start to organize the code around certain bits of utility that are like this. Maybe those are in objects, maybe they're in function libraries. On the other side, by having reduce handle the iteration logic, we hand off that requirement to the language and compiler. We could possibly gain some benefit from this in the future, like perhaps a performance benefit if reduce learned to take advantage of multiple cores (possibly a pie in the sky hope).

---

2.   https://www.objc.io/books/functional-swift/

Finally, here's the same functional approach with a somewhat more readable implementation, taking advantage of Swift's trailing closure syntax.

```
let act1SceneCount =
  romeoAndJuliet.reduce(0){ count, title in
      title.hasPrefix("Act 1") ? count + 1 : count
  }
```

However you feel about the ternary operator, I personally find that to be a very clean, readable solution with the right balance of terseness and information density.

But my point here is not to critique code. It's to encourage you to explore Swift's functional programming capabilities and to think functionally. If, as you're learning Swift, you try to solve problems of this type using higher-order functions instead of procedural code, you'll maximize your learning experience.

Of course, there are a lot of problems where the object-oriented paradigm still makes sense to use. For instance, dealing with view code still works best in the OO paradigm we're all used to. However, when you get to problems dealing with lists of data, transforming data, deriving answers from data sets, and so forth, that's where the functional paradigm really shines. Languages like Swift that offer a multi-paradigm approach are often the pragmatic way to go because they give you a variety of tools for different types of problems.

But you have to pay attention to the functional programming paradigm. It's the hot new thing, and important advances in computer science are going to be made available to functional and hybrid languages. So explore the functional tools that Swift gives you, make functional thinking part of your skill sets, and start looking at where you can use it to improve how you solve problems, more flexibly, safely, and with cleaner code.

This concludes our overview of functional programming in five languages. In the rest of the book, we'll dig deeper into functional programming with extended examples and advanced analyses.

Part VII

Going Deeper

In the preceding chapters, you've seen how functional programming works in five languages: Scala,
Clojure, Elixir, Haskell, and Swift. In this final
section, you'll get more hands-on exposure to functional programming in each of these languages.
And for fun, we've slipped in a chapter on functional
programming in one more language: Lua, the
lightweight embeddable scripting language popular
in game development.

## CHAPTER 17

Protocols in Swift vs. Ruby and Elixir

by José Valim

When Apple announced its new language, Swift, I started reading the docs and playing with the language with great curiosity. I was pleasantly surprised with many features in Swift, like the handling of optional values (and types) and the immutability being promoted throughout the language.

The language also feels extensible. For extensibility, I am using the same criteria we use for Elixir, which is the ability to implement language constructs using the language itself.

For example, in many languages, the short-circuiting && operator is defined as a special part of the language. In those languages, you can't reimplement the operator using the constructs provided by the language.

In Elixir, however, you can implement the && operator as a macro:

```
defmacro left && right do
  quote do
    case unquote(left) do
      false -> false
      _ -> unquote(right)
    end
  end
end
```

In Swift, you can also implement operators and easily define the && operator with the help of the @auto_closure attribute:

```
func &&(lhs: LogicValue, rhs: @auto_closure () ->
                          LogicValue) -> Bool {
    if lhs {
        if rhs() == true {
            return true
        }
    }
    return false
}
```

The @auto_closure attribute automatically wraps the tagged argument in a closure, allowing you to control when it is executed and therefore implement the short-circuiting property of the && operator.

However, one of the features that I suspect will actually hurt extensibility in Swift is the extensions feature. I have compared the protocols implementation in Swift with the ones found in Elixir and Clojure on Twitter. That explanation evolved into a blog post[1] and this chapter.

The Problem with Extensions

The extensions feature in Swift has many use cases. You can read them all in more detail in their documentation. Here we'll just deal with the general case and the protocol case.

Following the example in Apple documentation:

```
extension Double {
    var km: Double { return self * 1_000.0 }
    var m: Double { return self }
    var cm: Double { return self / 100.0 }
    var mm: Double { return self / 1_000.0 }
    var ft: Double { return self / 3.28084 }
}

let oneInch = 25.4.mm
println("One inch is \(oneInch) meters")
// prints "One inch is 0.0254 meters"

let threeFeet = 3.ft
println("Three feet is \(threeFeet) meters")
// prints "Three feet is 0.914399970739201 meters"
```

In this example, we are extending the Double type, adding our own computed properties. Those extensions are global and, if you're a Ruby developer, will remind you of monkey patching in Ruby. However, in Swift, extensions are always explicit (which I personally consider to be a benefit).

---

1.   http://blog.plataformatec.com.br/2014/06/comparing-protocols-and-extensions-in-swift-and-elixir/

What complicates extensions is exactly the fact that they are global. While I understand that some extensions would be useful to define globally, this always comes with the possibility of namespace pollution and name conflicts. Two libraries can define the same extensions to the Double type that behave slightly differently, leading to bugs.

This has always been a hot topic in the Ruby community, with refinements being proposed in late 2010 as a solution to the problem. At this moment, it's unclear if extensions can be scoped in any way in Swift.

The Case for Protocols

Protocols are a fantastic feature in Swift. Per the documentation, "a protocol defines a blueprint of methods, properties, and other requirements that suit a particular task or piece of functionality."

Let's see their example:

```
protocol FullyNamed {
    var fullName: String { get }
}

struct Person: FullyNamed {
    var fullName: String
}

let john = Person(fullName: "John Appleseed")
// john.fullName is "John Appleseed"
```

In the preceding example, we defined a FullyNamed protocol and implemented it while defining the Person struct. The benefit of protocols is that the compiler can now guarantee the struct complies with the definitions specified in the protocol. In case the protocol changes in the future, you'll find out immediately by recompiling your project.

I have long been advocating this feature for Ruby. For example, imagine you have the following Ruby code:

```
class Person
  attr_accessor :first, :last

  def full_name
    first + " " + last
  end
end
```

And imagine you have a method somewhere that expects an object that implements full_name:

```ruby
def print_full_name(obj)
  puts obj.full_name
end
```

At some point, you may want to print the title too:

```ruby
def print_full_name(obj)
  if title = obj.title
    puts title + " " + obj.full_name
  else
    puts obj.full_name
  end
end
```

Your contract has now changed, but there is no mechanism to notify implementations of the change. This is particularly cumbersome because sometimes such changes are done by accident, when you don't want to actually modify the contract.

This issue has happened multiple times in Rails. Before Rails 3, there was no official contract between the controller and the model or between the view and the model. This meant that, while Rails worked fine with Active Record (Rails' built-in model layer), every Rails release could possibly break integration with other models because the contract suddenly became larger due to changes in the implementation.

Since Rails 3, we actually define a contract for those interactions, but there is still no way to:

- Guarantee that an object complies with the contract (without extensive use of tests).

- Guarantee that controllers and views obey the contract (without extensive use of tests).

Similar to real-life contracts, unless you write it down and sign it, there is no guarantee that both parties will actually maintain it.

The ideal solution is to be able to define multiple, tiny protocols. Someone using Swift would rather define multiple protocols for the controller and view layers:

```swift
protocol URL {
    func toParam() -> String
}

protocol FormErrors {
    var errors: Dict<String, Array[String]>
}
```

The interesting aspect about Swift protocols is that you can define and implement protocols for any given type, at any time. The trouble, though, is that the implementations of the protocols are defined in the class/struct itself and as a result they change the class/struct globally.

Protocols and Extensions

Since protocols in Swift are implemented directly in the class/struct, during definition or via extension, the protocol implementation ends up changing the class/struct globally. To see the problem with this, imagine that you have two different libraries relying on different JSON protocols:

```
protocol JSONA {
    func toJSON(precision: Integer) -> String
}

protocol JSONB {
    func toJSON(scale: Integer) -> String
}
```

If the preceding protocols have different specifications on how the precision argument must be handled, we will be able to implement only one of the two previous protocols. That's because implementing any of the protocols above means adding a toJSON(Integer) method to the class/struct, and there can be only one of them per class/struct.

Furthermore, if implementing protocols means globally adding methods to classes and structs, it can actually hinder the use of protocols as a whole, as the concerns to avoid name clashes and to avoid namespace pollution will speak louder than the protocol benefits.

Let's contrast this with protocols in Elixir:

```
defprotocol JSONA do
  def to_json(data, precision)
end

defprotocol JSONB do
  def to_json(data, scale)
end

defimpl JSONA, for: Integer do
  def to_json(data, _precision) do
    Integer.to_string(data)
  end
end

JSONA.to_json(1, 10)
#=> 1
```

Elixir protocols are heavily influenced by Clojure protocols, where the implementation of a protocol is tied to the protocol itself and not to the data type implementing the protocol. This means you can implement both JSONA and JSONB protocols for the same data types and they won't clash!

Protocols in Elixir work by dispatching on the first argument of the protocol function. So when you invoke JSONA.to_json(1, 10), Elixir checks the first argument, sees it is an integer, and dispatches to the appropriate implementation.

What is interesting is that we can actually emulate this functionality in Swift! We can define the same method multiple times, as long as the type signatures don't clash. So if we use static methods and extensions, we can emulate the preceding behavior:

```
// Define a class to act as protocol dispatch
class JSON {
}

// Implement it for Double
extension JSON {
    class func toJSON(double: Double) -> String {
        return String(double)
    }
}

// Someone may implement it later for Float too
extension JSON {
    class func toJSON(float: Float) -> String {
        return String(float)
    }
}
```

```
JSON.toJSON(2.3)
```

The preceding example emulates the dynamic dispatch ability found in Elixir and Clojure, which guarantees no clashes in multiple implementations. After all, if someone defines a JSONB class, all the implementations would live in the JSONB class.

Since dynamic dispatch is already available, I hope protocols in Swift are improved to support local implementations instead of changing classes/structs globally.

Swift is a new language and in active development. I would love it if Swift protocols evolved to support non-global implementations. Protocols are a very extensible mechanism to define and implement contracts, and it would be a pity to see their potential hindered due to the global side effects their use might cause to the codebase.

## CHAPTER 18

Pattern Matching in Scala

by Venkat Subramaniam

You've seen some examples of Scala's expressive and concise nature in Chapter 5, *Creating Higher-Order Functions in Scala*, on page 31. Pattern matching is another area where you'll appreciate the elegance of Scala. As you saw in Chapter 10, *Patterns and Transformations in Elixir*, on page 69, pattern matching is a natural fit for functional programming, and Scala provides simple yet powerful facilities for pattern matching, as you'll see in this chapter.

Counting Coins

To explore the expressive power of pattern matching, let's write a function that will count the number of nickels, dimes, and quarters in a given collection:

```
val coins = List(25, 10, 5, 10, 5, 25, 10, 5, 5, 25)
```

Using the traditional if-else construct, the code would look like this:

```
def countCoins(coins : Seq[Int], nickels : Int = 0,
  dimes : Int = 0, quarters : Int = 0)  : Map[String, Int] = {

  if (coins.isEmpty)
    Map("nickels" -> nickels, "dimes" -> dimes,
      "quarters" -> quarters)
  else {
    if (5 == coins.head) {
      countCoins(coins.tail, nickels + 1, dimes, quarters)
    }
    else {
      if (10 == coins.head) {
        countCoins(coins.tail, nickels, dimes + 1, quarters)
      } else {
        if (25 == coins.head) {
          countCoins(coins.tail, nickels, dimes, quarters + 1)
        } else {
```

```
          countCoins(coins.tail, nickels, dimes, quarters)
        }
      }
    }
  }
}

println(countCoins(coins))
//Map(nickels -> 4, dimes -> 3, quarters -> 3)
```

The function accepts a collection of coins as the first parameter, followed by the known number of nickels, dimes, and quarters, all set to 0 by default. Within the method, if there are no coins, you return a map of the known counts. Otherwise, you check the first coin using a series of simple if-else statements and recursively process the rest of the coins. You could have used the collection's filter method for this also, but in this example, we'll see how to use patterns instead.

That's quite a bit of code and it appears noisy. But we can use pattern matching to make this function concise. Scala provides a match method that appears something like a switch statement, but is more powerful. It's an expression that can filter or match the target object against different types and data values. The previous code will reduce to a few lines that are easier to follow.

```
def countCoins(coins : Seq[Int], nickels : Int = 0,
  dimes : Int = 0, quarters : Int = 0)  : Map[String, Int] = {

  if (coins.isEmpty)
    Map("nickels" -> nickels, "dimes" -> dimes,
      "quarters" -> quarters)
  else coins.head match {
    case 5 => countCoins(coins.tail, nickels + 1,
      dimes, quarters)
    case 10 => countCoins(coins.tail, nickels,
      dimes + 1, quarters)
    case 25 => countCoins(coins.tail, nickels,
      dimes, quarters + 1)
    case _ => countCoins(coins.tail, nickels,
      dimes, quarters)
  }
}

println(countCoins(coins))
//Map(nickels -> 4, dimes -> 3, quarters -> 3)
```

Here you replaced the outermost else block with a call to the match method on the first element or the head of the coins collection. Scala matches the value of the first element with each case of literals you have provided and takes the appropriate route.

The underscore in case _ represents a wildcard, used if all of the other cases fail to match. Scala does not insist that you provide the wildcard case, but without it any mismatch would result in a runtime exception.

The match operation does not restrict you to simple literals. You can replace the top-level if with a match in the coins count example:

```
coins match {
  case Seq() =>
    Map("nickels" -> nickels, "dimes" ->
      dimes, "quarters" -> quarters)
  case _ =>
    coins.head match {
      case 5 => countCoins(coins.tail, nickels + 1,
        dimes, quarters)
      case 10 => countCoins(coins.tail, nickels,
        dimes + 1, quarters)
      case 25 => countCoins(coins.tail, nickels,
        dimes, quarters + 1)
      case _ => countCoins(coins.tail, nickels, dimes, quarters)
  }
}
```

The first case takes effect if the collection is empty, and the wildcard case takes effect otherwise. You used two levels of match in this example, but that's not required. The list match also permits you to probe into the contents of the list. Using this, you can let the top-level match check the values of the list and eliminate the nested match.

```
  coins match {
    case Seq() =>
      Map("nickels" -> nickels, "dimes" ->
        dimes, "quarters" -> quarters)
    case Seq(5, _*) => countCoins(coins.tail, nickels + 1,
      dimes, quarters)
    case Seq(10, _*) => countCoins(coins.tail, nickels,
      dimes + 1, quarters)
    case Seq(25, restOfTheCoins @ _*) =>
      countCoins(restOfTheCoins, nickels, dimes, quarters + 1)
    case _ => countCoins(coins.tail, nickels, dimes, quarters)
  }
}
```

The pattern Seq(5, _*) matches a list whose first element is a value 5. The remaining elements in the list are represented by _* and may be captured into a reference, as in the case for 25. Capturing the values is optional, as you can see in the case expressions.

Matching All the Things

So far we've just scratched the surface of pattern matching. Scala allows you to match based on values and types; you can even use guarded cases using if, as you'll see next.

```
def process(message : Any) = {
  message match {
    case "hello" => println("received hello")
    case x : String => println("received a string " + x)
    case (a, b) => println("received tuple (" + a + ", " + b + ")")
    case 22 => println("received 22")
    case x : Int if x < 0 => println("received a negative number " + x)
    case y : Int => println("received number " + y)
  }
}

process(1, 2) // received typle (1, 2)
process("hello") // received hello
process("test")   // received a string test
process(22)       // received 22
process(12)       // received number 12
process(-32)      // received a negative number -32
```

The patterns "hello" and 22 look for an exact match. The patterns that specify the type, like x : String and y : Int, will accept any value of the appropriate type. The guarded case expects the value to satisfy the pattern in the case—type Int in this example—and the if statement to evaluate to true. You can also match tuples, which are lightweight immutable collections of values. In this example, you match any tuple with two values of any type. You can also dictate the type, like so: (a : Int, b : Double, c : String).

The order in which you place the case expressions matters. For example, if you reverse the last two cases, Scala will raise an unreachable code compile-time error. In a sense, the pattern matching in Scala is like a coin sorter: the data falls into a matching slot as it flows over the cases.

You can match against various values and types, including your own types. Scala's special type of classes named *case classes* are very useful for this. The instances of case classes are immutable, and they allow easy matching and extraction of data, as in the next example.

```
case class Sell(symbol : String, quantity : Int)
case class Buy(symbol : String, quantity : Int)
```

```
def processTrade(trade : Any) {
  trade match {
    case Sell(symbol, quantity) =>
      println("Selling " + quantity + " stocks of " + symbol)
    case Buy(symbol, quantity) if (quantity > 1000) =>
      println("Buying lots..." + quantity + " stocks of " + symbol)
    case Buy(symbol, quantity) =>
      println("Buying " + quantity + " stocks of " + symbol)
  }
}

processTrade(Sell("AAPL", 200)) // Selling 200 stocks of AAPL
processTrade(Buy("AAPL", 2000)) // Buying lots...2000 stocks of AAPL
processTrade(Buy("GOOG", 200))  // Buying 200 stocks of GOOG
```

When you create an instance of a case class, the values for the parameters flow in. For example, Sell("AAPL", 200) sends AAPL for the symbol and 200 for the quantity. When you use a case class in a pattern match, the values flow out. For example, in case Sell(symbol, quantity), the values present in the instance of case class are extracted into these parameters. So, if the case class contained GOOG and 200 for these two fields, these values are extracted into the variables s and q, respectively, if the pattern is defined as case Sell(s, q). This direction in which the data moves is referred to as apply (invoking a function and sending data to it) and unapply (extracting the data from the object, moving the data in the opposite direction). The unapply operation is quite useful in pattern matching, as you'll see next.

Using Extractions

If you want to perform more powerful extractions and apply a series of pattern matching, you can use Scala extractors. In the next example, you'll write an extractor to parse the details of a Task. First define a Task singleton class with an unapply method.

```
object Task {
  def unapply(taskInfo : String) = {
    val parts = taskInfo.split("---")
    if(parts.size != 2) None else Some(parts(0), parts(1))
  }
}
```

The unapply method expects the given string to contain one delimiter ---, and if the parameter conforms to that, unapply returns as a tuple the two parts before and after this delimiter. If the format does not conform, it returns a None, indicating a failure of extraction. The unapply method can signal a failure by returning either a None or a false.

The values in the tuple returned from the unapply will be assigned to individual parameters you place in the case. You can use the Task as an extractor.

```
def processTask(detail : String) = {
  detail match {
    case Task(day, task) => println("Task for " + day + ":" + task)
    case _ => println("invalid task format")
  }
}
```

If the detail parameter conforms to the format that the Task extractor expects, the day and task parameters will contain the day and the task item for the day.

Exercise this function with a few calls:

```
processTask("Monday --- integrate with the payment system")
//Task for Monday : integrate with the payment system

processTask("Wednesday -- hack code with no tests")
//invalid task format

processTask("Frday --- discuss discount rates")
//Task for Frday : discuss discount rates
```

In the first call, the Task conformed to the format and the extractor provided you the day and the task. In the second call, you ended up with a format error since the parameter did not conform to the expected format. The last call has the right format, but the day of week is messed up. This went undetected, but it's really easy to fix.

Create a DayOfWeek extractor to check the day of the week. The unapply method for this extractor can simply return a true or false to indicate if the string matches a day of the week.

```
object DayOfWeek {
  def unapply(day : String) = {
    List("Sunday", "Monday", "Tuesday", "Wednesday",
      "Thursday", "Friday", "Saturday") contains day.trim
  }
}
```

Let's improve the processTask method to use this extractor in combination with the extractor we already have.

```
def processTaskImproved(detail : String) = {
  detail match {
    case Task(day @ DayOfWeek(), task) =>
      println("Task for " + day + ":" + task)
    case _ => println("invalid task day or format")
  }
}
```

In the first case expression, you first invoke the Task extractor. This parses the content and splits the day part from the task information part. You further invoke the DayOfWeek extractor on the day part. The value of day is stored in the day reference, but the case match is not completed until the DayOfWeek extractor signals a success. If the day matches the format for a day of the week, as indicated by the unapply method of DayOfWeek, then the pattern match succeeds. If either the Task extractor signals a failure by returning None or the DayOfWeek extractor signals a failure by returning false, the match will not succeed. Exercise this improved version with the same arguments as you have sent to the first version of processTask and ensure that the validation of the data also happens.

```
processTaskImproved("Monday --- integrate with the payment system")
// Task for Monday : integrate with the payment system

processTaskImproved("Wednesday -- hack code with no tests")
// invalid task day or format

processTaskImproved("Frday --- discuss discount rates")
// invalid task day or format
```

That's pattern matching the Scala way, an elegant style of functional programming. But the ultimate payoff for functional programming is concurrency, and we'll explore that in Chapter 19, *Concurrency in Scala*, on page 157.

Concurrency in Scala

by Venkat Subramaniam

We've seen the object-oriented paradigm and the functional style of programming interplay in Scala in the previous Scala chapters. In this chapter, we'll use the functional purity for greater good—programming concurrency.

We all desire to make our applications faster and more responsive. There's no shortage of resources with multiple cores in our hands. The hard part is writing the code correctly to reap the benefits of the power on hand.

To fully exploit the power of concurrency and perform various complex tasks, concurrency libraries like Akka[1] are quite helpful. (See also *Programming Concurrency on the JVM [Sub11]* by one of our favorite authors -ed.) However, in this chapter, we'll stay within the facilities provided directly in the Scala language and make use of *parallel collections*.

Using Parallel Collections

We want our applications to be responsive and faster, but we don't want to compromise their correctness. The purity of functional programming is our ally in this area. When we set out to make code concurrent, we must ensure the purity of operations, making sure they don't have side effects. This means using vals (rather than vars) and immutable objects. For avoiding side effects, Scala rewards us with faster response without compromising the correctness of the results.

Let's first create a utility function that will allow us to measure the time operations will take. This will help us compare the sequential processing and its concurrent counterpart.

---

1. http://akka.io

```
object Time {
  def code(block: () => Unit) = {
    val start = System.nanoTime
    try {
      block()
    } finally {
      val end = System.nanoTime
      println("Time taken: " + (end - start)/1.0e9)
    }
  }
}
```

The code function of the Time singleton accepts a function value and measures the time it takes to apply or execute the function value (code block). For example, to report the time for a simple block of code that takes a short nap, we can write the following:

```
Time.code { () => Thread.sleep(1000) }
//Time taken: 1.00088
```

We've seen different Scala collections in the previous chapters. The collections provide a special method named par that returns to us a parallel collection.

Let's create a list of names and get a parallel collection from it.

```
val names = List("Jane", "Jacob", "Brenda", "Brad")
println(names)
//List(Jane, Jacob, Brenda, Brad)

println(names.par)
//ParVector(Jane, Jacob, Brenda, Brad)
```

Certain operations on parallel collections have parallel implementations, and we can make use of these to speed up operations that take significant time. Suppose we're creating a messenger application and want to check the status of multiple people we're interacting with. The function for this operation might look like the following:

```
def checkStatus(name : String) = {
  Thread.sleep(1000) //simulate the delay to communicate
  String.format("%s's status", name)
}
```

Sequential calls to this function will incur delay in proportion to the number of elements in the list.

```
Time.code { () => println(names.map { checkStatus }) }
//List(Jane's status, Jacob's status, Brenda's status,
//  Brad's status)
//Time taken: 4.005623
```

We can enjoy a speedup if we apply the map function on the parallel collection we created.

```
Time.code { () => println(names.par.map { checkStatus }) }
//ParVector(Jane's status, Jacob's status, Brenda's status,
//  Brad's status)
//Time taken: 1.021915
```

Unlike the execution of the map function on the List, the map function on the parallel collection ran the given function value in parallel for each element. The number of parallel executions depends on the number of threads in a pool that Scala allocates, which in turn depends on the number of cores available. This is simple, but it's somewhat limiting. If we need finer control on the thread pool, libraries like Akka provide some good solutions.

Suppose we want to find if all our meeting participants are connected. We can do this sequentially.

```
def isConnected(name : String) = {
  Thread.sleep(1000) //simulate the delay to communicate
  name.length < 6 //simulated response
}

Time.code { () =>
  println("All connected? :" + names.forall { isConnected })
}
//All connected? :false
//Time taken: 3.017145195
```

Unlike the map function, the forall function needs to collect the result of the evaluation of the function value for all the elements. However, the evaluations can be performed in parallel as in the next code.

```
Time.code { () =>
  println("All connected? :" + names.par.forall { isConnected })
}
//All connected? :false
//Time taken: 1.018888
```

Knowing When to Use Concurrency

We saw how the parallel collection runs some operations in parallel. Not all operations have parallel implementations, however. For example, the parallel collection provides the foldLeft, foldRight, and reduce methods so we can conveniently invoke them on these kinds of collections like we do on regular collections. Based on the context, we have to keep in mind that such operations will be sequential and not parallel.

```
def addToConnected(connected : Int, name : String) =
  connected + (if (isConnected(name)) 1 else 0)

Time.code { () =>
  println("Number of folks connected: " +
    names.foldLeft(0) { addToConnected })
}
//Number of folks connected: 3
//Time taken: 4.005546

Time.code { () =>
  println("Number of folks connected: " +
    names.par.foldLeft(0) { addToConnected })
}
//Number of folks connected: 3
//Time taken: 4.014092
```

There is another caveat with parallel collections: the parallel version may do
more work. Suppose we want to find the first connected person. We could
use the find function, like so:

```
Time.code { () =>
  println("A connected person: " + names.find { isConnected })
}
//A connected person: Some(Jane)
//Time taken: 1.003007775
```

The sequential version evaluated the isConnected function for only the first
person in the list before it found a matching element. Let's take a look at the
parallel version.

```
Time.code { () =>
  println("A connected person: " + names.par.find { isConnected })
}
//A connected person: Some(Jane)
//Time taken: 1.039542311
```

The parallel version gave the same result as the previous version and took
approximately the same time, but there's a catch. To understand this, let's
introduce a print statement, an impurity, to make visible the actual tasks
executed.

```
names.find { name => println("seq: " + name); isConnected(name) }
//seq: Jane

names.par.find { name => println("conc: " + name); isConnected(name) }
//conc: Jane
//conc: Jacob
//conc: Brad
//conc: Brenda
```

The parallel version ends up doing more work than the sequential version, as it's trying to evaluate all the cases in parallel. We have to weigh this in and ensure the extra executions are not prohibitively high and impact either the performance or the outcome.

Revisiting an Earlier Example

Let's put the parallel collection to a practical use. In Chapter 3, *Scala and Functional Style*, on page 15, we looked at concise code to fetch and process stock prices from Yahoo. Let's revisit that code and make it run parallel.

For this example, we'll use the following tickers:

```
val tickers = List("AAPL", "AMD", "CSCO", "GOOG", "HPQ", "INTC", "MSFT", "ORCL")
```

The code to fetch the price and construct it into a StockPrice object is repeated from that chapter here.

```
case class StockPrice(ticker : String, price : Double) {
  def print = println("Top stock is " + ticker + " at price $" + price)
}

def getPrice(ticker : String) = {
  val url = s"http://download.finance.yahoo.com/d/quotes.csv?s=${ticker}&f=snbaopl1"
  val data = io.Source.fromURL(url).mkString
  val price = data.split(",")(4).toDouble
  StockPrice(ticker, price)
}
```

The helper functions we needed to check if the stock prices are less than $500 and to pick the higher-priced stock are shown next:

```
def isNotOver500(stockPrice : StockPrice) = stockPrice.price < 500

def pickHigherPriced(stockPrice1 : StockPrice, stockPrice2 : StockPrice) =
  if(stockPrice1.price > stockPrice2.price) stockPrice1 else stockPrice2
```

Finally, here's the sequential code to compose all these to produce the desired result. We'll measure the time to execute this code.

```
Time.code { () =>
  tickers map getPrice filter isNotOver500 reduce pickHigherPriced print
}
//Top stock is ORCL at price $30.01
//Time taken: 17.777705
```

The code took around seventeen seconds to get the prices from Yahoo and determine the highest-priced stock not over $500.

Let's make a small change to the code to turn this into parallel execution.

```
Time.code { () =>
  tickers.par map getPrice filter isNotOver500 reduce pickHigherPriced print
}
//Top stock is ORCL at price $30.01
//Time taken: 3.805312
```

We inserted the call to par and invoked the map on the resulting parallel collection. All the requests to Yahoo and the subsequent calls to isNotOver500 are done in parallel. The only sequential part is the reduce operation and the resulting calls to pickHigherPriced. The parallel version took only around three seconds to produce the same result.

The functional programming style combined with powerful libraries make concurrent programming not only easier but also fun.

## CHAPTER 20

Clojure's Exceptional Handling of Exceptions

by Stuart Halloway

If you don't know about *conditions*, you should. Conditions are basically exception handling, but with greater flexibility. Many Lisps feature a condition system, and Clojure is no exception (pun inflicted by editor). Clojure's condition system is called error-kit. In this chapter, you will learn how to use error-kit, and why you will prefer it to plain old exception handling.

You don't need to have bought my book[1] to understand this article, but why wouldn't you want to? ;) You can follow along throughout this article by entering the code at Clojure's REPL. To install a REPL on your local machine, you can download the sample code from the book. The sample code has its own home page.[2]

The sample code includes a prebuilt version of Clojure and the clojure-contrib library that contains error-kit. To launch a REPL, execute bin/repl.sh (Unix) or bin\repl.bat (Windows) from the root of the sample code project. You should see the following prompt:

```
Clojure
user=>
```

For your reference, the completed sample is included in the download at examples/error_kit.clj.

---

1. *Programming Clojure (2nd edition) [HB12]*
2. http://github.com/stuarthalloway/programming-clojure

A Simple Example

To see how error-kit handles exceptions, we'll create a simple application and perpetrate some errors. Let's write an app that parses log file entries. Our log file entries will look like this:

```
2008-10-05 12:14:00 WARN Some warning message here...
```

In this imperfect world, it is inevitable that some miscreant will pass bad data to the log file parser. To deal with this, we will define an error:

```
(use 'clojure.contrib.error-kit)
(deferror malformed-log-entry [] [msg]
  {:msg msg
   :unhandled (throw-msg IllegalArgumentException)})
```

The error takes a single argument, a msg describing the problem. The :unhandled value defers to a normal Clojure (Java) exception in the event that a caller chooses not to handle the error. (The empty vector [] could contain a parent error, but we won't need that in this example.)

Now, let's write a parse-log-entry function:

```
(defn parse-log-entry [entry]
  (or
    (next (re-matches #"(\d+-\d+-\d+) (\d+:\d+:\d+) (\w+) (.*)" entry))
    (raise malformed-log-entry entry)))
```

The first argument to or uses a regular expression to crack a log entry. If the log entry is not in the correct format, the second argument to or will *raise* an error. Try it with a valid log entry:

```
(parse-log-entry
  "2008-10-05 12:14:00 WARN Some warning message here...")
-> ("2008-10-05" "12:14:00" "WARN" "Some warning message here...")
```

Of course, we could do more than just return a simple sequence, but since we are focused on the error case, we'll keep the results simple.

What happens with a bad log line?

```
(parse-log-entry "some random string")
-> java.lang.IllegalArgumentException: some random string
```

An unhandled error is converted into a Java exception, and propagates as normal.

The Problem with Exceptions

So why wouldn't we simply throw and catch exceptions? The problem is one of context. At the point of an exception, you know the most intimate details about what went wrong. But you do *not* know the broader context. How does the calling subsystem or application want to deal with this particular kind of error? Since you don't know the context, you throw the exception back out to someone who does.

At some higher level, you have enough context to know what to do with the error, but by the time you get there, you have lost the context to continue. The stack has unwound, partial work has been lost, and you are left to pick up the pieces. Or, more likely, to give up on the application-level task that you started.

A Solution: Conditions

Conditions provide a way to have your cake and eat it too. At some high-level function, you pick a *strategy* for dealing with the error, and register that strategy as a *handler*. When the lower-level code hits the error, it can then pick a handler *without unwinding the call stack*. This gives you more options. In particular, you can choose to cope with the problem and continue.

Let's say that you are processing some log files that include some garbage lines, and that you are content to skip past these lines. You can use with-handler to execute the code with a handler that will replace bad lines with, for example, a simple nil.

```
(defn parse-or-nil [logseq]
  (with-handler
    (vec (map parse-log-entry logseq))
    (handle malformed-log-entry [msg]
      (continue-with nil))))
```

The call to continue-with will replace any malformed log entries with nil. Despite the structural similarity, this is *not at all* like a catch block. The continue-with is specified by an outer calling function (parse-or-nil) and will execute inside an inner called function (parse-log-entry).

To test parse-or-nil, create a few top-level vars, one with a good sequence of log entries, and one with some corrupt entries:

```
(def good-log
  ["2008-10-05 12:14:00 WARN Some warning message here..."
   "2008-10-05 12:14:00 INFO End of the current log..."])
```

```
(def bad-log
  ["2008-10-05 12:14:00 WARN Some warning message here..."
   "this is not a log message"
   "2008-10-05 12:14:00 INFO End of the current log..."])
```

The good-log will parse without any problems, of course:

```
(parse-or-nil good-log)
-> [("2008-10-05" "12:14:00" "WARN" "Some warning message here...")
    ("2008-10-05" "12:14:00" "INFO" "End of the current log...")]
```

When parsing hits an error in bad-log, it substitutes a nil and moves right along:

```
(parse-or-nil bad-log)
-> [("2008-10-05" "12:14:00" "WARN" "Some warning message here...")
    nil
    ("2008-10-05" "12:14:00" "INFO" "End of the current log...")]
```

OK, but what if you wanted to do more than just return nil? Maybe the original API signals an error, but doesn't do any logging. No problem, just impose your own logging from the outside:

```
(defn parse-or-warn [logseq]
  (with-handler
    (vec (map parse-log-entry logseq))
    (handle malformed-log-entry [msg]
      (continue-with (println "****warning****: invalid log: " msg)))))
```

Now, parsing the bad-log will log the problem.

```
(parse-or-warn bad-log)
****warning****: invalid log:  this is not a log message
-> [("2008-10-05" "12:14:00" "WARN" "Some warning message here...")
    nil
    ("2008-10-05" "12:14:00" "INFO" "End of the current log...")]
```

Of course, a production-quality solution would use a real logging API, but you get the idea. Slick, huh?

Make Life Simple for Your Callers

It gets even better.

If you know in advance some of the strategies your callers might want to pursue in dealing with an error, you can name those strategies at the point of a possible error, and then let callers select a strategy *by name*. The bind-continue form takes the name of a strategy, an argument list, and a form to implement the strategy.

So, continuing with our log example, you might choose to provide explicit skip and log strategies for dealing with a parse error:

```
(defn parse-or-continue [logseq]
  (let [parse-log-entry
    (fn [entry]
      (with-handler (parse-log-entry entry)
        (bind-continue skip [msg]
          nil)
        (bind-continue log [msg]
          (println "****invalid log: " msg))))]
    (vec (map parse-log-entry logseq))))
```

parse-or-continue has no continue-with block, so a bad log entry will default to a Java exception:

```
(parse-or-continue bad-log)
-> java.lang.RuntimeException: java.lang.IllegalArgumentException:
    this is not a log message
```

Callers of parse-or-continue can select a handler strategy with the continue form. Here, the call selects the skip strategy:

```
(with-handler (parse-or-continue bad-log)
  (handle malformed-log-entry [msg] (continue skip msg)))
-> [("2008-10-05" "12:14:00" "WARN" "Some warning message here...")
    nil
    ("2008-10-05" "12:14:00" "INFO" "End of the current log...")]
```

And here it selects the log strategy:

```
(with-handler (parse-or-continue bad-log)
  (handle malformed-log-entry [msg] (continue log msg)))
****warning****: invalid log:  this is not a log message
-> [("2008-10-05" "12:14:00" "WARN" "Some warning message here...")
    nil
    ("2008-10-05" "12:14:00" "INFO" "End of the current log...")]
```

Notice the continue forms pass an argument to the bound continues. In these examples, we just passed the error message, but the parameter list could be used to implement arbitrary coordination between continue calls and bound continue forms. This is powerful.

Laziness and Errors

Most Clojure data structures are *lazy*, which means that they are evaluated only as needed. To make these lazy structures play nicely with conditions (or even plain old exceptions, for that matter), you have to install your handlers around the code that actually *realizes* the collection, not around the code that *creates* the collection.

This can be confusing at the REPL. Can you spot the problem here?

```
(with-handler
  (map parse-log-entry bad-log)
  (handle malformed-log-entry [msg]
    (continue-with nil)))
-> java.lang.IllegalArgumentException: this is not a log message
```

This code is trying to add a handler, but it isn't working. Stepping through the sequence of events will show why:

1. The with-handler block sets a handler.

2. The map creates a lazy sequence.

3. The handler block exits, returning the lazy sequence to the REPL.

4. The REPL realizes the sequence to print it, but by now the handler is gone. Oops.

In the earlier examples, we avoided this problem by explicitly realizing the sequence with calls to vec. Here's the takeaway: in your own applications, make sure to install handlers around *realization*, not instantiation.

Traditional exception handling gives you two points of control: the point of failure, and the handler. With a condition system, you have an all-important third point of control. Handlers can make *continues* available at the point of failure. Low-level functions can then raise an error, and higher-level functions can deal with the error *at the point it occurred, with full context.*

If you have ever found a large project staggering under the weight of exception-handling code, you might want to consider giving conditions a shot.

The choice of log file parsing for the example was inspired by a similar example[3] in Peter Seibel's excellent book *Practical Common Lisp [Sei05].*

---

3.   http://gigamonkeys.com/book/beyond-exception-handling-conditions-and-restarts.html

## CHAPTER 21

A Testing Framework for Elixir

by Bruce Tate

As Dave Thomas shared in Chapter 10, *Patterns and Transformations in Elixir*, on page 69, I too fell in love with Elixir. I fell so hard that my business, icanmakeitbetter,[1] began a year-long transition from Ruby on Rails to Elixir. That's one hell of a commitment to sell to your boss, but in truth, many in our industry have to make the same commitment to address new multicore architectures and increasingly distributed designs. We believe the payoff will be significant. In this chapter, I'm going to walk you through one aspect of that process: testing. I hope that in the process, you'll get a deeper sense of what it's like to solve real problems in Elixir.

Investing in Testing

At icanmakeitbetter, we have a test-heavy philosophy that strongly embraces this fundamental rule:

- Test all of your code with pretty, isolated, fast tests.

That's a dense sentence. Let's break it down.

- Test *all* of your code: we do test every single line we write, and we measure that coverage in Elixir with coveralls.[2] If a line of code is worth writing, it's worth testing.

- with *pretty*: we believe test cases should be first-class citizens. Because we write so many tests, every single tick of punctuation counts, and the vocabulary we choose is important to us. Tests are stories, and should read like them.

---

1. http://icanmakeitbetter.com
2. https://github.com/parroty/excoveralls

- *isolated, fast tests*: we believe isolated tests are easier to maintain. Setup code should be isolated, too. Isolated tests have another significant benefit in Elixir: Elixir can run them concurrently, making them very fast.

Out of the box, the Elixir language comes with a nice testing tool called ExUnit. We believe that ExUnit provides an excellent start, but does not go far enough to promote the second and third values. Tests should also be pretty and isolated. Take the following example.

Let's start with the anatomy of a typical Elixir ExUnit test:

```elixir
defmodule AppTest do
  use ExUnit.Case

  test "setup works" do
    context = %{ setup: :done}

    assert context.setup == :done
  end
end
```

Believe it or not, this test case represents a huge improvement over test cases in some languages. You can see the test and setup macros are shorter and cleaner than typical test cases based on functions.

One Experiment, Several Measurements

We can do better, though. We think the setup block should run an experiment, and each test block should run measurements. Combining setup code with test code makes it hard to isolate single-purpose code. The experiments and measurement concerns can become too entangled.

Let's rewrite that:

```elixir
defmodule AppTest do
  use ExUnit.Case

  setup( context ) do
    context
    |> Map.put( :setup, :done)
  end

  test "setup works", context do
    assert context.setup == :done
  end
end
```

That's a little better. We have a setup block that can run an experiment and test code that can run measurement. That's a potential improvement, but since there's typically only a single setup, the improvements can only take you so far.

Optimizing Setup with TrueStory

In our testing experience, we believe when testing commercial applications, the bulk of the work you'll do is building setup code, but that's precisely the code that gets the least amount of attention in a typical test.

Around October of last year, we began working on a testing library called TrueStory.[3] By restructuring our tests using macros into clear areas of responsibility, we can do a better job of writing single-purposed tests.

For this philosophy, we find that a story metaphor works well. We chose to use the noun story to define the setup and run our experiment. In short, we tell a story. Then, in another block called verify, we measure the impact on the real world with straight ExUnit assertions.

Then, your intentions are crystal clear. In the story, your code impacts our world, or context, in some way. This section can have impure functions, and can modify our context. In the verify block, we measure the impact of the story. Everything in the verify block must be a pure function.

We adopted this strategy after about a year of practice writing tests with various frameworks in Ruby and Elixir. Let's rewrite our test with our more descriptive macro:

```
    defmodule AppTest do
  use ExUnit.Case
  use TrueStory

  def set_map_key(c) do
    Map.put :setup, :done
  end

  story "run a simple story", c
    |> set_map_key
  verify
    assert context.setup == :done
  end
end
```

It's a tiny change, but our intentions are clear. Look at the advantages:

- We make it easy to reuse test setup collateral, leading to DRY code.
- By taking and returning a map—our context—our setup code composes well.
- We segregate the pure and impure with our story and verify blocks.
- Each component of our test has a single purpose.

---

3. https://github.com/ericmj/true_story

In fact, the idea of multiple setup blocks from named functions has made it into ExUnit as *named setups*. We're seeing an important idea in play here. The function names we've chosen participate in the overall thought for that line of code:

```
>   story "run a simple story", c
>     |> set_map_key,
```

Since we can build a clear pipe of functions, the story block can tell you everything about your test that you need to know. Let's get a little more complicated.

Condense and Combine the Measurements

We can still do better. In the previous test, we have only one measurement. Typically, we'll have more than one. When that happens, our verify block can group several different measurements together, like this:

```
defmodule AppTest do
  use ExUnit.Case
  use TrueStory

  use ExUnit.Case
  use TrueStory

  def set_map_key(c) do
    Map.put :setup, :done
  end

  def set_second_key(c) do
    Map.put :test, :true_story
  end

  story "two context keys", c
    |> set_map_key
    |> set_second_key,
  verify do
    assert :setup in Map.keys(c)
    assert :test in Map.keys(c)
    refute :not_present in Map.keys(c)
  end
end
```

The grouping is an improvement. It does two things for the reader:

- It tells readers that these tests are related.
- It segregates pure and impure code.

Sometimes, when you can segregate pure functional code, good things happen. Let me tell you what I mean.

Let's say you want to organize your code by adding some common setup functions in a setup block. This organization would allow you to eliminate repetition in your tests, but we have a problem. Since your tests that use that setup are not guaranteed to be pure, you must run the setup function for each test.

In this case, our verify block is pure, so we're guaranteed that our pure code will not change our environment, so *we can run all of the assertions in a verify block without needing to run the story setup again.* Our tests are faster, and the execution is clear. We don't have to teach users of TrueStory that setups will run multiple times, one for each test. The flow is explicit.

With another tiny tweak, we can get a second benefit as well. In TrueStory:

Failures are data; errors are exceptions.

Remember, our strategy is to run our experiments in the story block, and then multiple measurements. Our stateless measurements are pure assertions, and whatever pure functional code makes those assertions clear.

Not only are our measurements in verify independent of our story, but they are independent of each other. That means we can run *all of our measurements*, whether or not any single measurement fails.

That's a tremendous win.

Keep in mind that this behavior is exactly what you want as a developer. If your setup fails, you get an error—an exception that halts a given test in its tracks, because without a complete setup, *the system cannot continue.* On the other hand, if you get a failure, TrueStory will continue to run, telling you which assertions pass and which ones fail. You can get more information, and you can put it all to use at once if you see fit.

We've found that this small difference can mean a great difference to an individual developer's flow, allowing several fixes in a single test pass.

An error would stop this test as you would expect. You can also do all of the typical things you'd like to do in a context comparison, because you're dealing directly with ExUnit assertions.

Controlling Setup Repetition with Nested Contexts

When you're working with a bare-bones testing framework like ExUnit, you'll experience significant repetition when you set up code. Consider this testing script:

```
    ...
setup context do
  set_up_web_app
end

test "index, logged in" do
  user = new_user context
  log_in user

  response = get("/")
  assert response.code == 200
  assert response.template == "index"
end

test "profile, logged in" do
  user = new_user context
  log_in user

  response = get("/#{user.id}")
  assert response.code == 200
  assert response.template == "profile"
end

test "profile, logged out" do
  response = get("/")
  assert response.code == 404
end
```

This hypothetical code runs some simple tests and correctly uses the setup macro to control the duplication of the code to set up the web application. Still, you can see more duplication. Every test that has to log in replicates code to log in and create a user. The problem is that in real-world testing situations, you'll always have significant setup code, and this code causes a lot of duplication.

Controlling Setup Repetition with Story Pipes

We can eliminate this code in TrueStory with story pipes, like this:

```
    ...
# this example is simplified for clarity
def configure_web_app(c, ...) do
  c
  |> Map.put :conn, set_up_test_conn(...)
end

def logged_in(c, user) do
  c
  |> Map.put :session, log_in(new_user, c.conn)
end
```

```elixir
def get_root(c) do
  c
  |> Map.put :response, get_root(c.conn)
end

story "getting /", c
  |> configure_web_app
  |> get_root,
verify do
  assert c.conn.response == :redirect
  # more assertions about an unauthorized get
end

story "getting /, logged in", c
  |> configure_web_app
  |> logged_in(create_user)
  |> get_root,
verify do
  assert c.conn.response == :success
  # more assertions about a successful get of /
end
end
```

and so on.

The stories are the way we think when we're testing. We simply run a scenario, and then make assertions about whether that operation worked. By segregating each logical, meaningful piece of the setup in a story pipe segment, we can build more and more reusable test collateral.

The preceding code may leave you unsatisfied, because maybe it's better to actually have the application do the logging in. Such a test is an *integration test*. Since our testing components compose, integration tests are easy. We can write the preceding test like this:

```elixir
# this example is simplified for clarity
def configure_web_app(c, ...) do
  c
  |> Map.put :conn, set_up_test_conn(...)
end

def post_login(c, user) do
  c
  |> Map.put :conn, post("login", c.conn)
end

def get_root(c) do
  c
  |> Map.put :response, get_root(c.conn)
end
```

```elixir
  story "getting /", c
    |> configure_web_app
    |> get_root,
verify do
  assert c.conn.response == :redirect
  # more assertions about an unauthorized get
end

def integrate do
  story "logging in", c
    |> configure_web_app
    |> post_login(create_user),
  verify do
    assert c.conn.response == :redirect
    # more assertions about a successful login
  end

  story "getting /, logged in", c
    |> configure_web_app
    |> get_root,
  verify do
    assert c.conn.response == :success
    # more assertions about a successful get of /
  end
end
end
```

That's much more satisfying. By making our tests compose well, it's much easier to test flows that flow from one request into the next, verifying each step along the way.

As you can see, we've built on the foundation of ExUnit. We've defined a testing language with an overarching philosophy of one test, multiple experiments. We've isolated pure and impure functions. We've layered onto that motif composition of setup code and tests.

What you're left with is an excellent testing framework for the types of problems we typically solve for commercial applications: those with heavy setup, multiple steps, and verifications after each individual step.

We've found that our tests run quickly, and we're able to code much more quickly because our framework is encouraging us to build tests in nice bite-sized pieces.

In Chapter 22, *Building Test Data with Elixir*, on page 177, I'll walk you through Blacksmith, another testing tool that can help you create data templates for testing.

Building Test Data with Elixir

by Bruce Tate

In Chapter 21, *A Testing Framework for Elixir*, on page 169, I described a new unit and functional test framework we've built. In this article, I'll describe how we use macros to build fake test data.

At icanmakeitbetter, Elixir has made a huge difference. Because it is a functional language that fully supports concurrency and distribution, we are able to get much more performance out of our website. Elixir is also one of the first languages to support both a higher-level syntax and macros, and I'm going to talk about putting those features to good use to build beautiful test data.

Yes, I said beautiful.

Business applications need business data, and tests for those applications need fake data. Make that data plausible, and you'll find debugging much easier. Creating plausible testing data is relatively simple, but often leads to repetitive, tedious code. That's exactly the type of programming that my team works to avoid.

The Typical Approaches

Most typical test cases use one of a handful of approaches.

- Explicit: an application can simply explicitly generate test data, leading to code that looks like this:

```
~~~
Person.create first_name: "Paul", last_name: "Revere"
~~~
```

The downside is that such code will get awkward once you're creating enough entities with enough attributes. In short order, *the data overwhelms the test.*

- Through Fixtures: an application can create test data in tabular form, and then load all of that data into the application.

```
~~~
# person.csv
first_name, last_name
Paul, Revere
~~~
```

This strategy works all right, but leads to code that is hard to maintain as applications grow, because *foreign keys are difficult to manage.*

- Through templates: an application can use some kind of template to create fake data. This is the approach we chose. I'll show you many examples of this type of code as we go. This approach *adds complexity, and the tradeoff is not worth it for simple applications.* But once your application grows in complexity, the gains you can make in managing foreign keys and simplifying the creation of test data can be huge!

Beautiful Data for Beautiful Tests

In the preceding chapter, you saw first-hand our strong desire to make the repetitive tasks we do on a day-to-day basis *beautiful.* If I'm going to express a concept once or twice, I might be willing to live with the evil twins Ugly and Repetitive, but tests and the data that make them go will be expressed hundreds of times. I'm going to do everything I can to strip away all of the layers of tedium.

With Blacksmith, we want to be able to express these concepts with the best possible syntax:

- Templates: the central premise of Blacksmith is that we express a template in a module called Forge. That template describes an entity. This foundation will feed the many different data forms that we need. Users can then override any of the map's keys as needed.

- Flexible back ends: an entity may be a map, a struct, or even a JSON map. A persistent store might be a CSV file, a relational database, or some other type of database.

- Prototypes: sometimes, one entity is based on another. For example, an employee may be a user with an employee number.

- Saved and unsaved data: sometimes, our data is database-backed, and sometimes not.

- Single items and collections: we want to be able to create a list just as easily as a single record.

- Composite collections: databases have primary and foreign keys, and keeping those aligned with test data is sometimes tedious.

- Sequences to keep elements unique: sometimes, a test scenario may need a unique email or identifier. Blacksmith makes it easy.

Let's dig into each one of these elements in detail.

Registering Templates and Prototypes with Forge

You'll register each data template in a module usually called Forge. This is a template for a Person. Notice the Faker framework that we use to fake individual elements:

```
~~~
defmodule Forge do
  use Blacksmith
  register :user,
    first_name: Faker.Name.first_name,
    last_name: Faker.Name.last_name,
    email: Sequence.next(:email, &"test#{&1}@example.com")

  register :admin,
    [prototype: user],
    roles: ["admin"]
end
~~~
```

We're registering each type of entity in our Forge module. The first entry registers users. The Faker library supplies plausible values for first_name and last_name. We use a sequence to create an email so that each email for a new user will be unique. Blacksmith registers four different functions for creating users:

- Forge.user(overrides \\'%{}) creates a user, overriding any keys.
- Forge.user_list(n, overrides \\ %{}) creates a list of n users.
- Forge.saved_user(repo, overrides \\ %{}) creates a user, saved to repo.
- Forge.saved_user_list(n, repo, overrides \\ %{}) creates a list of n users, saved to repo.

By default, calling user and user_list creates a map, though you can change this behavior. You'll need to customize Blacksmith to use the saved versions. I'll show you how to override that behavior later, as well as how to use the override values.

Also in the previous listing, you can see an admin registration. In the three-argument form of register, you have the name, fields, and options. We're passing the prototype option, which allows us to register one model based on another. For admins, Blacksmith will create a new user with a roles field set to ["admin"].

Instantiating Template Entries

Now, you can create new users or admins. Just use your Forge module and the macros that Blacksmith creates for you, like this:

```
user =  Forge.user
```

Or, you can create a list of five users, like this:

```
users = Forge.user_list 5
```

You can override any of the registered attributes, like this:

```
user = Forge.user first_name: "Will", last_name: "Override"
```

Simple and powerful. Now, your tests can quickly create new entities with many elements, with the ability to override or create new attributes as needed.

Mutual Attributes and Having

You can also create several entities together with a mutual list of attributes. Let's say we want to create a few users, all sharing the same country_id attribute. We could use the having macro, like this:

```
Forge.having country_id: usa_id do
  user = Forge.user
  admin = Forge.admin
end
```

Now, both user and admin will have a country_id equal to usa_id. This advantage is small here, but will grow significantly with the number of attributes and entities that you need to manage. For example, in our tests, we may have dozens of questions and choices, all which have the same survey_id and company_id.

What if we need to create some other type of entity, like, say, an Elixir struct?

Creating Structs

We had a pleasant surprise when we built this API. We'd accidentally built in support for structs! Since an Elixir struct is just a map with the extra _struct_ key, just adding the key _struct_: User to the existing User record would create users that satisfy a struct called User like this:

```
register :user,
  __struct__: User,
  first_name: Faker.Name.first_name,
  last_name: Faker.Name.last_name,
  email: Sequence.next(:email, &"test#{&1}@example.com")
```

Creating Custom Entities

You can create something other than maps or structs. To do so, you just need to tell Blacksmith how. Elixir has a JSON library called Poison. Let's create a Forge that tells Blacksmith how to create a new JSON hash from an Elixir map, like this:

```
defmodule JsonForge do
  use Blacksmith

  @new_function &Blacksmith.Config.new_json/2

  register :user,
    name: "John Henry",
    email: Faker.Internet.email
end
defmodule Blacksmith.Config do
  def new_json(attributes, overrides) do
    attributes
    |> Dict.merge( overrides )
    |> Poison.Encoder.encode([])
  end
end
```

You can see a Forge with two specific enhancements. The first is the attribute variable, @new_function. Blacksmith creates maps, and that function tells Blacksmith how to create a JSON hash from a map.

Second, you can see the function new_json defined in Blacksmith.Config. That function simply takes the attributes (the ones generated by Blacksmith), merges in the overrides, and then calls Poison.Encoder.Encode on the result. The result is that each new entity will create a new JSON entity.

Customizing Persistence

If you want to create persistent entities, you need to show Blacksmith how to save single entities and lists of entities. For example, you might want to save records using Ecto, a persistence engine for Elixir. Here's how you'd go about it. Let's say you're starting with an Ecto schema, like this:

```
defmodule User do
  use Ecto.Model

  schema "users" do
    field :first_name, :string
    field :last_name, :string
    field :email, :string
  end
end
```

We're creating a simple database-backed entity. The database schema and model will both have corresponding fields.

Next, we create a Forge. Our Forge will specify the User struct for Ecto, as well as a couple of functions that Ecto could use to save one or many entities, like this:

```
defmodule Forge do
  use Blacksmith

  @save_one_function &Blacksmith.Config.save/2
  @save_all_function &Blacksmith.Config.save_all/2

  register :user,
    __struct__: User,
    first_name: Faker.Name.first_name,
    last_name: Faker.Name.last_name,
    email: Sequence.next(:email, &"jh#{&1}@example.com")
end
```

Now all that remains is to create a couple of functions to show Blacksmith how to persist Ecto data:

```
defmodule Blacksmith.Config do
  def save(repo, map) do
    repo.insert(map)
  end
```

```
  def save_all(repo, list) do
    Enum.map(list, &repo.insert/1)
  end
end
```
~~~

If you have a repo called UserRepo, with this Forge you can create one or many rows with:

~~~
```
user = Forge.saved_user UserRepo
party = Forge.saved_user_list 5, UserRepo
```
~~~

It's that easy.

If we had to create one or two database records for our tests, or if all of our entities had a handful of fields, we would probably opt for a different approach. We'd simply create them explicitly by hand. Similarly, if we had to create one database with complex relationships, we'd just use our software to create the database and save that data as fixtures.

Unfortunately, when you're testing business software, neither of these conditions are true. We have to create plausible data for each one of the thousands of test cases we run. With this simple little strategy for creating flat entities and lists, saved or not, we can take the tedium out of running tests.

## CHAPTER 23

Haskell's Type System

by Paul Callaghan

Imagine an approach to programming where you write down some description of what your code should do, then before running your code, you run some automatic tool to see if the code matches the description. That's test-driven development, you say!

Actually, this is what you're doing when you use static types in most languages too. Types are a description of the code's inputs and outputs, and the check ensures that inputs and outputs match up and are used consistently. Modern type systems—such as in Haskell—are very flexible and allow these descriptions to be quite detailed; plus, they aren't too obtrusive in use and often very helpful.

One point I'll investigate here is how advances in types are converging with new ideas on testing, to the point where (I claim) the old distinctions are starting to blur and advances are starting to open up exciting new possibilities—hence my suggestion that *we need a new word to describe what we're doing* that is free from preconceptions and outdated thinking.

So put aside your bad experiences from Java, and prepare to be amazed!

TL;DR

Apologies for length, but it's a big topic and I want to give a high-level view of the whole area. Here are the essential points:

- Haskell's type system is pretty flexible and mostly unobtrusive (unlike some static systems).

- A good type system is a powerful design language, too.

- We can also work with types in a "type-driven development" style.

- Parametric polymorphism is about using the same code for everything.

- Interfaces provide clean overloading and encourage and support approaches like DCI.

- Often Haskell feels like a dynamically typed language, though with a good safety net in reserve.

- Haskell has its limits, but the cost-benefit trade-off is probably in our favor.

- There are several options beyond Haskell, such as dependent types.

- Dependently typed languages are an elegant combination of computation *and* reasoning.

- Many TDD specs can be encoded as (dependent) types, and vice versa.

- I believe the distinction between tests and types is blurring, and each side can learn much from the other to capitalize on this.

What Are Types For?

Types do sometimes get some bad press. Many people will say types are about nailing details down and trying to avoid errors. This sounds to me a bit dry and negative, too much like a straitjacket, too *conservative.*

Some type systems undoubtedly are too restrictive and just don't give enough return for the work required to use them (Java is a prime example), but I'm talking about Haskell's type system here, which are quite a different kettle of fish. In this context, I prefer to see and use types as both *a design language and a safety net.* That is, they are more about help and opportunity rather than constraint, and this is pretty much how the type systems have been designed into these modern languages.

Design-wise, I can sketch some of the ideas in my mind as types, add some code, and have the compiler tell me when I'm missing some details or trying something silly. Quite often, I only write down types for the hard stuff when I want to be sure about it, and I let the compiler work out the rest. In this mode, the type checker is definitely the slave and not the master! When my code gets past the type checker, this gives high confidence that the code isn't going to have problems at runtime, at least not in the aspects described via the types. It's a highly valuable tool in development, with obvious similarities to TDD. Many functional programmers even refer to *type*-directed development (and observe that we've been doing it for a while...).

Type systems vary a lot, from minimal (like C) to cumbersome (like Java) to flexible (like Haskell) to awesome (like dependent type theory). The differences involve how articulate the descriptions (that is, types) can be, and how much reasoning (or inference) power can be applied. That is, how much useful stuff we can say directly in the types, rather than in separate tests or comments or documentation, and how much the tools can exploit this richer knowledge. The more advanced systems offer new ways of using types as well, such as semantic-directed editing and increased automation of the routine aspects of programming.

A Concrete Example: Sorting

Let's look at various types for a sort routine/method/function. We'll look at how this is handled in several languages and consider what the type is saying. Obviously, these library routines are reliable; the point here is what the types can tell us or help us do.

- Ruby: The types in Ruby don't say much, maybe just to indicate what can be sorted by virtue of some object being able to respond to a method called *sort*. There's a general expectation (though no requirement) that sorting will return an Array. We will, however, get runtime exceptions if the sorting can't proceed—for example, with [2, "a"].sort, it won't permit comparisons of Fixnum and String, or my personal favorite gotcha, [[], nil].sort.

- C: C allows something like int sort(int *vals, int num_vals) for sorting an array of ints in place. Typically, we want to generalize our sort routine to work with arbitrary types, so we will find in stdlib.h something like void qsort(void *vals, int num_vals, int size_vals, int comp_fn(void *, void *)), which allows in-place sorting of an array of items by using a supplied comparison function.

- Java: This language has several options, but the basic pattern is this for general sorting: void sort(T[] a, Comparator<T> c), which allows sorting of an array of some underlying element type T, using some comparison function on T values, wrapped up in a comparator object. The T construction is a placeholder in Java's so-called "generics" mechanism, and gets instantiated when the preceding code is applied to a concrete array. One effect of the generics is to guarantee that the comparison function is suitable for use on the element types. Earlier versions of Java provided a method sort(Object[] a, Comparator c); this would allow sort to be called on an array containing anything. Notice that the generics version moves some of the expensive runtime checking to a single check at compile time, and provides a bit more confidence that the resulting array hasn't got funny data added.

- Haskell: The Haskell version is sort :: Ord a => [a] -> [a], which basically says "given a type 'a' for which ordering is defined, we can sort a list of such 'a's to provide another list of the same element type." It says pretty much what the Java generics version does, albeit (IMHO) more succinctly and with no OO overhead. We could replace the Ord a => part with an explicit function argument, to give (a -> a -> Bool) => [a] -> [a]; in other words, we could require a function that takes two arguments to indicate whether a swap of elements is needed. (The Ord a stuff is effectively wrapping up a particular comparison function; we'll come back to this.)

But consider now, what is missing? Nothing? We're saying something about the data structures expected as input, and about the output type, plus ensuring that the ordering test can be used with the data. However, it still can't rule out bad definitions like sort xs = [] (always return an empty list) or sort xs = reverse xs (return a reversed copy of the list). Do we want to rule these out?

If we're sensible, then we'll probably sketch out some tests, maybe boiling down to checking assertions like sort [] == [] (empty list case) or sort [2,1] == [1,2] or sort [2,1,2] == [1,2,2]. We can even define some properties using the QuickCheck library and run automatic checks on a few hundred random examples to try to uncover counter examples. Perhaps we'll look at the code and identify some edge cases that need particular attention (depending on the algorithm), or want to check that the implementation has the stability property, such as sort_by first [[1,"b"],[1,"a"]] == [[1,"b"], [1,"a"]] and similar cases.

Do these have to be encoded as separate tests? Why can't we move some of this thinking into the code itself?

It turns out, we can! And in several ways. Possibilities include the approach called "design by contract" or some extensions to Haskell. However, I'm going to focus on a more general approach that subsumes all of the others. It is based on "dependent type theory," and effectively it's about *merging types and programs into a single language*. With this advanced language, we have the tools to encode our tests *inside* our program in a sensible way.

We can also encode conditions or invariants that are hard to express as tests —such as requiring that the code will never lose elements or duplicate any, and that indeed it does always return a sorted result.

First, we need to understand how Haskell's type system works, and see how it can be used for good in programming.

The Language of Haskell's Type System

I suggested that one important feature for a type system is how much it allows us to describe, so we'll start looking at the *language* of Haskell types first. It's perfectly accurate and appropriate to describe a type system as a language—it has words, grammar rules, and meanings. However, languages differ in what they can be used to express (or articulate), by virtue of the forms of sentences available.

Propositional logic can only talk about atomic propositions, like "Rubies are red," and combinations of these via the logical operators—for example, "Rubies are red and not(Rails is written in C)." Predicate logic allows some more flexibility by allowing the ability to quantify over entities, hence enabling sentences like, "For all m, m is mortal -> father_of(m) likes Rails" (in other words, every mortal's father likes Rails—probably untrue but we're not talking truth here, just talking about what we can articulate). In this example, we speak of the variable m being bound by the for-all quantifier. We can have many other kinds of logic, such as modal logic where we talk about possibility vs. necessity, or second-order logic where we can quantify over properties of elements, or...well, whatever we want.

Simple type systems (such as Pascal) can be like propositional logic, only able to say basic things such as, "This method takes two Ints and returns a String." Typically, we'd express this as (Int, Int) -> String, using the thin arrow symbol as a kind of implication, in the sense of, "If you give me two Ints, then you get a String back."

Programmers can add new type names—for example, a Person record to contain name, age, and address—and use these type names among the ones supplied in the language.

C allows references to functions to be passed around, and these can be represented using nesting—for example, (Int, Int -> Int) -> String for taking an Int and a function (from Int to Int) and returning a String. This is OK for basic work, but clearly more flexibility is needed.

Haskell's core type system is a restricted form of predicate logic. It allows variables in the type expressions to stand for arbitrary types, enabling a feature called *parametric* polymorphism. This kind of polymorphism (for there are several) is about *using the same piece of code whatever the actual input types*. For example, taking the length of a list has type [a] -> Int, and can be computed without considering the type of list elements: all it needs to do is walk through the list structure counting the nodes. It's completely irrelevant what is in the list, and no choice of element type can affect how the counting works! Similarly, list reversal has type [a] -> [a]; again, it is parametrically polymorphic and able to work with any list. Notice that type variable 'a' appears twice; this means that the input type is the same as the output list, so it can never, for example, convert a list of Ints to a list of Strings.

Stepping back a bit, this "it works for everything, and works consistently" view is often precisely what we want to articulate, and the benefits for checking code should be clear. For example, the mapping operation on lists has type

```
(a -> b) -> [a] -> [b]
```

meaning in English, "Give me a function from some a to some b, and a list of some 'a's, and you'll get back a list of some 'b's." Notice how it says something useful about what map does, that we no longer need to explain in the documentation? Furthermore, when we use map, the compiler can check automatically that its use is appropriate.

Similarly, function composition f . g = \x -> f (g x) has type (b -> c) -> (a -> b) -> a -> c, translated as "If we can convert 'b's to 'c's and 'a's to 'b's, then we can convert 'a's to 'c's, for whatever choice of a,b,c." Again, the type clearly says what the requirements are and indicates what we can expect back.

We can use polymorphism when defining our own data types too; for example:

```
data SamePair a = MkSamePair a a
```

has a constructor that combines two values of the same type. You saw some other examples last time. Let's now look at how the type language is used.

Type Inference and Type Checking

A language by itself isn't much use—we need some reasoning rules and algorithms to make it useful. That's what we'll cover here. The core inference rule is actually quite simple: if you have a function f that expects some value of type A, and you have a value x of type C such that A and C match in some way, then f(x) is firstly OK and also it has type B.

```
f : A -> B      x : C
------------------- if A = C
      f(x) : B
```

Notice that this rule doesn't "do" anything—it just says how we can relate bits of information. So next we can think about the two key algorithms: type *inference* and type *checking*.

Inference takes a piece of code and works out what the type could be, and most versions walk through a syntax tree and apply the preceding rule from the bottom up.

Checking takes a piece of code and a type, and decides whether the type is appropriate. There are several techniques we can use, such as using the code alone to infer a second type and seeing if it matches the original, or using a top-down tree walk that basically uses the preceding rule in reverse (which is also great for inferring omitted type information).

Many compilers (quite reasonably) use a mixture of inference and checking when compiling the code, so don't get too hung up on the differences. Just be aware of the options, and that we have several techniques to work with the types in our code.

Extra features like type variables fit easily into this framework, with the main change being that our A = C test might need to do *unification* (just as in Prolog) on two expressions, and anything learned from the unification needs to be applied to B. For example, where reverse :: [a] -> [a] and foo :: [Int], then A is [a] and C is [Int], which matches with the substitution a := Int. So we can conclude reverse foo :: [Int] because the B part is updated from [a] to [Int] because of the substitution. If you're happy with this example, then you've just understood the heart of Haskell's type checking.

Some Examples

```
foo1 text = unlines (map reverse (lines text))
```

Will this definition pass the type checker? What is its type? Given that lines :: String -> [String] and unlines :: [String] -> String, then it can infer that text should be a String, can approve the use of map, and can conclude that the result is going to be a String—in other words, conclude foo1 :: String -> String. No programmer annotations are needed, and our safety net has passed the code for use.

Let's try some type-driven development now. Suppose I want a function group_on that works a bit like Ruby's group_by—for example, where (1..10).group_by {|x| x % 2 == 0 } gives {false=>[1, 3, 5, 7, 9], true=>[2, 4, 6, 8, 10]}. For the sake of making the example a bit more complex, I'm going to do it via a wrapper around one of the Haskell library functions. (It could also be done as a fold loop that adds one element to a hash table on each step.) A Haskell List library function groupBy :: (a -> a -> Bool) -> [a] -> [[a]] can group *adjacent* equal elements—for example, groupBy (==) "Mississippi" gives ["M","i","ss","i","ss","i","pp","i"], but it's not quite what we want, so we need some wrapping. Let's get the type system to help us.

To start with, what's the type we want? Informally, we split a list of something into a hash or map, where the key is the result of some operation and the value is a list of the original items that gave that value. Notice that we're not talking concrete types, so we can expect to make this (parametrically) polymorphic; we can use the same piece of code no matter what the actual payload data is. Instead of a Hash, I'll use a simpler type of a list of pairs. For the preceding example, we expect [(false, [1,3,5,7,9]), (true, [2,4,6,8,10])].

First attempt: list in, list of pairs out, so we come up with something like group_on :: [a] -> [(b, [a])] as the type to aim for. But we need a way to generate the keys in the result, so we need to pass in a function for this. Hence group_on :: (a -> b) -> [a] -> [(b, [a])] as the next guess. But, how do we know when two 'b' values are the same? We'll need this to be able to group properly. Basically, we don't know yet. At present, all we know is how to get 'b' values from 'a' values (with the first argument) and that we want to put 'b' values as the keys in the result.

This is actually a key point about polymorphism and worth exploring. Polymorphism in types encodes the minimum we can expect or require, *and does not let us know anything else.*

More concretely, such polymorphic code can't mess around with the data it is working on, because it knows very little about it. This is great for enforcing modularity, among other things.

So how do we get to compare 'b' values? Well, we have to give the code a way to do it, and to keep it simple, I'll pass in another function. Hence we now have group_on :: (b -> b -> Bool) -> (a -> b) -> [a] -> [(b, [a])]. Notice how the type now shows the minimum we have to supply in order to use it, and how it succinctly expresses the main aspect of what it's going to do—convert our list into a hash. (Of course, it doesn't say everything; we'll discuss that later.) Note how it's also acting like part of a specification as well. What we have makes sense, and so next we can develop some code to match the type.

In an ideal world, our Haskell code editor could use the type information to help us build the definition from top to bottom, with us doing the creative parts and it managing the small, inferable details. In our example here, we know we want to use the groupBy library function wrapped up in some way, so we could start by writing ? (groupBy ? (? input)), where ? marks the bits we don't know yet, and see what the editor infers for the unknowns, after which we can attack each unknown in turn. (This is a divide and conquer approach, of course.) The preceding is basically saying we want to do something before and something after the groupBy, but we're not sure yet what it is.

We do have this technology now for dependent type languages like Agda, but as far as I know, it hasn't quite made it down to Haskell yet (which is a shame).

Back to the old-fashioned ASCII text file mode!

However, there is a nice trick to get some targeted support from your type checker: instead of your unknowns, just use value () (empty parentheses) where you don't know what to put. This is Haskell's dummy or placeholder value, the one we use when some value is needed, but we don't want to use anything meaningful. It's also the zero case for the range of notations for pairs ('a', True), triples ('a', True, 3), quads ('a', True, 3, [Nothing]), and so on. () is a tuple with nothing in it. When you use it for unknowns in your code, the type checker will produce a type error indicating that ()'s type (which is also written as ()) doesn't match the type expected at that part of the code. So we could write the following in our Haskell file and compile it:

```
group_on :: (b -> b -> Bool) -> (a -> b) -> [a] -> [(b,[a])]
group_on same eval inp = () (groupBy () (() inp))
```

We would instantly get a type error complaining that () :: () (the right-most one) doesn't have a type a -> b because it's being used as a function in the context of () inp (applied to the inp argument), but it doesn't match the general a -> b type pattern for functions. We can then start trying to refine the () values with more concrete versions, and work through the consequences. For example, we might guess () should be a map of something, so we would replace with map (). Then, we might realize that the new () should be a function, hence map (\x -> ()). At this point, the checker is satisfied here and it will now get us to work on the argument to groupBy. This technique might help some of you.

There are other techniques. In Chapter 13, *Functional Thinking and Haskell*, on page 97 I said "think data!," so we can think about the input (a list of 'a' things) and the fact that we want to group them on the basis of some 'b' result, then consider various ways we can do this while using the library's groupBy function.

If you're not happy with the abstract view, it's perfectly OK to think of concrete data instead and work through some examples on paper, and maybe even draw pictures of the various stages of the operation. It's also useful to work with a concrete example in the interpreter's REPL and see what you can build up. This technique really does work in FP, since many of your definitions will turn out to be short-ish anyway! It also works in Ruby, of course, so do try it if you haven't already. So let's do that. We know we want groupBy in there somewhere, and we can still use the () trick, so we can write the following at the prompt and see what it does:

```
groupBy () [1..10]
```

A type error, of course, but it suggests that () should be a function of two arguments. Next iteration:

```
groupBy (\a b -> ()) [1..10]
```

Another type error, because () needs to be a Boolean, so let's think about some test here. By luck, Haskell has even in its standard library. We want to group elements if they are both even or both not even, so try this:

```
groupBy (\a b -> even a == even b) [1..10]
```

Finally, we get something, but [[1],[2],[3],[4],[5],[6],[7],[8],[9],[10]] is not what we want. But, groupBy groups adjacent equal elements, so we need to do a bit more work, maybe trying to sort the list first.

Time passes.

Eventually, we find that the following works for our example:

```
map (\xs -> (even $ head xs, xs))
    $ groupBy (\a b -> even a == even b)
    $ sortBy (\a b -> even a `compare` even b) [1..10]
```

And then we can adapt it to code by pulling out the concrete details, hence:

```
group_on same eval inp
    = map (\es -> (eval $ head es, es))
      $ groupBy (\x y -> eval x `same` eval y)
      $ sortBy  (\x y -> eval x `compare` eval y) inp
```

We can simplify this in various ways—for example, by avoiding repeat runs of the eval function, or by using more overloading (as introduced later)—but this will do for now. (One extra detail has slipped in—that we need to know how to order 'b' values, and I'm quietly allowing Haskell's overloading to handle this.) It passes the type checker, and we can see pretty clearly how it works—a combination of sorting into a suitable order, grouping adjacents, then post-processing the result. One for you to consider: what testing should we do now?

Comfort Break

We're certainly not there yet, and we—everyone—have plenty more to explore first. Always reflect on what you'd like in a language rather than sticking to what existing languages give you and soldiering on. Thinking about type systems is part of this.

Here's a relevant and poignant example from Java. If you've used Java, you might have needed the .clone() method a few times. Recall how it gets used, though—typically like this:

```
Foo orig = Foo.new();
Foo copy = (Foo) orig.clone();
```

Why is that cast needed on the second line? Is it just because that's the Java way and you've gotten used to it? Or does it point to a weakness in the language? It is rather annoying to have to write down information that is very obvious to the programmer, which also adds to the "noise" in the program and obscures the "signal."

Sadly, it is a language weakness: Java's type system imposes certain constraints in order to get its version of inheritance to work "safely," and this means that inherited methods get restricted types. An overridden method must return the same type as the method in its ancestors.

Like most interesting aspects of life, designing a type system is a bit of a balancing act or trade-off, of juggling flexibility and articulacy with being able to retain useful properties and still be usable by programmers.

Some languages have a good balance, others not, and I'd place Java in the latter camp: the benefits are quite modest, and the costs too high. I would like to put Haskell in the first camp.

However, Java's issues don't mean that type checking in OOP is inherently problematic, or that the only alternative is dynamic checking—even if some people try to sell you this argument. There is much good work in the area that develops alternative approaches. I recommend Kim B. Bruce's *Foundations of Object-Oriented Languages* (2002) as a useful starting point. It has a highly readable first section that surveys the main languages, including some illuminating discussion of Java's design and implementation. Then it proposes several attractive alternatives to Java. A key aspect of Bruce's approach is keeping data and functionality separate, making serious use of interfaces for the latter.

Interfaces and Type Classes

Interfaces, in the sense used here, work on several levels. Here's a standard example from Haskell that will be familiar to Java programmers: the "comparable" interface. I'll explain it in two stages—first, an underlying equality test, then the wider less-than-or-equal test.

```
class Eq a where
  (==) :: a -> a -> Bool

class Eq a => Ord a where
  (<=)    :: a -> a -> Bool
  compare :: a -> a -> Ordering     -- LT or EQ or GT
```

The technical term for entities like the preceding is "type class," intuitively identifying a set of types that provide the listed functionality. I prefer the more informal term "interfaces," since what we're doing is describing some functionality that can be assumed for some type, or a promise of what a value in that type can provide. When you have that interface or promise, you can then write code that uses that interface.

The first definition describes an interface called Eq, which promises a binary operator == that takes two values and returns a Boolean. We can use this operator freely in other code—for example, counting how many items in a list are equal to a given target by scanning the list and selecting (filtering) which items are "the same" as some target, i.e., by returning True when compared to it.

```
count_same target list = length [ x | x <- list, x == target ]
```

There are other ways to write this definition—for example, length . filter (\x -> x == target)—but that's off topic. Now, how flexible is this code? Which types can we use it with? Well, the only thing we need to know or assume is that the underlying type has == defined for it. For the whole definition, we can say informally: we can count how many values in a list are the same as some target, as long as the target and list elements are the same type, and assuming we can compare values of that type. More formally, expressing this as a type in Haskell, we have:

```
count_same :: Eq a => a -> [a] -> Int
```

This literally says, assuming Eq is defined for some 'a', and given a value of type 'a' and a list whose elements are in the same base type, then we can produce an Int. The "fat arrow" is used to separate the "preconditions" part from the main type.

Like with the preceding parametric polymorphism, this type signature can be *inferred automatically* by the Haskell compiler; we don't have to work it out.

This is a huge difference from Java, where the compiler is just checking the type information, so the programmer needs to write in all of the type information explicitly. Haskell instead is doing some *type inference* first, to work out what the type should be, then does some type checking to ensure that your code is being used appropriately.

I'll say it again, because it's very important: for a lot of code in Haskell, you can just write down the code, and the compiler will infer what the types should be, then check that the types are being used consistently. You don't need to write down lots of type information. It's a bit like programming in Ruby (little or no type baggage) and enjoys some of the benefits of dynamic languages—but with a good safety net in the background.

There's one more detail to explain from the definition of Eq, and that's the type signature of Eq a => a -> a -> Bool required for (or that can be assumed for) the equality test. That is, assuming Eq is defined for some type 'a', then the equality test can compare two 'a' values and return a Bool. So True == False is fine type-wise, since replacing 'a' with Bool gives Bool -> Bool -> Bool, and this matches how we're using it. But, we can't do True == (True,True) since Bool and (Bool, Bool) are different types. It doesn't make sense (in this context) to compare different things for equality. Note also that this restriction is being checked at compile time, not at runtime, and we certainly don't have to write the code to check this for this ourselves as we do in Java. Neither do we need to add in type casts either, which is another limitation of Java's type system. Incidentally, Kim B. Bruce's OO-style LOOM and LOOJ languages lift this restriction by adopting similar techniques to Haskell's type classes.

So, that's equality. The next interface provides ordering tests, and it's introduced as a sub-interface of equality. That is, we're extending the equality interface with a <= test, with the effect that we can assume == is defined if <= is defined. Alternatively, if we want to define <=, then we have to define == too. It's a reasonable convention, but you can define a different version if you want—in other words, it's not permanently baked in. (The type class also prescribes an often-useful general comparison test compare, which distinguishes between less-than, equals, and greater-than cases. This is the detail that snuck into my group_on example, as a result of wanting to sort on the 'b' values.)

There are several ways to equip types with suitable definitions for the interface functions, similar to Java's "implements" mechanism. Firstly, we can do it explicitly by providing code for the functions. In the following code, we just give a direct definition of equality testing for Booleans. For certain standard type classes, the compiler can automatically *derive* functions (including the following code), thus saving us work (and avoiding mistakes), though we won't use it here.

```
instance Bool where
  True  == True  = True
  False == False = True
  _     == _     = False
```

Here's a slightly more complex instance definition, concerning equality of lists.

```
instance Eq a => Eq [a] where        -- 1
  []     == []     = True            -- 2
  (x:xs) == (y:ys) = x == y && xs == ys  -- 3
  _      == _      = False           -- 4
```

Line 1 indicates that this code provides a definition of equality for a list with element type 'a', *assuming* that we already have equality defined for 'a' itself, which is quite reasonable. The definition by cases says (2) empty lists are equal; (3) that when both lists are non-empty, then they are equal only if the two head (or first) elements match and the list tails (the rest) match as well; and finally, (4) any other case is not equal.

Notice how == is being used with different types on line 3; the first is comparing elements of the list, and the second is comparing lists. This is overloading, where the same name (==) is being used safely with different types, and in particular, the language mechanism is selecting appropriate code to run for each case depending on what the types are. Haskell's class mechanism was originally designed to handle such overloading in a convenient and sound way, though we've since found it has other great uses too.

Consider what happens when we compare [[[True], [False]]] and [[[True],[True]]]—in other words, a three-deep nested list of Boolean values, or [[[Bool]]]. Behind the scenes, Haskell constructs a "dictionary" that contains code for doing the comparison, and effectively uses the list equality code three times plus equality on Bool to build code that runs the precise code we need. Put another way, it uses the type information to build the code it needs, without us having to spell it out. This adds a lot of power and flexibility.

What do these interfaces provide?

I think there are several related benefits for programming:

- Great documentation facility: Haskell allows us to clearly say what we're assuming for certain concepts, and to say what assumptions are behind the code using the interfaces. This alone is worth the price of admission!

- Rationalization by programming to an interface: We say exactly what we can assume, and our code is only able to use what we've said it can. In particular, it limits the scope for exploiting other details of the data, which greatly helps with modularity and security.

- Simplicity of assumptions: By assuming only as much as we need, then the code is less likely to contain unnecessary details, and hence be more suitable for use elsewhere. Plus, if it's simpler, then it will be easier to change (in fact, if it's suitably abstract, then perhaps no changes will be needed, since it has isolated various aspects from each other).

- Safety: compare some uses of modules in Ruby, where code is included and has to rely on the free variables (or external references) in code being available in the class it's included into. The interface says precisely what is assumed, and the type checker ensures only that is used. (This kind of finger-crossing in Ruby is a detail I find particularly concerning; it is quite a bad code smell in my view. I don't believe we have to accept this weakness.)

- Convenience and overloading: quite often, we want to use the same concept, like equality, with various types, but we don't want to pollute our namespace with type-specific names. One name should do for all. Haskell's type system retrieves the particular piece of code to use with a type, just by examining the type of the values involved.

- Ad hoc polymorphism: parametric polymorphism is about using the same code for everything, and can be contrasted against a kind of polymorphism where everything "behaves" the same by virtue of responding to the same interface, usually via type-specific code. This is known as "ad hoc" polymorphism, in the sense of "determined by case."

Ruby can simulate some of the behavior, but do notice the value of being explicit and clear about interface use, and not relying on certain implicit features of Ruby. So, is it worth adding some kind of explicit interface feature to Ruby? Is the trade-off favorable, particularly if DCI or similar patterns get more popular? Answers on a postcard, please.

It's useful to consider what kind of language feature Interfaces are and how they works.

Firstly, it's not magic, in the sense that we can represent the underlying mechanisms inside Haskell itself and do some of the legwork ourselves. Interfaces are basically records (or dictionaries) whose fields are (mostly) functions, and dependence on interfaces equates to requiring relevant records to be passed in to provide the needed implementations. We can build such records by constant records, or using functions to convert records for small types into records for larger types (such as the preceding list equality code). The type checker contains an inference component that ensures that relevant dictionaries get created. Secondly, there is some syntactic sugar to allow these dictionaries to be used smoothly and consistently (with some efficiency too).

In summary, Interfaces are a mechanism that can mostly be programmed within the language, and just uses some extra support to make it more usable and convenient. I thought it worth highlighting this, just to help you visualize how such ideas might apply in other languages—it's not too big a job to simulate it in Ruby.

Some Real-World Examples with Interfaces

There has been a lot of interest recently in DCI (Data, Context, Interaction). DCI is an architectural idea developed by Trygve Reenskaug—who also proposed model-view-controller (MVC)—for simplifying and decoupling components in OO programming, basically by encouraging the separation of an object's data from the various roles that it plays, and only equipping the object with the role functionality it needs in a particular context. For example, a person could have a role as an employee and a role as a parent, and the employee part of the application will rarely need to know about the parent role.

This DCI approach echoes some of the ideas from Bruce's work in its separation of data and functionality. It's reassuring to see the same core idea arise from different approaches—from Reenskaug trying to make OO programs more intelligible, and from Bruce trying to rationalize and improve OO type systems.

Now, we can write Ruby code in a DCI style with some extra legwork. Roles can be encoded as modules, then imported into particular instances to equip that instance with the appropriate functionality. We reduce the size of model classes, and gain reusable components too. It works, but language-wise, this seems a bit "Heath Robinson."

Can we do better? Can we add type information in a useful way that also aids checking of the code and doesn't eat into the flexibility? I believe yes to both. We can set up Haskell-style interfaces to make clear what we are assuming about the source data, and type checking ensures that we use these interfaces appropriately. Furthermore, the dictionary building process *automatically* assembles the relevant combination of roles needed for any piece of code.

The next example was inspired by a talk on Hexagonal Rails at the 2012 Scottish Ruby conference. Delivered by Matt Wynne, Steve Tooke, and Kevin Rutherford, this talk discussed the need for avoiding deep hierarchical architectures and encouraging a flatter style that is conceptually simpler and also leads to less coupling in code. More modularity and less coupling tends to make code easier to maintain and to understand. They also presented some experiments in restructuring Rails code along these lines, and the experimentation continued into a popular follow-on session where groups of us tried out our own ideas.

It struck me how such experiments and related thinking were being limited by the constructs available in Ruby. The attempts at abstracting controller functionality had to be represented directly in code and were partly being obscured by code details, and there was no easy way to take a more abstract view. Put another way, a good type system is a powerful language for design too, and in the discussions the lack of such a system was telling.

My response was to start sketching out some code that used interfaces and polymorphism to enforce a clean separation of concerns. The persistence role can be managed via an interface that just allows saving and loading of data. Validity of data can be separated off to a layer independent of persistence. Mapping to URLs can also be abstracted out.

Finally, the update action at the controller level can just pull together the functionality from the interfaces (aka, roles in DCI terms) and provide a simple connection between them. Such code would only know that (a) it can build some domain-specific data from the form, (b) it can try to persist it or get an error message back, and (c) it can determine the URLs for the next step. Such code will never be able to access domain details or business logic.

By virtue of the overloading, we can also use the same piece of code for most or all controllers in the app. Here's a brief and informal excerpt.

```
-- provides ability to save etc
class Valid a => Persist m a where
  save :: a -> m (Either ErrorMsg a)

-- allows mapping to a URL
class Url r where
  show :: r -> Url
  [...]

create_ constr args
 = do res <- save (constr args)              -- 1
      case res of                            -- 2
         Right r    -> redirect (show r)      -- 3
         Left  msg  -> render (template (Just msg)) -- 4
```

Line 1 builds an object from the incoming params, given a suitable constructor; line 2 checks the outcome of persisting the new object; then if OK (line 3) execution jumps to the show page, else (line 4) sends the user back to the form with some error message.

Notice how the details of persistence are very separate from details of URL routes, and there's no chance of interference. The controller layer is restricted to mediating between the core app (for building data and saving it) and its web interface. Quite naturally, the interactions are flatter and indeed only use the minimum info allowed through the interfaces. Notice the DCI feel to this too, where the data's roles are separate and only combined when required. It will be interesting to convert this approach back into Ruby code.

Pros and Cons—the 80/20 Rule

So, that covers the main ideas from Haskell 98's type system. Let's evaluate it.

I described the design of type systems (and programming languages) as a balancing act: you want the articulacy (freedom to say interesting things) but want to retain some useful automation, ease of use, and conceptual consistency. It is very rare to get both.

Haskell manages a pretty good balance, though, I believe. The type system is pretty versatile, and only requires explicit hints when you're using complex overloading. What can't Haskell do, or do nicely?

Well, most of the things I'll cover soon under dependent types! But there are some aspects of traditional OOP that don't translate nicely, primarily the ability to build lists of objects of unrestricted mixed types ("heterogeneous lists"); in other words, we can't write [2, 'a', False] in standard Haskell. There are some extensions that allow various cases of such lists, each with their own advantages and disadvantages. If we know in advance which types to expect, then we can code it up as a tagged union and do the decoding ourselves. There are other techniques like reducing the values to a common interface, so they all look the same and respond to the same methods, even if they are different underneath.

It is appropriate to invoke an 80/20 rule here.

In my experience, comparing Haskell to its mainstream peers, (much) more than 80 percent of my code fits adequately inside Haskell, and the remaining fraction isn't too painful—certainly no deal breakers. So I'd rather have the convenience and benefits for the 80 percent part and live with a few awkward bits for a small section of the code. It's certainly not worth discarding the benefits for the 80 percent and moving to a dynamic language just because of some issues with a minority part of the program. The 80/20 rule also applies to the programming side of Haskell too—more than 80 percent of my code works nicely in a pure functional setting, and the awkward stuff takes up less than 20 percent, and often is much less.

So, what does this say about dynamic typing?

My claim is that Haskell & Co. are approaching a level of flexibility and unobtrusiveness that they are becoming a credible alternative, and so many of the traditional objections to static types and traditional justifications of dynamic types are starting to lose their force and so need to be re-evaluated.

Some of these objections are a bit wooly—for example, drawing conclusions about Haskell from conclusions about Java. One recent Ruby book spends a few pages arguing in favor of dynamic typing because it doesn't need extensive type annotations. It's a good advertisement for Haskell too(!)

There are still some phenomena that even the very advanced type systems can't handle well, but these tend to be rare or contrived. I personally would prefer help with the 80 percent or more of my program that can be covered, and do the best I can on the rest. The alternative—abandoning help on the 80 percent just to accommodate the minority aspects—is not too appealing from an engineering standpoint.

Now, what do you think?

Beyond Haskell: Dependent Types

Haskell is something of a "sweet spot" in language design, balancing a reasonably flexible type system with useful inference properties, but it is by no means the best we can do. So what else is there?

Language designers continually experiment with modest extensions to Haskell's basic system, to see if they can eke out any extra functionality without making the language too hard to use, and mileage varies here.

Instead, let's look at the next big step in language sophistication, where we allow types to become full first-class citizens of our language. The Haskell we've seen so far still keeps the world of data separate from the world of types. Types are a description of happenings in data-land and they do not meet, and this puts some limits on what we can articulate.

Dependent type theory lifts many of the limits. Data and code can appear in types, and types can appear inside code as data. We end up with a single uniform language, not two (data vs. types), and can start to do some very interesting things in this uniform language. Quick, let's see some practical examples!

```
reverse :: (A:Type)(n:Nat) Vec A n -> Vec A n
```

Haskell's reverse just promised to give a list of the same type back. With dependent types, we can include information about list length too, hence encode that reverse preserves type *and* input size.

The signature literally says, given some type A (for elements) and a length n, then reverse takes a vector (our name for a sized list) of size n and returns a vector of the same size. So it's a guarantee that we don't add or lose elements.

How about appending one vector to another?

The following says that appending vectors of size m and n gives a vector of their combined size, m + n!

```
vappend :: (A:type)(m,n:Nat) Vec A m -> Vec A n -> Vec A (m + n)
```

So, notice how we've taken a step up in the kinds of information we can represent inside our types, with consequences for what the compiler can do with it. We get more articulacy in data definitions too. For example, to build a sized vector, we need only the following: a vnil constructor that produces a vector of size 0, and a vcons constructor that adds an element onto a vector of size n to get one of size (n + 1).

```
vnil :: (A:Type) Vec A 0
vcons :: (A:Type)(n:Nat) A -> Vec A n -> Vec A (n+1)
```

It's now impossible to get the size of the vector wrong, and we can never use vnil where a vector of size 1 or more is expected (since 0 != n + 1).

This has implications for pattern matching too. For example, if we define the head function for a non-empty vector (size n + 1), then the vnil pattern is impossible and never needs to be handled.

This next bit may seriously blow your mind.

Propositions Are Types, and Proofs Are Programs

We can use any values of arbitrary complexity inside type expressions, not just simple values like numbers. We can even encode logical propositions too, and use these to express pre and post conditions, and more. For example, the following represents a property of equality—that when two things are equal, then what we can do with one thing, we can do with the other.

```
foo2 :: (A:Type)(P:A -> Type)(a,b:A)Eq A a b -> P(a) -> P(b)
```

We can do more than just encode logical propositions: we can work with *proofs* of them *entirely inside the language* as well. If you've done any logic before, you may recognize the following as a statement of transitivity of implication. "If B implies C, and A implies B, then A implies C."

```
(B -> C) -> (A -> B) -> (A -> C)
```

How do we "prove" this? The usual way is to find the combination of inference rules that yield the preceding statement as the final conclusion. Here's a better proof:

```
f . g = \x -> f (g x)
```

No, this isn't a typo. It *is* the definition of function composition. Recall that its polymorphic type in Haskell is (b -> c) -> (a -> b) -> (a -> c). Look familiar?

This is no accident. There is a striking similarity between how functions work and how logical implications work, and we can use this as a way to encode proofs of propositions as programs. It has a name too—in fact, several names because the idea appeared in several places independently around sixty years ago. I'll use the conventional "Curry-Howard Correspondence" for now.

Pause to consider the huge significance of this idea!

Checking validity of a proof is then a case of checking the type of the program. Finding a proof equates to developing a program with the required type (go tease some mathematicians!). We can also think of the program as a way to generate proofs of the conclusion from proofs of the hypotheses. For example, if we have a proof of B -> C and one of A -> B, then we can use the definition of function composition to build a proof of A -> C! So function composition is a bit like a theorem we can apply to get from one stage of reasoning to another.

How about mathematical induction? Ever noticed that it's simple recursion? We can write down the principle as a type that says a lot of what we understand about induction. We have some property P to establish for all numbers; then a proof that P holds for 0 (the base case); and a proof that if P holds for some m, then it holds for m + 1 (the step case). Finally, if given some n, then the overall result is a proof of P for that n.

```
nat_induction :: (P : Nat -> Prop)
                 (base : P 0)
                 (step : (m:Nat)P m -> P (m+1))
                 (n : Nat) P n
```

What does the proof of this look like? It's a recursive function that works through n to generate the proof it requires! In other words, nat_induction P base step 3 yields step 2 (step 1 (step 0 base)).

So, the more powerful language allows us to encode complex logical propositions as (dependent) types, and the programming language inside it allows us to develop and use proofs, all inside the same language, no external tools needed. This really does represent a language that combines—in a clean, elegant, and powerful way—both computation *and* reasoning.

Another Look at Sorting

We started off looking at the type of sort and now know enough to see what we can really do with dependent types.

```
    A:Type              n:Nat              v:Vec A n
    lteq:Sigma[f: A -> A -> Bool]is_ordering(f)
-----------------------------------------------------------
sort A n lteq v : Sigma[w:Vec A n] is_permutation_of(v,w)
                        && is_sorted(w,lteq)
```

Don't panic! Let's take it piece by piece. As before, sorting is polymorphic, so we can use it on vectors of any element type. Input length can be anything, and the result contains a vector of the same length—in other words, length is preserved. We also have an argument, lteq, that supplies the information about comparing A values. And, as you may have guessed, this will be our less-than-or-equal test, where a result of True means "don't swap," and False means "do swap."

The extra pieces are to do with properties we require from the input, and properties that will hold for the result. For the lteq function, not just any 2-ary predicate will do. Using a function that always returns True will not produce a sorted result. Briefly, the construct Sigma[x:T]P(x) is pairing some data x with some more data P(x) that depends on x. Above, we're pairing the lteq function with a proof that it has the properties required for less-than-or-equal. And in the result, we get the result of sorting plus proofs that the output is a permutation of the input (in other words, we're rearranging data) and that the result really is in the sorted order implied by our choice of lteq.

So yes, this is more detailed than the types we saw at the start, but if these are the properties of sorting that we care about, then no further testing is required. The type checker has it covered. And if we change the code, then either the code still type checks, or we have to justify why the change is safe by modifying the code so it does type check.

Are dependent types more verbose? Yes, because there is more going on. However, there are ways to hide away some of the obvious information and push the core ideas to the fore. In the preceding, A and n are easily inferred from the context, and thus rarely shown, so leaving the important inputs of the comparison function and the vector to be sorted. One thread of research in this area looks at other kinds of abbreviation mechanisms to help with practical programming, such as making it easier to bridge between simple data and more complex types (which was one of my specialities).

We're also making great progress with tool support. It's often suggested that type information can be used by code editors to make informed decisions about editing support, and this is particularly true with dependent types. There is much more information available in a processable format (not just in comments or in the programmer's head), and this can be used to great effect: really powerful type-directed development. Such tools begin with some statement of what we want to develop, represented as a type. Then we use a mix of backwards and forwards reasoning to develop the program. We can leave some details as unknown too—kind of what we simulated in Haskell with the () value, but here the tools provide much more powerful handling of unknowns, inferring immediately obvious values and providing kinds of automatic inference for the more complex steps.

Here's a quick example: developing a proof of (B -> C) -> (A -> B) -> (A -> C). This type is set as our initial goal, and the corresponding proof (program) as the first unknown. We can shift the arguments into the context to get f : B -> C, g : A -> B, x : A with a new goal of ? : C. That is, we need some combination of f,g,x that generates a C value. We can fill in the full answer if we want, or we can build it up in pieces. For example, we can suggest f ? as the solution to the goal, and get a second goal ? : B (in other words, the argument we need to pass to f). That goal is solved by g x. The editor will then show the final result, that our proof/program is \ f g x -> f (g x). Some editors can also do advanced analysis on the structure of goals and fill in some of the code automatically, such as presenting us with only the data patterns that can occur and leaving the right-hand sides to us.

These tools are very powerful, and have been used to help fully and completely build formal proofs of real results like the four color theorem. They also represent a very different and powerful way to program, and have much potential.

If you want to know more about dependent types right away, I suggest you start looking at the Idris language for a language in the Haskell style. There are more advanced languages (and tools), such as Agda or Epigram or Coq or Cayenne, though they can be a bit steep as an introduction.

Back to Earth

I hope you appreciate now that advances in type systems are starting to converge with ideas in TDD. More work is needed, of course, but the exciting possibilities are clear.

What can TDD learn from tests? What can types learn from TDD? Personally, I'm in the strange position of using TDD for Rails work but also being aware of the possibilities in types. It's, um, interesting. And annoying, at times. In the long term, I envision a framework where the distinction between types and tests isn't so significant, and we are all able to work flexibly and confidently with good support from our tools. I have no idea what we should call this, though!

In the meantime, I think types work can benefit from TDD in several ways:

- We should be encouraged by the great ideas and range of work in this area, particularly real-world code.

- We should appreciate alternative perspectives on code verification and development practices.

- We should be glad there are lots of case studies to think about, analyze, and maybe adapt/translate.

And how about this for TDD?

- Stronger DSL use to encode the properties we care about, and making that DSL more flexible. Specs encoded as types tend to be more succinct than TDD specs, and I believe it's worth considering how the DSL for specs can be streamlined in a similar way.

- Encouraging more decomposition of code to promote testability. Types get unwieldy if we try to do too much in a piece of code, so functional programmers often break such code into pieces and develop them independently. It's well known in TDD that some code is more testable than other code—typically code that is smaller, more modular, and less reliant on side effects. Can we promote this in TDD by orienting the DSL for specs toward such code, making the more complex cases less attractive?

- Approach to side effects. Side-effects can be a pain in type checking, and it seems people are realizing this in tests too, as they make it harder to isolate the things that need to be tested. Again, can the DSL be designed to promote this aspect of testability?

- Other approaches to mock objects? Mocks seem to cause a lot of confusion. The purpose is to set up fake inputs to some test with predictable behavior such that certain paths in the tested code are exercised. Put another way, it's setting up some preconditions or assumptions under which the test should be run. We can do this in a dependent types setting in a more abstract way by passing in hypotheses of how such objects behave. For example, passing in a value of type $(x{:}A)$ Eq $(f\,x)\,(x + 3)$ indicates that some f adds 3 onto its input, and we can use this hypothesis inside the proof of the test to get values from uses of f. So, instead of building objects that have some runtime behavior, we instead frame that behavior via hypotheses. This view may also help simplify the DSL for mock-like behavior.

- Why do tests have to be in a separate file? Is this a practical detail or a theoretical detail? In the types world, we believe the types and code belong together. Is this possible for tests?

- Using tests to drive code generation. Given some type signature, the tools can sometimes predict what structure the corresponding code should have, and this is something dependent types people use often to cut down on work. Can the same be done for TDD specs? It seems feasible—for example, to parse a TDD spec and generate as much of the corresponding class as possible, maybe including code fragments, error messages, and helpful comments to simplify the development work and side-step certain transcription errors. Changes in the spec could automatically flag diff conflicts in the code. (I wish I had time to try this.)

Indeed, considering ideas such as these may pave the way to better interoperability in future.

Final thought: how far can existing tests be translated to types? Or existing types be translated to tests? I think the overlap is significant. That says something.

We've delved into some pretty heady Haskell concepts in this chapter. In Chapter 24, A Haskell Project: Testing Native Code, on page 211, you'll get to follow along as a programmer develops an application in Haskell.

A Haskell Project: Testing Native Code

by Aaron Bedra

This chapter will dive into a number of programming techniques at once. The goal is to explain an advanced form of testing that can be very useful. We're going to use a higher-level language, Haskell, to test some legacy C code. We do this because Haskell (or any more expressive language) takes less code to express the essence, or intended functionality, of a program. We will reimplement the code already built in our legacy codebase to determine if it is functioning as intended.

If you want to follow along with this chapter, you'll need a few tools installed. You'll need a C compiler capable of compiling C11 standard code. This can be a current GCC or Clang. You'll also need a Haskell environment. There are a few different ways to set up your Haskell environment. If you already have Glasgow Haskell Compiler (GHC), GHCi, and Cabal installed, you can continue to use your setup. If you're installing Haskell for the first time, stack[1] is highly recommended. We'll be using stack in this chapter, so if you wish to follow along exactly, you'll need to install it.

We'll start by making sure we have the necessary tools.

```
$ stack setup
... GHC will be installed ...
$ stack install QuickCheck
... QuickCheck will be installed ...
$ stack exec ghci
Prelude> import Test.QuickCheck
Prelude Test.QuickCheck> :q
```

This ensures that you have GHC, installed, along with the QuickCheck library. If for some reason this doesn't work for you, consult the stack documentation.

---

1.   http://docs.haskellstack.org/en/stable/README.html

Our Native Code

For our native code, we're going to create an implementation of the Caesar cipher.[2] This isn't something you would use for real encryption, but if you think about the implications of bugs in native crypto implementations, the impact is pretty huge.

Let's start with our legacy code:

```
caesar.c
#include <stdlib.h>
#include <string.h>
#include <ctype.h>

char *caesar(int shift, char *input)
{
  char *output = malloc(strlen(input));
  memset(output, '\0', strlen(input));

  for (int x = 0; x < strlen(input); x++) {
    if (isalpha(input[x])) {
      int c = toupper(input[x]);
      c = (((c - 65) + shift) % 26) + 65;
      output[x] = c;
    } else {
      output[x] = input[x];
    }
  }

  return output;
}
```

Like all substitution ciphers, this function accepts a number in which to shift each character. We'll be using the English alphabet, so our shift will be between 1 and 25.

This code has some bugs. They may or may not be obvious, but there's a good chance a simple unit test wouldn't expose them.

Our Model

```
caesar.hs
import Data.Char
import Data.Ix
import Foreign.C
import System.IO.Unsafe
import Test.QuickCheck
```

---

2. https://en.wikipedia.org/wiki/Caesar_cipher

```
caesar :: Int -> String -> String
caesar k = map f
  where
    f c
        | inRange ('A', 'Z') c = chr $ ord 'A'
          + (ord c - ord 'A' + k) `mod` 26
        | otherwise = c
```

In this example, we recreate the Caesar implementation. You can ignore the slew of import statements for now. They will all be used during this chapter, so we're putting them in place so we don't have to worry about them later.

Our Haskell implementation starts with a type signature. It accepts an Int and a String, and returns a String. The function maps over all the characters in the message and applies the shift as long as the character is in the range of uppercase A to Z.

A Brief Introduction to Haskell's FFI

Haskell, like many other languages, has the ability to call native code. It also has an interface for native code to call Haskell, but we aren't going to explore that in this chapter. We are interested in the ability for Haskell to call our native Caesar cipher implementation.

Haskell's Foreign Function Interface (FFI) can be invoked using the following construct:

caesar.hs

```
foreign import ccall "caesar.h caesar" c_caesar
    :: CInt -> CString -> CString
```

It starts with foreign import ccall, which signals our call. It's followed by the location where the function is defined and the name of the function we wish to call. Next we provide a name that we can use for this function inside our Haskell code. Since we already have a function named caesar, we will name this one c_caesar to help us keep track of it. Finally, we give it a type signature. This works like any other Haskell function, but you may notice that the types aren't familiar. Haskell's types are different from C. They are represented differently and in order to exchange information across the boundaries, we have to take some additional precautions.

Wrapping Our Native Code in Haskell

First things first, we need to provide a missing component. We haven't yet created our caesar.h file with the definition of our native caesar function. Let's take care of this before we continue.

```
caesar.h
#pragma once

char *caesar(int shift, char *input);
```

In order to smooth out the type differences in our code, let's write a wrapper function. This function will take standard Haskell types and return them, but inside the function, it will convert between the Haskell and C types appropriately so the types don't pollute the rest of our Haskell code. There is one exception here, but we will get to that soon enough.

```
caesar.hs
native_caesar :: Int -> String -> IO String
native_caesar shift input = withCString input $ \c_str ->
  peekCString(c_caesar (fromIntegral shift) c_str)
```

In our wrapper, we create a function that takes and returns standard Haskell types. Inside our wrapper function, we call our C code, converting the types before sending them along. We use the peekCString function to extract the data from the heap. This operation is examining memory on the heap that could be modified outside our ability to control it. This makes the operation inherently unsafe. You'll notice that the return value of our wrapper differs slightly from our model. The return value is wrapped in IO to provide a layer of protection against this.

Experimenting with GHCi

Before we begin, we need to make our C code accessible. All we have at the moment is some text files. Let's compile them into something we can use.

```
$ gcc -shared caesar.c -o caesar.so
# Depending on your OS and compiler version
# you may need to do the following
$ gcc -fPIC -shared caesar.c -o caesar.so
# You may also need to set LD_LIBRARY_PATH as well
$ export LD_LIBRARY_PATH=.
```

We can now invoke GHCi and try out our code.

```
$ stack exec ghci caesar.hs caesar.so
GHCi, version 7.10.3: http://www.haskell.org/ghc/  :? for help
[1 of 1] Compiling Main             ( caesar.hs, interpreted )
Ok, modules loaded: Main.
*Main> caesar 2 "ATTACKATDAWN"
"CVVCEMCVFCYP"
*Main> native_caesar 2 "ATTACKATDAWN"
"CVVCEMCVFCYP"
```

We can now use both functions from the REPL and see that they appear to be functionally equivalent.

A Brief Introduction to QuickCheck

QuickCheck was originally written in 2000 by Koen Claessen and John Hughes. Their paper on the subject[3] is a detailed introduction. We won't go into a lot of detail in this chapter, but reading this paper is highly encouraged. To get better acquainted, let's write a simple property. We'll use an example directly from the Haskell wiki.[4]

```
quickCheck ((\s -> s == s) :: [Char] -> Bool)
```

We can try it by firing up GHCi.

```
$ stack exec ghci
GHCi, version 7.10.3: http://www.haskell.org/ghc/  :? for help
Prelude> import Test.QuickCheck
Prelude Test.QuickCheck> quickCheck ((\s -> s == s) :: [Char] -> Bool)
+++ OK, passed 100 tests.
```

First, we import the QuickCheck module. You may have noticed that we did that in the preceding model in anticipation of this section. If you already have GHCi open and the previous code loaded, you won't have to add the import. This was a quick introduction, but it's enough for us to build on.

Writing an Equivalence Property

Now that we have the basics out of the way, let's begin to write a property on our code. Let's try an equivalence property.

```
quickCheck (\s -> (caesar 2 s) == (native_caesar 2 s))
```

If we try running this, we will quickly encounter a type error.

```
*Main> quickCheck (\s -> (caesar 2 s) == (native_caesar 2 s))

<interactive>:2:36:
    Couldn't match type 'IO String' with '[Char]'
    Expected type: String
      Actual type: IO String
    In the second argument of '(==)', namely '(native_caesar 2 s)'
    In the expression: (caesar 2 s) == (native_caesar 2 s)
```

This error comes from a discrepancy in the return types of our Caesar functions. The caesar function returns String, while the native_caesar function returns IO String. There are a few different ways to solve this. For the purpose of this chapter, we're going to take the easy way out.

---

3.   http://www.eecs.northwestern.edu/~robby/courses/395-495-2009-fall/quick.pdf
4.   https://wiki.haskell.org/Introduction_to_QuickCheck1

```
caesar.hs
unsafeEq :: IO String -> String -> Bool
unsafeEq x y = unsafePerformIO(x) == y
```

The `unsafeEq` function takes care of the type discrepancy by using the `unsafePerformIO` function to get the value inside the IO String monad and then do a comparison. Since all we really care about is if these two values are equivalent, this is good enough for us to continue. Let's modify our property and try again.

```
quickCheck (\s -> unsafeEq (native_caesar 2 s) (caesar 2 s))
```

When we run this, we no longer get a type error, but something else interesting comes up. Take note of the :l caesar.hs command. This will reload the file in the currently running REPL so you don't have to quit and start over after you make updates.

```
*Main> :l caesar.hs
*Main> quickCheck (\s -> unsafeEq (native_caesar 2 s) (caesar 2 s))
*** Failed! Falsifiable (after 4 tests and 1 shrink):
"a"
*Main> native_caesar 2 "a"
"C"
*Main> caesar 2 "a"
"a"
```

We see that in fact these values are not equivalent! How could we have such a simple issue? Let's take a look back at our model.

```
caesar :: Int -> String -> String
caesar k = map f
  where
    f c
        | inRange ('A', 'Z') c = chr $ ord 'A'
          + (ord c - ord 'A' + k) `mod` 26
        | otherwise = c
```

In our model, we expect uppercase English alphabet characters. When we feed it anything else, it just returns the character provided. Now we have a choice to make. We can either update our model to properly handle lowercase characters, or we can make sure that we only ever pass in what we expect. In order to ensure we only pass in valid values, we'll need to create a generator. For a brief overview of the generators available in QuickCheck, you can reference the documentation.[5]

---

5.   https://hackage.haskell.org/package/QuickCheck-2.8.2/docs/Test-QuickCheck.html#g:5

In our case, the standard generators won't get us exactly what we need. We need to create a custom generator for this task.

```
caesar.hs
genSafeChar :: Gen Char
genSafeChar = elements ['A' .. 'Z']

genSafeString :: Gen String
genSafeString = listOf genSafeChar

newtype SafeString = SafeString
        { unwrapSafeString :: String } deriving Show
instance Arbitrary SafeString where arbitrary =
        SafeString <$> genSafeString
```

First, we start by defining what a valid character is. We use the range A to Z as expected. From that we define what a valid string is by creating a list of valid characters. That's pretty straightforward, but what about the next two lines? We aren't going to go into a long explanation here, but essentially it is some Haskell housekeeping that will allow us to use the genSafeString function inside our property.

Now that we have a generator that ensures we will only provide valid values, let's update our property to use it.

```
caesar.hs
equivalenceProperty = forAll genSafeString $ \str ->
  unsafeEq (native_caesar 2 str) (caesar 2 str)
```

Things change a bit here. First, we're now defining this so we can reference it later without having to type the expression in every time. Next, we use the forAll function to start our expression. We then use our new generator to create a valid input string. Next we call our unsafeEq function using the generated value to test equivalence. Let's give it all a try.

```
*Main> quickCheck equivalenceProperty
*** Failed! Falsifiable (after 65 tests):
"WPOYGHOPUCNUKKKRRQXRNZNY"
*Main> caesar 2 "WPOYGHOPUCNUKKKRRQXRNZNY"
"YRQAIJQRWEPWMMMTTSZTPBPA"
*Main> native_caesar 2 "WPOYGHOPUCNUKKKRRQXRNZNY"
"YRQAIJQRWEPWMMMTTSZTPBPA\SOH"
```

We again find ourselves staring at a scenario where the outputs between the functions are not equivalent. This time we see a real bug in our native implementation. You may see different output when you run this, but the additional \SOH at the end of the native output signals a memory management issue in our C code.

Defect Smashing

We have a reproducible scenario that demonstrates the presence of a memory management bug in our C code. Now that we have a failing test, we need to figure out what is actually wrong with our code. Let's take another look.

```
caesar.c
char *caesar(int shift, char *input)
{
  char *output = malloc(strlen(input));
  memset(output, '\0', strlen(input));

  for (int x = 0; x < strlen(input); x++) {
    if (isalpha(input[x])) {
      int c = toupper(input[x]);
      c = (((c - 65) + shift) % 26) + 65;
      output[x] = c;
    } else {
      output[x] = input[x];
    }
  }

  return output;
}
```

A closer examination reveals the issue. As with most programming problems, there are a few different ways to address this. We will again take the easy way out. Fixing memory issues this way is not recommended for production code. We will fix this by simply changing the bounds of the for expression.

```
for (int x = 0; x <= strlen(input); x++) {
```

Let's compile and run our property again.

```
$ gcc -fPIC -shared caesar.c -o caesar.so
$ stack exec ghci caesar.so caesar.hs
GHCi, version 7.10.3: http://www.haskell.org/ghc/  :? for help
[1 of 1] Compiling Main             ( caesar.hs, interpreted )
Ok, modules loaded: Main.
*Main> quickCheck equivalenceProperty
+++ OK, passed 100 tests.
```

Much better! We don't see any more equivalence issues. We can't really be satisfied with this yet, though. Running only one hundred tests doesn't give us enough confidence to continue. Let's crank up the number of tests we run before calling this ready.

```
caesar.hs
deepCheck p = quickCheckWith stdArgs { maxSuccess = 100000 } p
```

Here we define deepCheck, which runs a given property with modified arguments to QuickCheck. This particular example runs 100,000 tests.

```
*Main> deepCheck equivalenceProperty
+++ OK, passed 100000 tests.
```

Running our deepCheck version still passes, increasing our confidence that there are no differences between our native and Haskell implementations. As you develop properties for your code, choose the number of tests that makes the most sense. It is common to use the defaults for rapid development and larger numbers on continuous integration or the production build process.

This chapter demonstrated the basics of Haskell's QuickCheck library along with Haskell's FFI support. It combined them to explain an advanced testing technique that can be used to test the essence of legacy code. There are QuickCheck libraries available in almost every programming language. If Haskell isn't your cup of tea, you can still use this technique in any language that has a QuickCheck-style library and FFI support. Using property-based testing is a great technique that can leave you much more confident in your code.

## CHAPTER 25

The Many Faces of Swift Functions

by Natasha Murashev

The standard against which Swift is evaluated is Objective-C, which Apple intends to replace with Swift for its developers. Although Objective-C has some strange-looking syntax compared to other programming languages, the method syntax is pretty straightforward once you get the hang of it. Here's a quick throwback:

```
+ (void)mySimpleMethod
{
    // class method
    // no parameters
    // no return values
}
- (NSString *)myMethodNameWithParameter1:(NSString *)param1
             parameter2:(NSNumber *)param2
{
    // instance method
    // one parameter of type NSString pointer,
    // one parameter of type NSNumber pointer
    // must return a value of type NSString pointer
    return @"hello, world!";
}
```

In contrast, while Swift syntax looks a lot more like other programming languages, it can also get a lot more complicated and confusing than Objective-C.

Before I continue, I want to clarify the difference between a Swift method and function, as I'll be using both terms throughout this article.

Methods are functions that are associated with a particular type. Classes, structures, and enumerations can all define instance methods, which encapsulate specific tasks and functionality for working with an instance of a given type. Classes, structures, and enumerations can also define type methods, which are associated with the type itself. Type methods are similar to class methods in Objective-C.

TL;DR: Functions are standalone, while methods are functions that are encapsulated in a class, struct, or enum.

Anatomy of Swift Functions

Let's start with a simple "Hello, World!" Swift function:

```
func mySimpleFunction() {
    println("hello, world!")
}
```

If you've ever programmed in any other language aside from Objective-C, the preceding function should look very familiar:

- The func keyword denotes that this is a function.
- The name of this function is mySimpleFunction.
- There are no parameters passed in—hence, the empty ( ).
- There is no return value.
- The function execution happens between the { }.

Now on to a slightly more complex function:

```
func myFunctionName(param1: String, param2: Int) -> String {
    return "hello, world!"
}
```

This function takes in one parameter named param1 of type String and one parameter named param2 of type Int and returns a String value.

Calling All Functions

One of the big differences between Swift and Objective-C is how parameters work when a Swift function is called. If you love the verbosity of Objective-C, like I do, keep in mind that parameter names are not included externally by default when a Swift function is called:

```
func hello(name: String) {
    println("hello \(name)")
}

hello("Mr. Roboto")
```

This may not seem so bad until you add a few more parameters to your function:

```
func hello(name: String, age: Int, location: String) {
    println("Hello \(name). I live in \(location) too.
            When is your \(age + 1)th birthday?")
}
hello("Mr. Roboto", 5, "San Francisco")
```

If you only read hello("Mr. Roboto", 5, "San Francisco"), you would have a hard time knowing what each parameter actually is.

In Swift, there is a concept of an *external parameter name* to clarify this confusion:

```
func hello(fromName name: String) {
    println("\(name) says hello to you!")
}
hello(fromName: "Mr. Roboto")
```

In the preceding function, fromName is an external parameter, which gets included when the function is called, while name is the internal parameter used to reference the parameter inside the function execution.

If you want the external and internal parameter names to be the same, you don't have to write out the parameter name twice:

```
func hello(name name: String) {
    println("hello \(name)")
}
hello(name: "Robot")
```

Instead, just add a # in front of the parameter name as a shortcut:

```
func hello(#name: String) {
    println("hello \(name)")
}
hello(name: "Robot")
```

And of course, the rules for how parameters work are slightly different for methods...

Calling on Methods

When encapsulated in a class (or struct or enum), the first parameter name of a method is *not* included externally, while all following parameter names are included externally when the method is called:

```
class MyFunClass {

    func hello(name: String, age: Int, location: String) {
        println("Hello \(name). I live in \(location) too.
            When is your \(age + 1)th birthday?")
    }

}

let myFunClass = MyFunClass()
myFunClass.hello("Mr. Roboto", age: 5, location: "San Francisco")
```

It is therefore best practice to include your first parameter name in your method name, just like in Objective-C:

```
class MyFunClass {

    func helloWithName(name: String, age: Int, location: String) {
        println("Hello \(name). I live in \(location) too.
            When is your \(age + 1)th birthday?")
    }

}

let myFunClass = MyFunClass()
myFunClass.helloWithName("Mr. Roboto", age: 5, location: "San Francisco")
```

Instead of calling my function *hello*, I renamed it helloWithName to make it very clear that the first parameter is a name.

If for some special reason you want to skip the external parameter names in your function (I'd recommend having a very good reason for doing so), use an _ for the external parameter name:

```
class MyFunClass {

    func helloWithName(name: String, _ age: Int, _ location: String) {
        println("Hello \(name). I live in \(location) too.
            When is your \(age + 1)th birthday?")
    }

}

let myFunClass = MyFunClass()
myFunClass.helloWithName("Mr. Roboto", 5, "San Francisco")
```

Instance Methods Are Curried Functions

One cool thing to note is that instance methods are actually curried functions in Swift.

The basic idea behind currying is that a function can be partially applied, meaning that some of its parameter values can be specified (bound) before the function is called. Partial function application yields a new function.

So given that I have a class:

```
class MyHelloWorldClass {
    func helloWithName(name: String) -> String {
        return "hello, \(name)"
    }
}
```

I can create a variable that points to the class's helloWithName function:

```
let helloWithNameFunc = MyHelloWorldClass.helloWithName
// MyHelloWorldClass -> (String) -> String
```

My new helloWithNameFunc is of type MyHelloWorldClass -> (String) -> String, a function that takes in an instance of my class and returns another function that takes in a string value and returns a string value.

So I can actually call my function like this:

```
let myHelloWorldClassInstance = MyHelloWorldClass()
```

```
helloWithNameFunc(myHelloWorldClassInstance)("Mr. Roboto")
// hello, Mr. Roboto
```

Init: A Special Note

A special init method is called when a class, struct, or enum is initialized. In Swift, you can define initialization parameters, just like with any other method:

```
class Person {
    init(name: String) {
        // your init implementation
    }
}
Person(name: "Mr. Roboto")
```

Notice that, unlike other methods, the first parameter name of an init method is required externally when the class is instantiated.

It is best practice in most cases to add a different external parameter name—fromName, in this case—to make the initialization more readable:

```
class Person {
    init(fromName name: String) {
        // your init implementation
    }
}
Person(fromName: "Mr. Roboto")
```

And of course, just like with other methods, you can add an _ if you want your init method to skip the external parameter name. I love the readability and power of this initialization example from *The Swift Programming Language*:

```
struct Celsius {
    var temperatureInCelsius: Double
    init(fromFahrenheit fahrenheit: Double) {
        temperatureInCelsius = (fahrenheit - 32.0) / 1.8
    }
    init(fromKelvin kelvin: Double) {
        temperatureInCelsius = kelvin - 273.15
    }
    init(_ celsius: Double) {
        temperatureInCelsius = celsius
    }
}

let boilingPointOfWater = Celsius(fromFahrenheit: 212.0)
// boilingPointOfWater.temperatureInCelsius is 100.0

let freezingPointOfWater = Celsius(fromKelvin: 273.15)
// freezingPointOfWater.temperatureInCelsius is 0.0

let bodyTemperature = Celsius(37.0)
// bodyTemperature.temperatureInCelsius is 37.0
```

Skipping the external parameter can also be useful if you want to abstract how your class/enum/struct gets initialized. I love the use of this in David Owen's json-swift library.[1]

```
public struct JSValue : Equatable {

    // ... truncated code

    /// Initializes a new 'JSValue' with a 'JSArrayType' value.
    public init(_ value: JSArrayType) {
        self.value = JSBackingValue.JSArray(value)
    }

    /// Initializes a new 'JSValue' with a 'JSObjectType' value.
    public init(_ value: JSObjectType) {
        self.value = JSBackingValue.JSObject(value)
    }

    /// Initializes a new 'JSValue' with a 'JSStringType' value.
    public init(_ value: JSStringType) {
        self.value = JSBackingValue.JSString(value)
    }
```

---

1.   https://github.com/owensd/json-swift

```
/// Initializes a new 'JSValue' with a 'JSNumberType' value.
public init(_ value: JSNumberType) {
    self.value = JSBackingValue.JSNumber(value)
}

/// Initializes a new 'JSValue' with a 'JSBoolType' value.
public init(_ value: JSBoolType) {
    self.value = JSBackingValue.JSBool(value)
}

/// Initializes a new 'JSValue' with an 'Error' value.
init(_ error: Error) {
    self.value = JSBackingValue.Invalid(error)
}

/// Initializes a new 'JSValue' with a 'JSBackingValue' value.
init(_ value: JSBackingValue) {
    self.value = value
}
}
```

Fancy Parameters

Compared to Objective-C, Swift has a lot of extra options for what type of parameters can be passed in. Here are some examples.

Optional Parameter Types

In Swift, there is a new concept of optional types:

Optionals say either "there is a value, and it equals x" or "there isn't a value at all." Optionals are similar to using nil with pointers in Objective-C, but they work for any type, not just classes. Optionals are safer and more expressive than nil pointers in Objective-C and are at the heart of many of Swift's most powerful features.

To indicate that a parameter type is optional (can be nil), just add a question mark after the type specification:

```
func myFuncWithOptionalType(parameter: String?) {
    // function execution
}

myFuncWithOptionalType("someString")
myFuncWithOptionalType(nil)
```

When working with optionals, don't forget to unwrap!

```
func myFuncWithOptionalType(optionalParameter: String?) {
    if let unwrappedOptional = optionalParameter {
        println("The optional has a value! It's \(unwrappedOptional)")
    } else {
        println("The optional is nil!")
    }
}

myFuncWithOptionalType("someString")
// The optional has a value! It's someString

myFuncWithOptionalType(nil)
// The optional is nil
```

If you're coming from Objective-C, getting used to working with optionals definitely takes some time!

Parameters with Default Values

```
func hello(name: String = "you") {
    println("hello, \(name)")
}
hello(name: "Mr. Roboto")
// hello, Mr. Roboto

hello()
// hello, you
```

Note that a parameter with a default value automatically has an external parameter name.

And since parameters with a default value can be skipped when the function is called, it is best practice to put all your parameters with default values at the end of a function's parameter list. Here is a note from the *The Swift Programming Language* on the topic:

> Place parameters with default values at the end of a function's parameter list. This ensures that all calls to the function use the same order for their non-default arguments, and makes it clear that the same function is being called in each case.

I'm a huge fan of default parameters, mostly because it makes code easy to change and backward-compatible. You might start out with two parameters for your specific use case at the time, such as a function to configure a custom UITableViewCell. And you can add a new parameter with a default value if another use case comes up that requires another parameter, such as a different text color for your cell's label. All the other places where this function has already been called will be fine, and the new part of your code that needs the parameter can just pass in the non-default value!

Variadic Parameters

Variadic parameters are simply a more readable version of passing in an array of elements. In fact, if you were to look at the type of the internal parameter names in the following example, you'd see that it is of type [String] (array of strings):

```
func helloWithNames(names: String...) {
    for name in names {
        println("Hello, \(name)")
    }
}

// 2 names
helloWithNames("Mr. Robot", "Mr. Potato")
// Hello, Mr. Robot
// Hello, Mr. Potato

// 4 names
helloWithNames("Batman", "Superman", "Wonder Woman", "Catwoman")
// Hello, Batman
// Hello, Superman
// Hello, Wonder Woman
// Hello, Catwoman
```

The catch here is to remember that it is possible to pass in 0 values, just like it is possible to pass in an empty array, so don't forget to check for the empty array if needed:

```
func helloWithNames(names: String...) {
    if names.count > 0 {
        for name in names {
            println("Hello, \(name)")
        }
    } else {
        println("Nobody here!")
    }
}

helloWithNames()
// Nobody here!
```

Another note about variadic parameters: the variadic parameter must be the *last* parameter in your function's parameter list!

Inout Parameters

With inout parameters, you have the ability to manipulate external variables (in other words, *pass by reference*):

```
var name1 = "Mr. Potato"
var name2 = "Mr. Roboto"

func nameSwap(inout name1: String, inout name2: String) {
    let oldName1 = name1
    name1 = name2
    name2 = oldName1
}

nameSwap(&name1, &name2)

name1
// Mr. Roboto

name2
// Mr. Potato
```

This is a very common pattern in Objective-C for handling error scenarios. NSJSONSerialization is just one example:

```
- (void)parseJSONData:(NSData *)jsonData
{
    NSError *error = nil;
    id jsonResult =
        [NSJSONSerialization JSONObjectWithData:jsonData
        options:0 error:&error];

    if (!jsonResult) {
        NSLog(@"ERROR: %@", error.description);
    }
}
```

Since Swift is so new, there aren't clear conventions on handling errors just yet, but there are definitely a lot of options beyond inout parameters! Take a look at David Owen's recent blog post on error handling in Swift.[2]

Generic Parameter Types

I'm not going to get too much into generics in this chapter, but here's a very simple example for how you can make a function accept parameters of different types while making sure that both parameters are of the same type:

```
func valueSwap<T>(inout value1: T, inout value2: T) {
    let oldValue1 = value1
    value1 = value2
    value2 = oldValue1
}

var name1 = "Mr. Potato"
var name2 = "Mr. Roboto"
```

---

2. http://owensd.io/2014/08/22/error-handling-take-two.html

```
valueSwap(&name1, &name2)

name1 // Mr. Roboto
name2 // Mr. Potato

var number1 = 2
var number2 = 5

valueSwap(&number1, &number2)

number1 // 5
number2 // 2
```

Variable Parameters

By default, parameters that are passed into a function are constants, so they cannot be manipulated within the scope of the function. If you would like to change that behavior, just use the var keyword for your parameters:

```
var name = "Mr. Roboto"

func appendNumbersToName(var name: String, #maxNumber: Int) -> String {
    for i in 0..<maxNumber {
        name += String(i + 1)
    }
    return name
}

appendNumbersToName(name, maxNumber:5)
// Mr. Robot12345

name
// Mr. Roboto
```

Note that this is different than an inout parameter—variable parameters don't change the external passed-in variable!

Functions as Parameters

In Swift, functions can be passed around just like variables. For example, a function can have another function passed in as a parameter:

```
func luckyNumberForName(name: String, #lotteryHandler: (String, Int) ->
    String) -> String {
    let luckyNumber = Int(arc4random() % 100)
    return lotteryHandler(name, luckyNumber)
}

func defaultLotteryHandler(name: String, luckyNumber: Int) -> String {
    return "\(name), your lucky number is \(luckyNumber)"
}

luckyNumberForName("Mr. Roboto", lotteryHandler: defaultLotteryHandler)
// Mr. Roboto, your lucky number is 38
```

Note that only the function reference gets passed in—defaultLotteryHandler, in this case. The function gets executed later as decided by the receiving function.

Instance methods can also be passed in a similar way:

```
func luckyNumberForName(name: String, #lotteryHandler: (String, Int) ->
    String) -> String {
    let luckyNumber = Int(arc4random() % 100)
    return lotteryHandler(name, luckyNumber)
}

class FunLottery {

    func defaultLotteryHandler(name: String, luckyNumber: Int) -> String {
        return "\(name), your lucky number is \(luckyNumber)"
    }

}

let funLottery = FunLottery()
luckyNumberForName("Mr. Roboto",
    lotteryHandler: funLottery.defaultLotteryHandler)
// Mr. Roboto, your lucky number is 38
```

To make your function definition a bit more readable, consider type-aliasing your function (similar to typedef in Objective-C):

```
typealias lotteryOutputHandler = (String, Int) -> String

func luckyNumberForName(name: String, #lotteryHandler: lotteryOutputHandler) ->
    String {
    let luckyNumber = Int(arc4random() % 100)
    return lotteryHandler(name, luckyNumber)
}
```

You can also have a function without a name as a parameter type (similar to blocks in Objective-C):

```
func luckyNumberForName(name: String, #lotteryHandler: (String, Int) ->
    String) -> String {
    let luckyNumber = Int(arc4random() % 100)
    return lotteryHandler(name, luckyNumber)
}

luckyNumberForName("Mr. Roboto", lotteryHandler: {name, number in
    return "\(name)'s' lucky number is \(number)"
})
// Mr. Roboto's lucky number is 74
```

In Objective-C, using blocks as parameters is popular for completion and error handlers in methods that execute an asynchronous operation. This should continue to be a popular pattern in Swift as well.

Access Controls

Swift has three levels of access controls:

1. *Public access* enables entities to be used within any source file from their defining module, and also in a source file from another module that imports the defining module. You typically use public access when specifying the public interface to a framework.

2. *Internal access* enables entities to be used within any source file from their defining module, but not in any source file outside of that module. You typically use internal access when defining an app's or a framework's internal structure.

3. *Private access* restricts the use of an entity to its own defining source file. Use private access to hide the implementation details of a specific piece of functionality.

By default, every function and variable is internal. If you want to change that, use the private or public keyword in front of every single method and variable:

```
public func myPublicFunc() {

}
func myInternalFunc() {

}
private func myPrivateFunc() {

}
private func myOtherPrivateFunc() {

}
```

Coming from Ruby, I prefer to put all my private functions at the bottom of my class, separated by a landmark:

```
class MyFunClass {
    func myInternalFunc() {

    }
    // MARK: Private Helper Methods
    private func myPrivateFunc() {

    }
    private func myOtherPrivateFunc() {

    }
}
```

Hopefully, future releases of Swift will include an option to use one private keyword to indicate that all methods below it are private, similar to how access controls work in other programming languages.

Fancy Return Types

In Swift, function return types and values can get a bit more complex than we're used to in Objective-C, especially with the introduction of optionals and multiple return types.

Optional Return Types

If there is a possibility that your function could return a nil value, you need to specify the return type as optional:

```
func myFuncWithOptionalReturnType() -> String? {
    let someNumber = arc4random() % 100
    if someNumber > 50 {
        return "someString"
    } else {
        return nil
    }
}

myFuncWithOptionalReturnType()
```

And of course, when you're using the optional return value, don't forget to unwrap:

```
let optionalString = myFuncWithOptionalReturnType()

if let someString = optionalString {
    println("The function returned a value: \(someString)")
} else {
    println("The function returned nil")
}
```

The best explanation I've seen of optionals is from a tweet by @Kronusdark:[3] I finally get @SwiftLang optionals, they are like Schrödinger's cat! You have to see if the cat is alive before you use it.

Multiple Return Values

One of the most exciting features of Swift is the ability for a function to have multiple return values:

```
func findRangeFromNumbers(numbers: Int...) -> (min: Int, max: Int) {
    var min = numbers[0]
    var max = numbers[0]
```

---

3.   https://twitter.com/WestonHanners/status/496444128490967041

```
    for number in numbers {
        if number > max {
            max = number
        }

        if number < min {
            min = number
        }
    }

    return (min, max)
}
findRangeFromNumbers(1, 234, 555, 345, 423)
// (1, 555)
```

As you can see, the multiple return values are returned in a tuple—a very simple data structure of grouped values. There are two ways to use the multiple return values from the tuple:

```
let range = findRangeFromNumbers(1, 234, 555, 345, 423)
println("From numbers: 1, 234, 555, 345, 423.
        The min is \(range.min). The max is \(range.max).")
// From numbers: 1, 234, 555, 345, 423. The min is 1. The max is 555.

let (min, max) = findRangeFromNumbers(236, 8, 38, 937, 328)
println("From numbers: 236, 8, 38, 937, 328.
        The min is \(min). The max is \(max)")
// From numbers: 236, 8, 38, 937, 328. The min is 8. The max is 937
```

Multiple Return Values and Optionals

The tricky part about multiple return values is when the return values can be optional, but there are two ways to handle dealing with optional multiple return values.

In the preceding example function, my logic is flawed—it is possible that no values could be passed in, so my program would actually crash if that ever happened. If no values are passed in, I might want to make my whole return value optional:

```
func findRangeFromNumbers(numbers: Int...) -> (min: Int, max: Int)? {
    if numbers.count > 0 {
        var min = numbers[0]
        var max = numbers[0]

        for number in numbers {
            if number > max {
                max = number
            }
```

```
            if number < min {
                min = number
            }
        }

        return (min, max)
    } else {
        return nil
    }
}

if let range = findRangeFromNumbers() {
    println("Max: \(range.max). Min: \(range.min)")
} else {
    println("No numbers!")
}
// No numbers!
```

In other cases, it might make sense to make each return value within a tuple optional, instead of making the whole tuple optional:

```
func componentsFromUrlString(urlString: String) ->
    (host: String?, path: String?) {
    let url = NSURL(string: urlString)
    return (url.host, url.path)
}
```

If you decide that some of your tuple values could be optionals, things become a little bit more difficult to unwrap, since you have to consider every single combination of optional values:

```
let urlComponents =
  componentsFromUrlString("http://name.com/12345;param?foo=1&baa=2#fragment")

switch (urlComponents.host, urlComponents.path) {
case let (.Some(host), .Some(path)):
    println("This url consists of host \(host) and path \(path)")
case let (.Some(host), .None):
    println("This url only has a host \(host)")
case let (.None, .Some(path)):
    println("This url only has path \(path). Make sure to add a host!")
case let (.None, .None):
    println("This is not a url!")
}
// This url consists of host name.com and path /12345
```

As you can see, this is not your average Objective-C way of doing things!

Return a Function

Any function can also return a function in Swift:

```
func myFuncThatReturnsAFunc() -> (Int) -> String {
    return { number in
        return "The lucky number is \(number)"
    }
}

let returnedFunction = myFuncThatReturnsAFunc()

returnedFunction(5) // The lucky number is 5
```

To make this more readable, you can of course use type-aliasing for your return function:

```
typealias returnedFunctionType = (Int) -> String

func myFuncThatReturnsAFunc() -> returnedFunctionType {
    return { number in
        return "The lucky number is \(number)"
    }
}

let returnedFunction = myFuncThatReturnsAFunc()

returnedFunction(5) // The lucky number is 5
```

Nested Functions

And in case you haven't had enough of functions from this chapter, it's always good to know that in Swift, you can have a function inside a function:

```
func myFunctionWithNumber(someNumber: Int) {

    func increment(var someNumber: Int) -> Int {
        return someNumber + 10
    }

    let incrementedNumber = increment(someNumber)
    println("The incremented number is \(incrementedNumber)")
}
myFunctionWithNumber(5)
// The incremented number is 15
@end
```

Swift functions have a lot of options and a lot of power. As you start writing in Swift, remember: with great power comes great responsibility. Optimize for readability over cleverness!

Swift best practices haven't been fully established yet, and the language is still constantly changing, so get your code reviewed by friends and coworkers. I've found that people who've never seen Swift before sometimes teach me the most about my Swift code.

Happy Swifting!

## CHAPTER 26

A Functional Approach to Lua

by Josh Chisholm

If you write code in mainstream programming languages, you might never have heard of Lua. But I bet you've heard of Angry Birds, Wikipedia, or World of Warcraft. So what made their developers use Lua in those mainstream products? Perhaps it's because Lua is lightweight, cross-platform, embeds and extends well, performs well, and has a small memory footprint and a shallow learning curve. Those are good reasons. But I'd like to believe that *some* developers are attracted to Lua because it supports different paradigms and includes some pretty sweet functional programming capabilities.

You probably know some JavaScript. Although Lua has quite a different heritage, it shares many design ideas with JavaScript and feels similar. Syntactically, Lua is a bit less spiky:

```
function hello() {
    say("Hi there, I'm JavaScript");
}

function hello()
    say "Howdy, I'm Lua"
end
```

Just like JavaScript, Lua owes a lot to Scheme, a Lisp dialect. But because both JavaScript and Lua *appear* closer to Java and C, you wouldn't immediately recognize the Lisp underpinning either of them. Look beneath the syntax, though, and Lua has some features that make it great for using functional techniques as part of a multi-paradigm approach.

First-Class Functions in Lua

If you've come this far in this book, you know that saying functions are first-class just implies there's nothing special about them, so they can be treated like any other value. And you know that a higher-order function does at least one of two things: it either takes other functions as arguments, or it returns functions. These are important capabilities in functional languages, so let's see how they are implemented in Lua.

Suppose we have a handy list of cats. We can use Lua's *table* concept—a Swiss Army–style collection that behaves like both an array and a hash:

```
local cats = {
    { name = "meg", breed = "persian" },
    { name = "mog", breed = "siamese" }
}
```

A function that collects the names of all of our cats would look like this:

```
function namesOf (things)
    local names = {}
    for index, thing in pairs(things) do
        names[index] = thing.name
    end
    return names
end

print(namesOf(cats)[1])    --> meg
print(namesOf(cats)[2])    --> mog
```

Lua uses 1-based indexes, which are easy to think about but can be easy to get wrong.

We could write a very similar breedsOf(cats) function, but we'd have to repeat the logic for iterating over the collection of things. We'd also use special-purpose language syntax twice (for...in). Higher-order functions give us a uniform way of combining functions to reduce duplication, and we can exploit this in Lua:

```
function map (things, fn)
    local mapped = {}
    for index, thing in pairs(things) do
        mapped[index] = fn(thing)
    end
    return mapped
end

function namesOf (things)
    return map(things, function(thing)
        return thing.name
    end)
end

function breedsOf (things)
    return map(things, function(thing)
        return thing.breed
```

```
    end)
end

print(namesOf(cats)[1])    --> meg
print(breedsOf(cats)[2])   --> siamese
```

Via this sort of reuse, functional programs in Lua tend to consist of lots of very small things.

Recursion in Lua

Recursive functions eventually call themselves, like this:

```
function factorial (n)
    if n == 0 then
        return 1
    else
        return n * factorial(n - 1)
    end
end

print(factorial(5))    --> 120
```

Easy to follow, but executing this function for some values of n will result in a stack overflow error. That's because on each successive invocation of factorial(n-1), the machine must retain a reference to the previous iteration on its stack. The stack is finite, so it eventually runs out of space and the program explodes:

```
print(factorial(-1))

lua: factorial.lua:5: stack overflow
stack traceback:
    factorial.lua:5: in function 'factorial'
    factorial.lua:5: in function 'factorial'
    ...
```

Lua 5.0 added proper tail calls, a sort of functional goto that makes it possible to structure a recursive function such that it never runs out of stack space:

```
function factorial (n)
    return factorialUntil(n, 1)
end

function factorialUntil (n, answer)
    if n == 0 then
        return answer
    else
        return factorialUntil(n - 1, n * answer)
    end
end

print(factorial(-1)) --> Loops forever, but doesn't crash
```

Can you spot the difference? For a Lua function to benefit from tail call optimization, its return value needs to call a function (often itself) and do nothing else. Expressions are allowed to appear in the arguments, as in return factorialUntil(n - 1, n * answer) because function arguments are evaluated immediately. But expressions such as return n * factorial(n - 1) cannot be optimized because the * is the last operation, instead of the recursive function call.

Building with Functional Primitives

We had to define our own map() earlier, which we'll use again in a minute. Let's define a few more functional primitives that we can arrange into bigger and better things:

```
function each (things, fn)
    for i, thing in ipairs(things) do
        fn(thing)
    end
end

function filter (things, fn)
    local filtered = {}
    each(things, function(thing)
        if fn(thing) then
            table.insert(filtered, thing)
        end
    end)
    return filtered
end

function cons (things, ...)
    local all = {}
    each({...}, function(t)
        table.insert(all, t)
    end)
    each(things, function(t)
        table.insert(all, t)
    end)
    return all
end
```

I should point out that all of these are relatively slow, because they copy elements between Lua tables. We can guarantee immutability of these tables, so we could avoid copying and simply manipulate pointers into a limited set of underlying tables. That's what proper functional languages like Haskell do by default. But I want to focus on functional semantics rather than on performance, so we'll keep things simple.

A Simple Game Animation

With these preliminaries out of the way, we're ready to tackle an actual problem that a typical Lua hacker might face. Lua is often used as a scripting language for games. These days, games often include particle systems that generate organic-looking graphical effects. I've always wanted to build a particle emitter, so today I'm going to start a fire, functional style!

A functional particle system wouldn't retain mutable state, so it might be a function that accepts state (particles) as an argument and produces new state (new particles).

But before I can start writing my particle system, I need something capable of drawing. I was without my computer this weekend, so that gave me an excuse to use Codea,[1] a cute little iPad Lua development environment with a drawing API.

The Codea runtime calls a draw() function in your code, once per frame. After drawing each particle, I'll mutate the flame to acquire a new state of the flame as a whole. This bit is necessarily imperative, so let's keep it short and sweet:

```
f = flame({}, 0)
function draw()
    each(f.particles, function(p)
        drawParticle(p.style)
    end)
    f = f.next()
end
```

As we shall see, f = f.next() is in fact the *only* example of mutable state we'll need.

Next, a drawing adapter renders each particle as an ellipse in Codea's drawing API:

```
function drawParticle(style)
    fill(style.red, style.green, style.blue, style.alpha)
    ellipse(style.x, style.y, style.radius, style.radius)
end
```

So, what exactly is a "flame"? In my model, a flame comprises many particles, each of which "evolves" over time to make a new flame:

```
function flame(particles, t)
    local newParticles = evolve(particles, t)
    return {
```

---

1.   http://twolivesleft.com/Codea/

```
            particles = newParticles,
            next = function()
                return flame(newParticles, t + 1)
            end
        }
    end
end
```

Each particle changes style over time, taking a step function describing *how* it changes style over time:

```
function particle(step, style, t)
    local newStyle = step(style, t)
    return {
        style = newStyle,
        next = function()
            return particle(step, newStyle, t + 1)
        end
    }
end
```

I've used one object-oriented detail here, by keeping state (or style) close to behavior that manipulates that state (the next function). But since I'm keeping clear of *mutable* state, I don't think the pure functional police can bust me.

My model describes a step in the evolution of the whole flame in three parts:

```
function evolve(particles, t)
    return generate(mutate(prune(particles)), t)
end
```

Particles are generated at a point in time, then they repeatedly mutate until they die. Given a set of particles, we "prune" any dead particles, "mutate" each remaining particle, and "generate" new particles to keep the flame alive. Each operation produces a new set of particles—the state of the flame as a whole:

```
function mutate(particles)
    return map(particles, function(p)
        return p.next()
    end)
end

function prune(particles)
    return filter(particles, function(p)
        return p.style.alpha > 0
    end)
end
```

Before we can generate particles, we have to describe what it means to be a particle in a flame. I'm sure there are established models for this, but I have a vague mental image of how I want my fire to look, so I'm going to make an approximation based on my fuzzy knowledge. In my eyes, flames seem to consist of upwardly moving particles that also move smoothly from side to side, change color, get smaller, and gradually disappear. So my spark particle is this somewhat random-looking transformation of position, color, and size over time:

```
function spark(style, t)
    return {
        x      = style.x - math.sin(t * 0.5),
        y      = style.y + 1,
        red    = style.red   + (math.sin(t * style.seed) * 40),
        green  = style.green + (math.sin(t * style.seed) * 33),
        blue   = style.blue,
        alpha  = (style.alpha - 5 * style.seed) * 0.97,
        seed   = style.seed,
        radius = 5 - t * 0.03
    }
end
```

What are all these magic numbers? What's this "seed" thing? These are just some dials I came up with to tweak the "personality" of each spark and to give the overall flame a varied but consistent feel. The sparks I was fiddling with? Oh yes, those were generated by this last piece of my functional puzzle:

```
function generate(particles, t)
    return cons(particles,
        particle(spark, {
            x = 0,
            y = 0,
            red = 255,
            green = 40,
            blue = 10,
            alpha = 220,
            seed = 0.3
        }, 0),
        particle(spark, {
            x = 1,
            y = 2,
            red = 220,
            green = 30,
            blue = 10,
            alpha = 180,
            seed = 0.5
        }, 1)
        -- snip: lots more spark particles!
    )
)
```

Several more particles and lots more knob twiddling later (omitted for brevity), and the outcome is something like the smooth flame animation I was day-dreaming of:

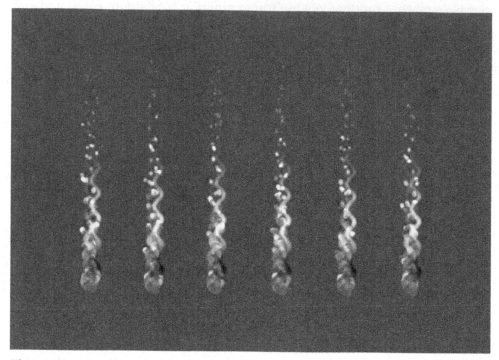

The individual frames don't do it justice, so you'll have to imagine the upwardly, side-to-side movement and color progression as each particle burns and fades into nothingness. Or you can grab the code from github[2] and fiddle with it in Codea or elsewhere.

Twiddle those knobs again, tweak the magic numbers, add different kinds of particles, and you'll generate a completely different effect. As it stands, this is about right for some jazzy looking torches in my new dungeon adventure game!

Oh, and I think it also works as a nice example of using functional code alongside iterative code in just one more programming language.

---

2.   https://gist.github.com/joshski/5429239

Meet the Authors

More than a dozen authors contributed to this volume, some of them language designers and all of them recognized experts in their programming craft. I think you should meet them.

Aaron Bedra

Aaron is the chief security officer at Eligible. He is the creator of Repsheet, an open source threat intelligence framework. Aaron is also the co-author of *Programming Clojure (2nd edition) [HB12]*.

Michael Bevilacqua-Linn

Michael has been programming computers ever since he dragged an Apple IIGS that his parents got for opening a bank account into his fifth grade class to explain loops and variables to a bunch of pre-teenagers. He currently works for Comcast, where he builds distributed systems that power infrastructure for their next-generation services, and he wrote *Functional Programming Patterns in Scala and Clojure [Bev13]*. He tweets occasionally at @NovusTiro.

Paul Callaghan

A keen functional programmer since 1986, Paul moved into Haskell during his PhD work on natural language processing, then into dependent type theory as part of his post-doc work with several pioneers of the field. Lured back to the real world via Rails and e-commerce after a decade of teaching, Paul currently works on a variety of bespoke web apps at TranscendIt, where he writes Ruby with a distinct accent. Paul also flies big traction kites and can often be found being dragged around inelegantly on the beaches of Northeast England. He blogs at free-variable.org and tweets as @paulcc_two.

Josh Chisholm

Josh is a co-founder of Featurist, a software development consultancy based in London. He started programming because he wanted to write games. After over a decade of serious programming, he is just getting back to where his fun began. His first commercial game will hit a device near you any day now. He occasionally tweets as @joshski but he regularly plays with code at github.com/featurist.

Mark Chu-Carroll

Mark is a PhD computer scientist and professional software engineer. He works as a server engineer at Foursquare. His professional interests include collaborative software development, programming languages and tools, and how to improve the daily lives of software developers. Mark blogs about math-related topics on Scientopia. Aside from general geekery and blogging, he plays classical music on the clarinet, traditional Irish music on the wooden flute, and folds elaborate structures out of paper.

Stuart Halloway

Stuart is a founder and president of Cognitect, Inc. He is a Clojure committer, and a developer of the Datomic database. Stuart has spoken at a variety of industry events, including StrangeLoop, Clojure/conj, EuroClojure, Clojure/west, SpeakerConf, QCon, GOTO, OSCON, RailsConf, RubyConf, JavaOne, and NFJS. Stuart has written a number of books and technical articles. Of these, he is most proud of *Programming Clojure (2nd edition) [HB12]*.

Rich Hickey

Rich is the creator of the Clojure language. He says that he developed Clojure because he wanted a modern Lisp for functional programming, symbiotic with the established Java platform, and designed for concurrency. He is the CTO at Cognitect.

Tony Hillerson

Tony is a technical manager at MapQuest. Tony has spoken at RailsConf, AnDevCon, and 360|iDev, and has created popular Android screencasts. He's written a few books, including a Pragmatic Programmer book about mobile app development in the Seven in Seven series. In his free time, Tony enjoys historical fencing, playing the bass and Warr Guitar, and making electronic music. Tony lives outside Denver, Colorado with his wife Lori and three kids.

Natasha Murashev

Natasha is an iOS developer by day and a robot by night. She blogs about Swift, watchOS, and iOS development on her blog, natashatherobot.com;[1] curates a fast-growing weekly Swift newsletter, This Week in Swift;[2] and organizes the try! Swift Conference around the world in Tokyo, New York, and Bangalore. She's currently living the digital nomad life as her alter identity: @NatashaTheNomad.[3]

Venkat Subramaniam

Venkat is an award-winning author, founder of Agile Developer, Inc., and an adjunct faculty at the University of Houston. He has trained and mentored thousands of software developers in the United States, Canada, Europe, and Asia, and is a regularly invited speaker at several international conferences. Venkat helps his clients effectively apply and succeed with agile practices on their software projects. Venkat is the author of *.NET Gotchas [Sub05]*, *Programming Groovy: Dynamic Productivity for the Java Developer [Sub13]*, and *Pragmatic Scala: Create Expressive, Concise, and Scalable Applications [Sub15]*, and the coauthor of 2007 Jolt Productivity Award winning *Practices of an Agile Developer [SH06]*. His latest book is *Programming Concurrency on the JVM: Mastering Synchronization, STM, and Actors [Sub11]*.

Bruce Tate

Bruce is a mountain biker, kayaker, and father of two from Austin, Texas. As the CTO of icanmakeitbetter.com, he writes Elixir and Ruby code to help his customers ask and answer questions through insight communities that will help each client improve a little more each day. He is the author of *Seven Languages in Seven Weeks [Tat10]* and the co-author of *Programming Phoenix [TV16]*. He is also the editor of Your Elixir Source, the line of books for the Elixir programming language at the Pragmatic Bookshelf.

Dave Thomas

Dave is a programmer who likes to evangelize cool stuff. He co-wrote The Pragmatic Programmer and was one of the creators of the Agile Manifesto. His book *Programming Ruby [FH04]* introduced the Ruby language to the world, and *Agile Web Development with Rails* helped kickstart the Rails revolution.

---

1. https://www.natashatherobot.com/
2. https://swiftnews.curated.co/
3. https://twitter.com/natashathenomad

José Valim

José is the creator of Elixir, a member of the Rails Core Team, and the author of the *Crafting Rails Applications [Val13]* book. He is the co-founder of Plataformatec, a software consulting company. At Plataformatec, he's the head of the R&D activities, where he leads Plataformatec's contributions to the open source world, mainly in Ruby, Rails, and Elixir.

Bibliography

[Bev13]   Michael Bevilacqua-Linn. *Functional Programming Patterns in Scala and Clojure*. The Pragmatic Bookshelf, Raleigh, NC, 2013.

[FH04]   Dave Thomas, with Chad Fowler and Andy Hunt. *Programming Ruby (2nd edition)*. The Pragmatic Bookshelf, Raleigh, NC, 2nd, 2004.

[HB12]   Stuart Halloway and Aaron Bedra. *Programming Clojure (2nd edition) (out of print)*. The Pragmatic Bookshelf, Raleigh, NC, 2nd, 2012.

[Lip11]   Miran Lipovaca. *Learn You a Haskell for Great Good!: A Beginner's Guide*. No Starch Press, San Francisco, CA, 2011.

[Sei05]   Peter Seibel. *Practical Common Lisp*. Apress, New York City, NY, , 2005.

[SH06]   Venkat Subramaniam and Andy Hunt. *Practices of an Agile Developer*. The Pragmatic Bookshelf, Raleigh, NC, 2006.

[Sub05]   Venkat Subramaniam. *.NET Gotchas*. O'Reilly & Associates, Inc., Sebastopol, CA, 2005.

[Sub11]   Venkat Subramaniam. *Programming Concurrency on the JVM*. The Pragmatic Bookshelf, Raleigh, NC, 2011.

[Sub13]   Venkat Subramaniam. *Programming Groovy 2*. The Pragmatic Bookshelf, Raleigh, NC, 2013.

[Sub15]   Venkat Subramaniam. *Pragmatic Scala*. The Pragmatic Bookshelf, Raleigh, NC, 2015.

[Tat10]   Bruce A. Tate. *Seven Languages in Seven Weeks*. The Pragmatic Bookshelf, Raleigh, NC, 2010.

[Tho16]   Dave Thomas. *Programming Elixir 1.3*. The Pragmatic Bookshelf, Raleigh, NC, 2016.

[TV16]   Chris McCord, Bruce Tate, and José Valim. *Programming Phoenix*. The
           Pragmatic Bookshelf, Raleigh, NC, 2016.

[Val13]   José Valim. *Crafting Rails 4 Applications*. The Pragmatic Bookshelf, Raleigh,
           NC, 2013.

Index

Put the "Fun" in Functional

Elixir puts the "fun" back into functional programming, on top of the robust, battle-tested, industrial-strength environment of Erlang. Add in the unparalleled beauty and ease of the Phoenix web framework, and enjoy the web again!

Programming Elixir 1.3

Explore functional programming without the academic overtones (tell me about monads just one more time). Create concurrent applications, but get them right without all the locking and consistency headaches. Meet Elixir, a modern, functional, concurrent language built on the rock-solid Erlang VM. Elixir's pragmatic syntax and built-in support for metaprogramming will make you productive and keep you interested for the long haul. Maybe the time is right for the Next Big Thing. Maybe it's Elixir. This book is *the* introduction to Elixir for experienced programmers, completely updated for Elixir 1.3.

Dave Thomas
(362 pages) ISBN: 9781680502008. $38
https://pragprog.com/book/elixir13

Programming Phoenix

Don't accept the compromise between fast and beautiful: you can have it all. Phoenix creator Chris McCord, Elixir creator José Valim, and award-winning author Bruce Tate walk you through building an application that's fast and reliable. At every step, you'll learn from the Phoenix creators not just what to do, but why. Packed with insider insights, this definitive guide will be your constant companion in your journey from Phoenix novice to expert, as you build the next generation of web applications.

Chris McCord, Bruce Tate, and José Valim
(298 pages) ISBN: 9781680501452. $34
https://pragprog.com/book/phoenix

Secure JavaScript and Web Testing

Secure your Node applications and see how to really test on the web.

Secure Your Node.js Web Application

Cyber-criminals have your web applications in their crosshairs. They search for and exploit common security mistakes in your web application to steal user data. Learn how you can secure your Node.js applications, database and web server to avoid these security holes. Discover the primary attack vectors against web applications, and implement security best practices and effective countermeasures. Coding securely will make you a stronger web developer and analyst, and you'll protect your users.

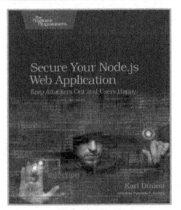

Karl Düüna
(230 pages) ISBN: 9781680500851. $36
https://pragprog.com/book/kdnodesec

The Way of the Web Tester

This book is for everyone who needs to test the web. As a tester, you'll automate your tests. As a developer, you'll build more robust solutions. And as a team, you'll gain a vocabulary and a means to coordinate how to write and organize automated tests for the web. Follow the testing pyramid and level up your skills in user interface testing, integration testing, and unit testing. Your new skills will free you up to do other, more important things while letting the computer do the one thing it's really good at: quickly running thousands of repetitive tasks.

Jonathan Rasmusson
(256 pages) ISBN: 9781680501834. $29
https://pragprog.com/book/jrtest

Long Live the Command Line!

Use tmux and Vim for incredible mouse-free productivity.

tmux 2

Your mouse is slowing you down. The time you spend context switching between your editor and your consoles eats away at your productivity. Take control of your environment with tmux, a terminal multiplexer that you can tailor to your workflow. With this updated second edition for tmux 2.3, you'll customize, script, and leverage tmux's unique abilities to craft a productive terminal environment that lets you keep your fingers on your keyboard's home row.

Brian P. Hogan
(102 pages) ISBN: 9781680502213. $21.95
https://pragprog.com/book/bhtmux2

Practical Vim, Second Edition

Vim is a fast and efficient text editor that will make you a faster and more efficient developer. It's available on almost every OS, and if you master the techniques in this book, you'll never need another text editor. In more than 120 Vim tips, you'll quickly learn the editor's core functionality and tackle your trickiest editing and writing tasks. This beloved bestseller has been revised and updated to Vim 8 and includes three brand-new tips and five fully revised tips.

Drew Neil
(354 pages) ISBN: 9781680501278. $29
https://pragprog.com/book/dnvim2

Past and Present

To see where we're going, remember how we got here, and learn how to take a healthier approach to programming.

Fire in the Valley

In the 1970s, while their contemporaries were protesting the computer as a tool of dehumanization and oppression, a motley collection of college dropouts, hippies, and electronics fanatics were engaged in something much more subversive. Obsessed with the idea of getting computer power into their own hands, they launched from their garages a hobbyist movement that grew into an industry, and ultimately a social and technological revolution. What they did was invent the personal computer: not just a new device, but a watershed in the relationship between man and machine. This is their story.

Michael Swaine and Paul Freiberger
(422 pages) ISBN: 9781937785765. $34
https://pragprog.com/book/fsfire

The Healthy Programmer

To keep doing what you love, you need to maintain your own systems, not just the ones you write code for. Regular exercise and proper nutrition help you learn, remember, concentrate, and be creative—skills critical to doing your job well. Learn how to change your work habits, master exercises that make working at a computer more comfortable, and develop a plan to keep fit, healthy, and sharp for years to come.

This book is intended only as an informative guide for those wishing to know more about health issues. In no way is this book intended to replace, countermand, or conflict with the advice given to you by your own healthcare provider including Physician, Nurse Practitioner, Physician Assistant, Registered Dietician, and other licensed professionals.

Joe Kutner
(254 pages) ISBN: 9781937785314. $36
https://pragprog.com/book/jkthp

The Pragmatic Bookshelf

The Pragmatic Bookshelf features books written by developers for developers. The titles continue the well-known Pragmatic Programmer style and continue to garner awards and rave reviews. As development gets more and more difficult, the Pragmatic Programmers will be there with more titles and products to help you stay on top of your game.

Visit Us Online

This Book's Home Page
https://pragprog.com/book/ppanth
Source code from this book, errata, and other resources. Come give us feedback, too!

Register for Updates
https://pragprog.com/updates
Be notified when updates and new books become available.

Join the Community
https://pragprog.com/community
Read our weblogs, join our online discussions, participate in our mailing list, interact with our wiki, and benefit from the experience of other Pragmatic Programmers.

New and Noteworthy
https://pragprog.com/news
Check out the latest pragmatic developments, new titles and other offerings.

Save on the eBook

Save on the eBook versions of this title. Owning the paper version of this book entitles you to purchase the electronic versions at a terrific discount.

PDFs are great for carrying around on your laptop—they are hyperlinked, have color, and are fully searchable. Most titles are also available for the iPhone and iPod touch, Amazon Kindle, and other popular e-book readers.

Buy now at *https://pragprog.com/coupon*

Contact Us

Online Orders:	*https://pragprog.com/catalog*
Customer Service:	*support@pragprog.com*
International Rights:	*translations@pragprog.com*
Academic Use:	*academic@pragprog.com*
Write for Us:	*http://write-for-us.pragprog.com*
Or Call:	+1 800-699-7764

CPSIA information can be obtained
at www.ICGtesting.com
Printed in the USA
BVOW04s2232260717
490379BV00004B/4/P